Anti-Drug Crusades
in Twentieth-Century China

Anti-Drug Crusades in Twentieth-Century China

Nationalism, History, and State Building

Zhou Yongming

ROWMAN & LITTLEFIELD PUBLISHERS, INC.
Lanham • Boulder • New York • Oxford

ROWMAN & LITTLEFIELD PUBLISHERS, INC.

Published in the United States of America
by Rowman & Littlefield Publishers, Inc.
4720 Boston Way, Lanham, Maryland 20706
http://www.rowmanlittlefield.com

12 Hid's Copse Road
Cumnor Hill, Oxford OX2 9JJ, England

British Library Cataloguing in Publication Information Available

Library of Congress Cataloging-in-Publication Data

Zhou, Yongming, 1963–
    Anti-drug crusades in twentieth-century China : nationalism,
history, and state building / Zhou Yongming.
        p.   cm.
    Includes bibliographical references and index.
    ISBN 0-8476-9597-2 (cl. : alk. paper). —ISBN 0-8476-9598-0 (pa.
: alk. paper)
    1. Drug abuse—China. 2. Drug abuse—China—Prevention. 3. Opium
trade—China—History. 4. Drug traffic—Political aspects—China.
5. Narcotics, Control of—China. I. Title. II. Title: Anti-drug
crusades in 20th century China.
HV5840.C6Z48   1999
363.45'0951—dc21   99-35068
                                                                             CIP

Printed in the United States of America

∞™ The paper used in this publication meets the minimum requirements of American
National Standard for Information Sciences—Permanence of Paper for Printed Library
Materials, ANSI Z39.48-1992.

For
Lan and Caroline

Contents

Illustrations

FIGURES   **PAGE**

Acknowledgments

In the long process of research and writing of this book, I have received help from many people and institutions. First of all, I am deeply grateful to Professor Richard G. Fox, whose direction and encouragement have been important at every stage of this study. I am also profoundly indebted to Professor Arif Dirlik, who is such a dedicated teacher and always has had time for me over the years. This study has benefited a great deal from his critical comments.

My deepest thanks also go to the other members of my dissertation committee, Professors Judith Farquhar, Orin Starn, Claudia Strauss, and Ralph Litzinger. During the period of dissertation write-up, Professor Farquhar was often the first person from whom I sought help and advice. Professor Starn has been a most caring, understanding, and insightful mentor over many years, and always gave me encouragement when I most needed it. I want to express my deepest appreciation for the support from them and from all members of my committee.

I am also grateful to all the people who provided me help during my fieldwork, although the number of names would be many long to list here in entirety. I owe special thanks to Professor Lin Chaomin at Yunnan University and Professor Ma Mozhen at Beijing Medical University for their advice. I wish to mention with gratitude Professor R. Bin Wong at the University of California—Irvine for his insightful comments on the draft of this work.

At various stages of this study, I have received financial support from a number of sources, including the Duke University Graduate Fellowship and Asian-Pacific Studies Fellowships. A Summer Grant from the Center for International Studies at Duke University enabled me to take a preliminary research trip to China in 1992, during which this study was first conceived. A Graduate Fellowship of the National Program for Advanced Study and Research in China from the Committee on Scholarly Communication with China, a Small Grant from the

Wenner-Gren Foundation, and a Young Scholar Award from the China Times Cultural Foundation supported my fieldwork in China. The Washington Center for China Studies, and Dr. Sun Yat-Sen Scholarship Foundation provided additional financial support; and a Fellowship from the Pacific Cultural Foundation helped to fund part of my write-up period. In addition, travel grants from both the Hoover Institution and the Harvard-Yenching Library supported library research at Stanford University and Harvard University.

Thanks also go to helpful librarians at Hong Kong Baptist College Library, Nanjing University Library, Yunnan University Library, Beijing Library, Beijing University Library, Duke University Library, Hoover Institution Library, Harvard-Yenching Library, and archivists at the Second National Historical Archives of China in Nanjing.

I would like to thank editor Susan McEachern and copyeditor Kathleen Silloway for their assistance in the stages of submission to and copyediting by Rowman & Littlefield. I also wish to thank the National Narcotics Control Commission of China for granting me permission to use ten photographs in this book. I am also grateful to Professor Zhu Qingbao at Nanjing University for providing me with an additional photograph.

Finally, I should thank my family. My daughter Caroline was born in the middle of the write-up and the joys of her birth gave me the final push to finish this book. My wife Lan has supported this project with her patience, understanding, and skillful help in typing the manuscript. I dedicate this book to them with love and appreciation.

1

Introduction

On June 26, 1992, more than 40,000 people held an anti-drug gathering in the municipal stadium in Kunming, capital city of Yunnan province, where the problem of heroin abuse was the most rampant in China. During the proceedings, a number of drug traffickers were publicly tried, and twenty-one of them were sentenced to death. They were immediately sent to the execution ground and killed by a firing squad. After the governor gave a speech proclaiming the government's resolve to fight drug problems, 4,000 kilograms of heroin and opium were set on fire in sixty immense electrical pots at a corner of the stadium. The flames rose as high as thirty feet in front of the excited spectators, who were applauding and cheering enthusiastically. The atmosphere was highly charged. On the same day, 160 kilograms of heroin, opium, and marijuana were publicly burnt at Humen, a small town near Guangzhou, where Lin Zexu destroyed thousands of pounds of seized British opium in 1839. In the meantime, thirty-one Guangdong drug offenders were sentenced to death and eighteen of them were immediately executed.

These are just two episodes from the latest anti-drug crusade, which is still under way in China. Since 1990, there have been annual public anti-drug trials and gatherings in China around June 26, which is the International Anti-Narcotics Day and also serves as the anniversary of the First Opium War (1840–1842). Both the timing and locations have been chosen with great deliberation for their symbolic importance. Looking further back into history, anti-drug gatherings and public burning of seized drugs have occurred countless times since the Opium War all over China. In fact, this practice has become a ritual of China's anti-drug campaign. The burning of opium at Humen in 1839 has become the archetype of the ritual and has been iterated, interpreted, practiced, and visualized to the general public. For example, the film *The Opium War* re-created that historic event in 1997. The film was made to

A scene from the film The Opium War *(produced in 1997), depicting the historical event of burning foreign opium in Humen in 1839 by Lin Zexu*

commemorate the reversion of Hong Kong, which the British gained from China as one of the results of the First Opium War, to Chinese rule. The burning of opium was presented full of extraordinary pageantry, making it one of the most impressive scenes of the film.

Many issues, however, are involved in the public anti-drug shows. Political ritual, state violence, nationalistic discourse, historic narrative, and emotional charge all play their parts to make the shows as spectacular as possible. Yet in the 160 years since the First Opium War, except for a twenty-year intermission under Communist rule, China never rid itself of drugs. The suppression of opium and other drugs in modern China has been a puzzling issue. Since the beginning of the twentieth century, anti-drug discourse has enjoyed widespread acceptance in society. Laws and regulations on drug suppression and control have increased in both quantity and the severity of punishment, and the state has engaged the issue by conducting nationwide anti-drug crusades. But drug abuse continues to worsen, and its effects on China are far-reaching. It is not exaggerated to say that drugs are inextricably related to every aspect of the economy, politics, society, and culture in modern China, yet this important phenomenon has not been fully studied.[1]

The main purpose of this study is to address the complexity of anti-drug campaigns by bringing the issues of nationalism and state building to drug studies in the context of twentieth-century China. I will demonstrate that modern Chinese nationalism and the needs of state building have shaped how these campaigns have been carried out. In modern China, the drug problem has been viewed not only as a kind of social deviance but also as an explosive issue closely related to the history of the Opium Wars, to the relationships between China and Western countries, and to the definition of national history and identity. Nationalism has thus played an important role in all anti-drug crusades in modern China.

However, anti-drug campaigns are also closely related to the internal politics of modern China. Since the fall of the Qing dynasty, China has witnessed changes of power among the Northern Warlords, the Nationalists, and the Communists. Anti-drug campaigns have been used by both the Nationalists and the Communists to build, consolidate, and demonstrate state hegemony through mass campaigns, nationwide mobilization, and use of state violence. This study examines how the state adopts multiple interpretations of the nationalist anti-drug discourse and then incorporates them into the state's hidden agenda of conducting anti-drug campaigns. The role played by the private sector and its relationship with the state are also explored within this context, with special attention to the National Anti-Opium Association (NAOA hereafter), an influential private organization that was very active from the mid-1920s to mid-1930s.

This book illustrates its arguments on nationalism and state building by exploring anti-drug movements in twentieth-century China. Aside from numerous regional and local anti-drug initiatives, there have been four nationwide, state-sponsored anti-drug crusades since 1906. The first one was conducted in the last years of the Qing dynasty, and was quite effective until it was disrupted by the fall of the dynasty in 1911. The second, conducted by the Nationalists from 1935 to 1940, as a part of the New Life Movement, just barely succeeded. The other two anti-drug campaigns occurred in post-1949 China. One was carried out in the early 1950s, and it took only three years to eliminate the drug problem, which had never been solved by previous regimes. Illicit drug use and trafficking reappeared as a social problem in the early 1980s, and since then China has become a major transit point in the heroin traffic from Southeast Asia to Hong Kong, and from there to the rest of the world where heroin is widely consumed. To deal with this issue, the Chinese government launched an anti-drug crusade at the end of the 1980s. So far its results have not been very effective.

This analysis centers on two inseparable aspects of anti-drug campaigns, namely, anti-drug discourses and anti-drug practices. As far as the anti-drug discourses are concerned, this book focuses on issues of nationalism, historical narrative, and anti-drug propaganda. With respect to anti-drug practices, it examines the relationship between state and society, especially how society uses the drug issue to create a public sphere in which it exercises its influences, and how the state tries to use anti-drug crusades to consolidate its power. By bringing nationalism and the theory of hegemony into the study of drugs, this study (1) constructs a brief cultural history of the campaigns, (2) explores how historical narratives of the Opium Wars and nationalism are used to make drugs an issue of public sphere, which in turn is used by the Chinese to legitimize the crusades, and (3) highlights how these anti-drug crusades became a means of state building under different historical circumstances.

This study has been accomplished through a combination of archival research, participant observation, and discourse analysis. It was first conceived during a preliminary field trip to China in the summer of 1992. From the winter of 1993 to the summer of 1995, I conducted archival research in Kunming, Beijing, and Nanjing, and fieldwork mainly in Yunnan province; I also conducted participant observation in Baoshan City and Dehong Prefecture during 1994 and 1995. Since this study's aim is to depict a broad picture of anti-drug crusades in modern China, its approach is macroscopic rather than microscopic, historically rather than locally oriented, and is supplemented with concrete case studies. This study is designed thus to contribute to a more sophisticated anthropology of drug studies, a subfield that so far has paid little attention to the issues of nationalism and state building.

ANTHROPOLOGY AND DRUG STUDIES

Much work has been done worldwide on substance abuse, which generally is viewed as merely a form of social deviance that affects public health and safety. Anthropologists have introduced a cultural perspective into the study of alcohol to go along with a biological and psychological perspective (Everett, Waddell, and Heath 1976). Since the 1970s, anthropological literature on drug studies has increased dramatically, yet several problems remain to be solved. First, traditionally, drug studies are often "by-products" of mainstream anthropological studies; consequently, most studies are merely descriptive, limited to historical reconstruction and geographical distribution (Marshall 1987).

The second problem is in a way the reverse of the first. Bringing a cultural perspective to drug studies often leads researchers to the "fallacy of culture" (Fox 1985). In concentrating on describing superficial or "exotic" drug customs, many studies have failed to explore the broader and deeper meanings attached to the issue. The incompleteness of most anthropological studies of drug use often derives from the misuse of the culture concept—the central concept of anthropology. Anthropological drug studies often treat culture as an organic, static structure rather than a complex, ever-changing set of human activities; as an entity powerful enough to determine behavior rather than a domain in which activities are defined and negotiated. Applied to drug studies, this "culturology" ends up with a one-size-fits-all explanation, that is, whatever the drug problem is, it is determined by the mighty force of the "culture."

Finally, based on the Eurocentric discourse on modern individuality, which views the phenomenon of drug use as a matter of individual experience and self-control (Dreher 1982; Alasuutari 1992), many drug studies focus on a limited "subculture" model. They neglect the fact that drug issues are related to much broader social and cultural contexts. Derived from the organismic culture concept, the concept of "subculture" refers to a specific setting where drug addicts live. Because drug addicts "share a common interest, they share certain characteristics and engage in certain common behaviors," and they naturally form a subculture that specifically belongs to themselves (Agar 1973, 3). The subculture is often seen as a self-sustained entity, isolated from the whole society. It is a replica of the "tyranny of culture" on a smaller scale.[2] Obviously, the subculture model cannot encompass the whole sphere of the anti-drug crusades in modern China. A new approach needs to be adopted to achieve two goals for this study: a better anthropological study on drugs, in general, and a better study of anti-drug campaigns in modern China, in particular.

NATIONALISM, HEGEMONY, AND THE PUBLIC SPHERE

The following chapters elaborate how, despite individual suffering being a part of modern Chinese anti-opium discourse, emphasis has been often placed in that discourse on opium's harmfulness to the state and the Chinese nation, especially since the late Qing. It is in this context that China's anti-drug campaigns have been closely related to modern Chinese nationalism. The drug issue has not been addressed in the "private" and "individual" spheres, where it has been traditionally defined in the West; rather it has been seen as something collective and public in modern China. Unfortunately, few anthropologists have paid attention to the issue of nationalism and its relationship to narcotics control movements around the world. This study tries to shed new light on this important yet understudied area.

When speaking of Chinese nationalism and anti-drug crusades, it is not very difficult to find a nationalistic narrative that blames foreigners for their role in the making of an opium epidemic in modern China. The history of the Opium Wars provides the Chinese a unique frame of reference within which to define their identity. In the anti-drug discourses of modern China, a striking point is that they are inextricably linked to the reinterpretation of national history. The Opium Wars play a prominent part in many anti-drug articles, pamphlets, films, and other forms of propaganda produced by both the Nationalists and the Communists.

Another striking point is that anti-drug crusades in modern China have been carried out mostly through mass mobilization and mass campaigns in which the state has played an active role. Conducting such mass campaigns has been the principal way of solving political and social problems in modern China (Bennett 1976). Under the Nationalists and Communists, all three state-sponsored anti-drug crusades have been carried out in this way, yet not one has had the sole aim of ridding the country of the drug epidemic. Rather, all have been integral parts of the state's attempts to consolidate its power. Several scholars have pointed out that the thrust of the New Life Movement went far beyond improving public health and individual morality, that it functioned, in fact, as a "controlled popular mobilization" to enhance the existing structure of authority through promoting disciplined behavior and a hygienic lifestyle (Dirlik 1975). In the current anti-drug campaign, the Communist leadership is reusing the techniques of mass campaigning, despite the fact that old techniques seem to have lost legitimacy after the Cultural Revolution.

In addition to the state, there have been many other agents involved in the anti-drug crusades. Sometimes, these agents are very active and influential, even challenging the state's authority directly, as in the case of the NAOA in the middle and late 1920s. Various private anti-drug organizations derive legitimacy for their initiatives from the pervasive sentiment of the whole society. Why has anti-opium discourse gained wide support among most strata of Chinese society? How has this discourse been used by both the state and private sectors to advance their causes? Answers to these questions are related not only to the rise of modern Chinese nationalism but also to the relationship between state and nonstate sectors in the efforts of drug suppression.

Several concepts, such as hegemony, civil society, and public sphere, developed mainly by Antonio Gramsci and Jurgen Habermas, provide the analytical framework for this study. Though anthropologists have shown growing interest in Gramsci's work in the past ten years, the concept of hegemony remains unclearly defined, and different scholars have presented various interpretations.[3] Acknowledging hegemony as a process, as emphasized by Raymond Williams (1977), this book uses the concept of hegemony in a manner as close as possible to its original context. According to Gramsci, "The supremacy of a social group manifests itself in two ways, as 'domination' and as 'intellectual and moral leadership' " (Gramsci 1971, 57). Taking into account that in modern China, the state has always played a key role in conducting anti-drug campaigns, the focus here is to examine how the state uses these anti-drug campaigns to dominate and, if possible, also to lead in its work to establish hegemony. This analysis looks closely at the "state" and its attempts to build and consolidate its own power in anti-drug campaigns. As Anne S. Sassoon argues, "The full range of concepts in *The Prison Notebooks* can only be appreciated by taking the 'State' as the starting point for analysis, and that the integral state, that is a formation of 'hegemony armored by coercion,' is the epistemological key to Gramsci's political thought" (Kurtz 1996, 113).

Unfortunately, an "integral state" has never been a reality in modern China; only the Communist state from 1949 to 1978 came closest to it. To build and sustain authoritarian and totalitarian regimes, the Nationalists and Communists used coercion more than hegemony, domination more than moral leadership. If the anti-drug discourse were ever hegemonic in modern China, its hegemony was often challenged. The absence of an integral state and the fact that anti-drug discourse is often open to ideological debate help explain the division between the anti-drug discourse and practice.

Given the fact that the state always wants to be dominant in China, how could the NAOA, a private organization, play such a powerful role against the state for almost a decade? This question brings us to another important issue of the theory of hegemony, that is, the relationship between the state and society. Gramsci differentiates "civil society" from "political society" to demonstrate the comprehensive range of hegemony. For him, coercive domination manifests itself mainly in "political society," which is represented by the various institutions of the state, but "civil society" consists of those "private" organizations separated from the state apparatuses, such as the church, school system, political parties, trade unions, mass media, and family. He realizes that no regime, regardless of how authoritarian it is, can sustain itself primarily through coercive state power. It is in civil society that the hegemony of the dominant group can be built up by means of persuasion and education.

Civil society is another complex concept, and its applicability to Chinese studies is a topic of ongoing debate.[4] Among scholars who have tried to use the concepts of hegemony and civil society to analyze various phenomena in China, some have pointed out two unique characteristics of modern China: the lack of a highly developed civil society like that of Western countries, and the active role of state power in the formation of hegemony (Blecher 1989, Yang 1989). Some argue that civil society, which developed and existed in China from the late Qing dynasty, has been gradually eroded by the state since the establishment of the Republic in 1912, and that it was not until the 1980s that elements of civil society re-emerged and increased along with the economic reforms (Rankin 1986, Yang 1989).

Introducing concepts such as hegemony and civil society into this study sets the stage to contextualize and re-examine them in the context of anti-drug campaigns. A more ambitious aim of this study is to examine the applicability of these concepts to the study of modern China. Realizing the danger of drawing a general conclusion from a concept that demands more critical elaboration, however, this study avoids using the term "civil society" to refer to those societal forces in the anti-drug campaigns. The activities of the NAOA in the 1920s point to there being elements of civil society in big cities like Shanghai, but their pervasiveness in small towns and rural areas has yet to be found. In any event, identifying discrete elements of civil society and then simply adding them up does not determine the existence of an actual civil society. Therefore, this study uses the concept of "public sphere" as the point of departure to describe the drug issue in Chinese society. The concept is elaborated by Jurgen Habermas:

> By "public sphere" we mean first of all a domain of our social life in which such a thing as public opinion can be formed. Access to the public sphere is open in principle to all citizens. . . . Citizens act as a public when they deal with matters of general interest without being subject to coercion; thus with the guarantee that they may assemble and unite freely, and express and publicize their opinions freely. (Habermas 1991, 398)

One can argue that in using this concept to analyze Chinese society, one faces the same dilemma as in using other Western-originated concepts. Yet as William Rowe argues, its applicability is derived from the fact that "the Chinese political lexicon did contain a term, *gong*, with meanings very similar to those of its Western counterpart *public*, with similar ambiguities, and subjected to similar contestations within the community of discourse" (Rowe 1993, 142). In addition, the enormous attention Chinese society has given to the drug issue makes it one of a few "public spheres" that provide room for broad participation of its members. As the following chapters will demonstrate, the drug issue has been a topic not only of general interest but also always subject to emotionally charged national debate. Drug suppression has been an issue where public opinion is able to exercise a great deal of influence.

STRUCTURE OF THE BOOK

Chapter 2 gives a brief history of opium suppression from the Opium Wars to the mid-1920s, with a focus on the anti-opium campaign of 1906–1911. The rise of modern Chinese nationalism helped in the making of a dominant anti-drug discourse nationwide. The success of the campaign can be explained by putting it in the reform context of the late Qing dynasty, which has been largely neglected by historians. Unlike other reform initiatives that often met strong resistance, because of the near consensus on the harm of opium, the anti-opium campaign witnessed not only the mobilization of the state but also of Chinese society, as demonstrated in the active role played by various Anti-Opium Societies.

Chapter 3 deals with the activities of the NAOA from 1924 to 1927. This case study shows that, along with the rise of the Chinese bourgeoisie and nationalism, the formation of the NAOA was a mobilization by an emergent Chinese bourgeoisie and its representative Shanghai elite to voice their concerns about the opium issue to both national and international audiences. Helped by the existing, hegemonic, anti-opium discourse, and drawing on their strong social and financial resources, as well as their mastery of modern mobilization skills, the NAOA quickly became the leader of the anti-opium movement in China's private sector.

Chapter 4 analyzes the relationship between the NAOA and the Nationalist government. The relationship involved confrontations as well as cooperation and negotiations, as the state and the NAOA adopted different strategies under different circumstances. The chapter shows how the war of public opinion waged by the NAOA against the opium monopoly put the NAOA in a position to influence the opium policies of Nanjing. This case study demonstrates how the hegemonic discourses on opium provided a special public sphere for private organizations to negotiate power with the state, even with an authoritarian one like the Jiang Jieshi (Chiang Kai-shek) regime.

Chapter 5 focuses on the opium policies of Jiang Jieshi and the Six-Year

Opium Suppression Plan. By putting the campaign in the context of the New Life Movement, this chapter demonstrates how the Six-Year Opium Suppression Plan was an integral part of Jiang's attempt to consolidate his personal power and to make him the spiritual leader of China. In the name of opium suppression, Jiang often used opium to fight local militarists. Though opium suppression became an effective way to bring local militarists under the control of the central government, Jiang also met strong resistance from them.

Chapter 6 reconstructs a brief history of the anti-drug crusade conducted by the Communists in 1949–1952, a campaign that had been kept invisible until recently. The chapter emphasizes the ways in which the campaign was carried out—including mass urban mobilization, oral propaganda, and public trials—to show how it was a deliberate effort by the Communists to consolidate their newly gained power. The campaign's effectiveness derived from the use of an existing anti-drug discourse and the formation of a comprehensive social control system, which no previous regime had ever enjoyed.

Chapter 7 discusses the changing discourse on drugs in contemporary China. The continuities and discontinuities of anti-drug rhetoric point to the identity crisis the authorities faced after the comeback of drugs in post-Mao China, and how the authorities tried to solve the problem by offering a new anti-drug discourse. The contemporary anti-drug discourse is constructed through demonizing drug offenders, and internationalizing or ethnicizing the drug issue.

Chapter 8 illustrates how the current campaign is being used by the government to relegitimize its use of state violence, and to strengthen social control in the historical context after 1989. It also examines how central and local authorities define and negotiate their roles in relation to each other in the campaign. Based on ethnological research, this chapter highlights several factors that contribute to the losing battle fought by the authorities in the war on drugs.

Chapter 9 explores how the Communists conducted anti-drug campaigns in Yi and Tibetan communities in southwest China in the 1950s, and a 1992 drug crackdown in a Hui community in Yunnan. The chapter focuses on how the Communists solved the drug problem by treating it as an integrated part of a larger strategy of gaining control of these communities. By comparing these campaigns with those conducted in the Han areas, and by comparing the campaigns in the 1950s with the crackdown in 1992, the chapter shows how the authorities adopted flexible and different policies in dealing with drugs in minority communities, and what has changed since the 1950s.

Chapter 10 presents conclusions of this study.

2

✛

Nationalism, Reform, and Anti-Opium Mobilization in Late Qing

From 1900 to the mid-1920s, China witnessed dramatic ups and downs in its efforts to control opium. There were two turning points during this period. One was the signing of the Ten-Year Opium Suppression Agreement between China and Britain in 1908; the other was the establishment of the Republic in 1912. Though a nationwide opium prohibition campaign began in 1906 and was supposed to last until 1917, the fall of the Qing dynasty in 1911 disrupted its momentum. But that short period between 1906 and 1911 marked the only time that China was able to make convincing progress in opium suppression since the First Opium War in 1840.

OPIUM AND OPIUM CONTROL PRIOR TO THE OPIUM WARS

The history of opium planting can be traced back further than a thousand years, but the massive consumption of opium as an addictive drug is a relatively new phenomenon, dating from the early nineteenth century. It is said that the opium poppy was introduced into China as early as the Tang dynasty (618–907 A.D.) by Arabian merchants. At first it was treated as a beautiful flowering plant, then as a kind of herbal medicine. It was not until the mid-fifteenth century, during the Ming dynasty (1368–1644 A.D.), that the name opium (*yapian*) and its methods of production were recorded. Then starting from 1589, opium was listed as an

*Blooming flowers of
the opium poppy*

*Fruits of the opium poppy, from
which raw opium is extracted*

item subject to tariffs imposed by the Ming dynasty's customs; although the tariff was raised several times in the following 130 years, the amount imported, principally through the Portuguese, increased steadily from negligible quantity to 200 chests in 1729 (Jiang and Zhu 1996, 5).

The popularity of opium in China had something to do with its unique consumption method by the Chinese. Unlike Europeans, who drank opium syrup or chewed it, the Chinese smoked opium mixed with tobacco. The method of smoking opium was first seen among Chinese in Jakarta, Batavia, and Java in the seventeenth century, and might have been introduced into Taiwan by the Dutch during their occupation in the early seventeenth century (Spence 1975, 147–49). Opium smoking gradually spread to China's southeast coastal area at the beginning of the eighteenth century, and in the 1760s, the Chinese started to smoke pure opium. The increased number of opium smokers, and the emergence of opium dens, prompted the Qing dynasty to take the opium issue seriously.

The emperors of the Qing dynasty saw opium's biggest threat as endangering the moral order of the "celestial dynasty." The opium suppression edict of 1729 by the Emperor Yongzheng (1723–1735) was the first of its kind to be issued during the Qing dynasty, signaling the start of China's opium-control efforts and the formation of an official anti-opium discourse. The edict was very simple. It targeted trafficking and operating opium dens as two main offenses. The traffickers were to be punished in the same way as those involved in transporting prohibited goods; the opium den operators, however, were treated as promoting heresy and were subject to capital punishment for their role in seducing "youngsters of good family" (Yu Ende 1934, 16).

Despite opium suppression edicts, the amount of opium imported increased constantly, from an average of 200 chests a year in 1729, to 1,000 chests in 1767, and to 1,813 chests in 1798—supplies to feed the increase in the number of smokers. The Qing Court banned the import of foreign opium in 1780, except for medicinal use, but the criteria for judging whether the imported opium was to be used for "medicinal purpose" was vague, and this provision became a loophole for opium smuggling. In 1796, the Qing Court ordered all opium importing haulted and removed the opium tax from its customs levies. This order was reiterated in 1800, and domestic poppy planting was also outlawed. From then on, all opium entering China was illegal (Jiang and Zhu 1996, 11–12).

Emperor Jiaqing (1796–1820) and Emperor Daoguang (1821–1850) both faced grave opium situations. In his 1813 opium suppression edict, Emperor Jiaqing characterized opium as "poisoning and confusing people's minds," and Emperor Daoguang in 1822 criticized its damage to "custom" and the "popular morale" of China. As opium smoking spread rapidly, anti-opium discourse began to touch on more concrete consequences of opium addiction than on morality concerns, such as opium's adverse effects to individual body and health. Emperor Jiaqing pointed out that opium also "deprives people of their livelihood, just like the effects of drinking poison wine" (Yu Ende 1934, 26). Emperor Daoguang issued another edict in 1830, declaring that opium would "waste a person's fortune and damage his health" (Yu Ende 1934, 47).

Both Jiaqing and Daoguang alleged that the government's customs houses were partially responsible for the spread of opium in not reporting opium trafficking for the purpose of tax collection. Daoguang even ordered a clandestine investigation of customs houses in Guangdong province. To him, protecting "custom" and "popular morale" was more important than anything else, including tax revenue (Yu Ende 1934, 39–40). But foreign opium merchants, local Chinese smugglers, and corrupt Qing officials saw making profits and ensuring bribery as priorities. Working together, a vast opium smuggling and distribution network was established gradually, resulting in the dramatic increase of illicit opium and the numbers of smokers in the reign of Emperor Daoguang. Opium smoking was common not only in the coastal areas but also in interior China; opium smokers were not only those ignorant youth and hooligans but also Qing officials and Manchu bannermen. The deterioration of opium suppression is reflected in Table 2.1.

Emperor Daoguang, who commenced his reign in 1821, worked diligently to solve the opium problem. Yet from 1820 to 1839, the amount of illicit opium entering China grew almost tenfold. This massive increase led to the outflow of a large quantity of silver, which posed a great threat to the financial stability of the Qing dynasty. Silver had been used as standard currency in China, and the exchange rate between silver and copper had been kept steady at one silver *tael* for 1,000 copper coins. China had enjoyed a large amount of surplus in its foreign trade before the nineteenth century, and the outflow of silver was never an issue. But the massive opium import trade changed the balance rapidly. For example, in 1817, the amount of opium imported cost 610,000 *taels*, or 4.1 percent of the total amount of import in Guangzhou. By 1825, the value was up to 9,782,000 *taels*, or 42 percent of total imports. From 1830 to 1834, the average annual amount of opium imported reached 13,953,000 *taels*, or 52 percent of all

Table 2.1. Foreign Opium Entering China, 1819–1839

Year	Chests	Year	Chests
1819–1820	4,186	1829–1830	16,257
1820–1821	4,244	1830–1831	19,956
1821–1822	5,959	1831–1832	16,650
1822–1823	7,773	1832–1833	21,985
1823–1824	9,035	1833–1834	20,486
1824–1825	12,434	1834–1835	21,885
1825–1826	9,373	1835–1836	30,202
1826–1827	12,231	1836–1837	34,776
1827–1828	11,154	1837–1838	34,373
1828–1829	13,868	1838–1839	40,200

Source: Jiang and Zhu 1996, 25.

imports (Zhu, Jiang, and Zhang 1995, 94–95). The outflow of silver caused its value to rise against copper coins, which in turn increased the tax burden of subjects of the dynasty, who had to pay their taxes in silver. Huang Juzi, a high-ranking official and an anti-opium advocate, pointed out the magnitude of the crisis in his petition to the Emperor in 1838:

> The value of silver has been increasing recently, with one tael exchanging for more than 1,600 copper coins. Since opium entered China, before the third year of Daoguang [1823], the annual outflow of silver was several million taels—from the third to the eleventh year, the annual outflow of silver was between 17 and 18 million taels. From the eleventh to the fourteenth year, the number was more than 20 million taels. From the fourteenth year to today, the number has increased to more than 30 million taels, not including numerous ports in Fujian, Jiangsu, Zhejiang, Shandong, and Tianjin, which, if added up, could reach tens of millions. We are using China's valuable financial resources to fill insatiable foreign greed by buying opium, which not only does great harm to the individual but also threatens to sicken the country. (Huang Juzi 1838, 463)[5]

After 1830, opium's damage to the Qing dynasty became more visible and concrete. In 1832, the Court was shocked to learn that opium addiction among troops sent to suppress the Yao uprising in northeast Guangdong province caused many desertions, and the angry Emperor Daoguang banished the governor-general of Guangdong and Guangxi to the far northwest of China (Yu Ende 1934, 49). The Qing Court faced a dilemma. On the one side, the Court had tightened laws on opium and forbidden the trafficking, as well as the planting and smoking of opium. On the other side, in spite of these measures, the problem of opium had only worsened and led, among other things, to an increased outflow of silver. It was in this context that a debate on opium policy, especially on how to curb the outflow of silver, broke out among the ruling elite.

In June 1836, Xu Naiji, a high-ranking official in Beijing, suggested relaxing opium regulations and applying more flexibility when dealing with the opium issue. His main purpose was to find ways to stop the silver outflow, a concern shared by most participants of the debate. Among his suggestions was to restore opium as a legal commodity subject to customs tariff, as it was before 1796. But once opium entered customs, it could only be traded on a barter basis. Believing it would be an effective way to deprive profits to foreign opium merchants, Xu also suggested that the Court should allow domestic opium planting so as eventually to drive out imported opium. As for opium smoking, Xu thought the Court should prohibit officials, scholars, and soldiers from smoking opium but relax the limits for the rest of the population. Since the opium smokers were those of no ability and will, he opined, opium addicts would not pose a great threat to the "celestial dynasty." Rather, the constant draining of China's financial resources should be the first priority of opium policy (Yu Ende 1934, 58–59).

It seemed that Emperor Daoguang was touched by Xu's arguments for relaxing prohibition, but not convinced. He sent Xu's suggestion to local officials in Guangdong for review, including the new governor-general of Guangdong and Guangxi, the governor of Guangdong, and the head of Guangzhou customs. Since they were persons dealing with opium issues on an everyday basis, the Emperor obviously wanted to hear their opinions. Their response came two months later in favor of Xu, claiming that the alternative opium policy would "benefit both the country and people's livelihood." They even drafted nine regulations to implement Xu's propositions. But Xu's opinions were rebutted by several high-ranking officials in Beijing, who in the end held sway. By November, the first phase of the debate on opium policy was over (Jiang and Zhu 1996, 56–61).

The debate was reopened by Huang Juzi, a staunch prohibitionist, in June 1838. Frustrated by the failure of opium suppression, Huang proposed draconian laws against opium smokers. He asked the Court to give a one-year grace period to all opium addicts to rid themselves of the habit, after which, anyone found smoking opium would be subject to the death penalty. Once again Emperor Daoguang sent Huang's petition to provincial governors for review. The majority of the provincial governors opposed it, viewing it as unenforceable and as unlikely to solve the problem, which they saw as suppressing the supply end, not the consumption end (Yu Ende 1934, 62–63). Among ruling elites who supported Huang and advocated a strict suppression of the illegal opium trade, Lin Zexu made an alarming petition to the Emperor: "If the situation doesn't improve, it will not be long before the whole country will lack the manpower and financial resources to defend itself" (Lin Zexu 1839, 142). His argument was backed by the fact that opium smoking had spread to a wide array of social strata and that a financial crisis due to the illegal opium trade had existed for quite a while. Lin's and Huang's concerns focused on the harm opium brought to the country and the dynasty, on the problem of enlisting healthy army recruits, as well as on maintaining funds for the adequate support of the army.

These points prompted Emperor Daoguang's decision to adopt a decisive anti-opium policy in 1838, which meant the victory of Huang Juzi and the other hardliners. Xu Naiji was reduced to a lower rank and ordered to retire, and even several imperial clan members were deprived their ranks of nobility because of their habits. At the end of 1838, Lin Zexu was sent to Guangdong as imperial commissioner supervising the suppression of opium, and local officials were under pressure to enforce opium suppression vigorously. By the time Lin arrived in Guangdong on March 10, 1839, most Chinese smugglers had been stopped and the smuggling boats dismantled. Suppression activities intensified after Lin's arrival. On March 18, Lin issued a letter to all foreigners in Guangzhou and ordered that all opium be handed over to Qing authorities (Jiang and Zhu 1996, 63–69).

In his famous memorial to Queen Victoria of 1839, Lin asked, "Where is your conscience? I have heard that the smoking of opium is very strictly forbidden by

Opium smokers in late Qing dynasty

Opium is often related to other social vices—an addict smokes opium while patronizing prostitutes

your country; this is because the harm caused by opium is clearly understood. Since it is not permitted to do harm to your own country, then even less should you let it be passed on to the harm of other countries—how much less to China" (Lodwick 1996, 27). Within two months of Lin's arrival in Guangdong, a total of 21,306 chests of foreign opium had been confiscated. Lin ordered the opium to be destroyed in the small town of Humen from June 3 to June 25, the event that became a catalyst of the First Opium War between Britain and China. China was defeated by British gunboats, and the Nanjing Treaty was signed in 1842. Under the terms of the Treaty, China was forced to cede Hong Kong to the British and to open five port cities to foreign trade, signaling the beginning of modern Chinese history.

Whether the power struggle of inner-circle political factions or the misjudgment of Lin Zexu caused the Qing to adopt a hard-line policy, it would be naive to assume they directly caused the Opium War and its subsequent consequences to China.[6] Western powers were determined to open China as a big commercial market for their industrial products, so sooner or later China was destined to fall prey, be the commodity opium, cotton, or sugar. Though defeated in the First Opium War, the Chinese still insisted on keeping the opium trade illegal, despite the British pressure to legalize it. It was not until the Second Opium War, at the Shanghai Tariff Conference between China and Britain in 1858, that opium was legalized at thirty taels per *picul*. The long-held wish of the British to legalize the opium trade was finally realized (Hsu 1995, 211–12).

NATIONALISM AND THE RISE OF ANTI-OPIUM DISCOURSE AT THE TURN OF THE CENTURY

From the First Opium War to the end of the nineteenth century, the Qing dynasty suffered a series of domestic upheavals and foreign defeats. The Taiping Rebellion of 1851–1864 almost overthrew the Manchu rule. The much weakened Qing dynasty was defeated again in the Second Opium War (the Arrow War) of 1858–1860, which led to the signing of the Tianjin Treaty and legalization of the opium trade. From the 1860s to 1890s, China initiated the Self-Strengthening Movement, hoping to deal with the crisis. These attempts at industrialization and military modernization were doomed by China's defeat at the hands of the Japanese in 1894. The reformers' hope of rejuvenating China vanished again along with the aborted "Hundred-Day" Reform in 1898. In 1900, the Boxer Rebellion and the subsequent Western military invasion gave another devastating blow to the Qing dynasty. Coincidentally, the final decades of the nineteenth century also saw opium consumption become a problem of alarming, even epidemic, proportions in China.

After 1842, though opium continued to be condemned, the outcome of the First Opium War ended any effective opium suppression by the Qing dynasty.

This failure did not spare the attention of the rebels against the dynasty. Hong Xiuquan, the leader of the Taiping Rebellion (1851–1864), not only blamed the "devil foreigners" but also the Manchus for poisoning the body and soul of the Chinese nation. Hong made opium suppression one of the central features of his social reform program and backed his word by executing opium smokers publicly. In 1853, Hong also proclaimed his position against opium trade with the British. But like the dilemma the Qing dynasty had faced before, there was a gap between anti-opium regulation and its enforcement in practice. It was evident that, except for the early period of the Taiping Rebellion, opium suppression was not strictly enforced (Wang Jinxiang 1996, 33–35; Howard 1997).

The mounting pressure to extract extra revenue to suppress the Taiping Rebellion finally induced the Court to levy taxes on opium. The practice started in 1856 in Shanghai by the governor-general of Jiangsu and Jiangxi, and was followed by the governor-general of Fujian and Zhejiang in 1857, before the legalization of the foreign opium was finalized in 1858. Unable to meet the financial needs of local officials, Emperor Xianfeng (1851–1861), who succeeded Emperor Daoguang in 1851, had to give tacit consent to their practices, and in 1859, approved taxes on native Yunnan opium to subsidize the suppression of the Muslim uprising. Taxation on native opium of other provinces followed, which symbolized the de facto legalization of domestic opium planting, though theoretically the Court still forbade it until the mid-1880s (Jiang and Zhu 1996, 83–88).

Rising to prominence for their role in suppressing the Taiping Rebellion, Li Hongzhang and Zuo Zongtang were arguably the two most influential officials in the Court in the 1870s and the 1880s. Their handling of the opium issue represented the changing attitudes adopted by the Qing officials, who often put fiscal concern over moral concern, thus generally supporting the legalization of opium. In 1874, Li advocated relaxing the prohibition of domestic opium planting and using native opium to drive pricier foreign opium out of the Chinese market. In 1881, Zuo proposed increasing taxes on both foreign and domestic opium, hoping to achieve opium suppression through taxation. Both Li and Zuo were advocates of the Self-Strengthening Movement. Opium revenues were used to pay for capital defense expenses; for the Beijing police; for new navy gunboats; for making machinery, guns, cartridges, and percussion caps; for soldier's wages and sundries; and to pay off foreign loans for new arms (Spence 1975, 170–71).

In addition to bringing in much-needed revenues, Li and Zuo both hoped the high taxation on opium would eventually curb both foreign opium import and domestic consumption. As Li Hongzhang wrote to a British anti-opium advocate in 1881, the "single aim of my Government in taxing opium will be in the future — as it has always been in the past, to repress the traffic — never the desire to gain revenue from such a source" (Lodwick 1996, 28). Though domestic opium production only started in the early 1800s, Li Hongzhang's wish to promote it as a way to suppress the foreign opium was rapidly materialized. By the 1870s, the output of domestic opium in southwest China had far surpassed imported foreign opium, which began to decline in the 1880s. Yet behind Li's ostensible success was a disaster: the unchecked and unprecedented increase in the level of opium production and consumption all over the country.

Though there were no modern statistics in the late Qing, and all estimates on numbers of Chinese opium output and smokers are subject to dispute, the estimates are startling. In 1896, Robert Hart, the inspector-general of customs, estimated the output of opium in Yunnan, Guizhou, and Sichuan at 80,000, 40,000, and 120,000 *piculs*, respectively, five times as much as was imported that year (Jiang and Zhu 1996, 113–15). China's total opium output was even harder to estimate. Hart put it at 334,000 *piculs* in 1896, and the estimates of 1906 ranged from 146,000 *piculs* by the Qing Court, to 325,000 *piculs* by British Minister John Jordan, to 584,400 *piculs* by the International Opium Commission (Jiang and Zhu 1996, 129). Since domestic opium was relatively affordable, many people, even poor peasants, became smokers. One widely cited estimate of the number of opium addicts in 1890 was about 15 million, or about 3 percent of the total population (Spence 1975, 154). At the same time, the public attitude toward opium smoking was ambiguous. According to the report of the International Opium Commission, before the anti-opium campaign of 1906–1911, it was customary to offer guests opium while discussing business in opium dens in Zhejiang province. And in Fuzhou, opium smoking was a fashionable pastime—a rakish habit that youth felt urged to acquire (International Opium Commission 1909, vol. 2, 75; Wong 1997). Shanghai leisure newspapers, though acknowledging the danger of becoming addicted, often praised opium smoking in a refined luxury hall as one of the highest pleasures that one could enjoy (Des Forges 1997).

Although anti-opium rhetoric never stopped from the 1860s to the 1890s, to Qing officials at various levels, who were constantly facing a fiscal squeeze, the anti-opium voice often fell on deaf ears. The tide started to change in the 1890s. The turning point was China's defeat in the Sino-Japanese War of 1894 and the subsequent signing of the Treaty of Shimonoseki, in which China was asked to cede Taiwan and to pay an indemnity of 200 million taels. This event greatly shook up the remaining confidence of the Chinese literati and gentry class, for this time China was defeated not by Western powers but by Japan, which had been seen as a modest imitator of Chinese civilization. As Song Jiaoren (later the head of the Nationalist Party in the early Republic) recalled in 1911: "The Sino-Japanese War was surely the turning point of our country. Before the war, though China repeatedly had conflicts with foreigners, her wounds were not fatal and, nobody dared to insult her openly. Since the defeat of this war, China was forced to secede one province, to pay a 200 million war indemnity. China's prestige was all of a sudden diminished, making the waiting-for-their-turn powers all come after her in threatening gestures. China was almost no longer China" (Liu Jialin 1995, 137).

Burgeoning Chinese nationalism surged after 1895 in the face of a crisis threatening China's very survival. As the Self-Strengthening Movement failed to ward off the Japanese, more and more Chinese came to realize that China needed a broad range of political, economic, military, and social transformations in order to survive. In this context, opium was singled out as a social evil significantly contributing to China's degeneration, weakness, and humiliation. Opium critics included high-ranking government officials, famous scholars, as well as reform advocates. Zhang Zhidong, a political adversary of Li Hongzhang and later Li's successor in the Court, had been critical of the government's opium policy. In 1898, in his influential book *Learn,* he devoted a chapter to denouncing opium as a main cause of the miserable quality of life faced by ordinary people. Zheng Guanying, a famous reform advocate, in a letter to a member of the Shanghai Opium Prohibition Association in 1894, pointed out that opium eradication, along with the abandonment of the classic eight-legged essay and foot binding, could serve as the basis for China's self-strengthening efforts and thus ward off foreign insults and humiliation (Zheng Guanying 1988, 1178). In addition to publishing anti-opium articles, anti-opium advocates also set up Anti-Opium Societies in various places in and outside China.

Nationalism attached a collective emotional charge to the emerging anti-opium discourse, thus enabling its acceptance by most members of the Chinese nation. The rise of anti-opium rhetoric, along with the appeal of reform and the formation of Chinese nationalistic consciousness, also contributed greatly to the spread of newspapers in China during the same period. Though modern newspapers were first published by foreigners in China in the 1810s, it was not until the 1850s that Chinese-published newspapers appeared in Hong Kong, and not until the 1870s on the mainland. According to one statistic, from 1840 to 1890, there were about 170 foreigner-published newspapers in both Chinese and foreign languages, for almost 95 percent of the total number of newspapers in China (Fang Hanqi 1981, 18). But after the Sino-Japanese War, from 1895 to 1898, there appeared about 120 new newspapers in Chinese, of which 80 percent were published by the Chinese themselves. The reformists alone put out about thirty newspapers to advocate their cause (Liu Jialin 1995, 137). During the "Hundred Day" Reform of 1898, Emperor Guangxu (1875–1908) issued an edict allowing officials and ordinary people to publish newspapers, which increased the total number of newspapers in China to three times as many as the number in 1895 (Fang Hanqi 1981, 86–87).

It was this rapid development of newspapers, often pro-reform, that provided a context in which both nationalism and anti-opium rhetoric placed the opium issue in the public domain. For example, between March 4 and 9, 1895, *Zhibao,* a newspaper based in Tianjin, published "On National Strength" by Yan Fu, a famous reformist who first introduced to China the Darwinian idea of the survival of the fittest. In the article, Yan argued that abolition of opium, foot-binding, and traditional imperial examinations, and the adoption of a modern education system and constitutional monarchy were the ways to regain China's strength (Fang Hanqi 1981, 99–100). The issue of opium was listed as a fundamental problem to be solved along with China's political and educational systems. *Zhibao* also published excerpts from Zhang Zhidong's book *Learn*, thereby spreading out its anti-opium opinion.

By the last days of the Qing dynasty, the process of constituting an anti-opium discourse, which would last into post-Qing China, had basically been completed. The main components of the discourse focused on the damage opium could do at three different levels: the individual, the state, and the Chinese nation. At the individual level, emphasis was placed on addiction's negative consequences to personal health, fortune, career, and family. At the next level, opium's damage extended to the strength of the country, with claims that opium posed a threat of depriving the state of both financial and manpower resources. At the third level, the vitality of the Chinese race or nation was the issue, reflecting the anxiety of the Chinese people about their physical existence at the turn of the century. This discourse confirmed that opium caused the degeneration of individual physical health, and the cultural, social, and economic health of the whole nation. These three core components were inherited by later anti-opium crusaders and have been used as a common and popular form of anti-opium propaganda throughout modern China.

Any discussion of the spread of anti-opium rhetoric in China would be incomplete without mentioning the role played by foreign missionaries, especially Protestants. The Protestant missionaries started their activities in 1807, around the same time that opium trade became a serious issue in China. The position of the earliest missionaries on opium was ambiguous. On the one hand, many of them arrived at China on opium clippers and were supported by the East Indian Company and big opium traders. Some of them were directly involved in helping the British army in the First Opium War (Gu 1981, 22–31, 47–53). On the other hand, missionaries found out that, as one pointed out in 1907, "the Gospel had suffered immeasurably at the hands of opium. Opium was brought into China many years ago, hundreds perhaps—but the ordinary Chinese regarded it as having been brought in by foreigners about the time of the introduction of Protestant Christianity; so that in the minds of many Chinese all over the Empire, opium and the Christian religion are associated together. 'Away with your opium and your missionaries' had been the cry" (Centenary Conference Committee, 1907, 64). Or, as the Rev. J. Hudson Taylor, founder of the China Inland Mission, put it in 1888, "I am profoundly convinced that the opium traffic is doing more evil in China in a week than Missions are doing good in a year" (Lodwick 1996, 50). From both a moral point of view and from the concern of converting Chinese, the vast majority of missionaries in China were outspoken opponents against opium and opium trade in China.

The missionaries' main weapon was to publicize the opium evil through their numerous publications to Chinese audiences as well as to audiences in their home countries. The earliest anti-opium publication in Chinese by the missions encountered during research for this study was a pamphlet titled *Six Commandments of*

Opium, dating back to 1848, which was published in Ningbo, a coastal city in Zhejiang province. According to the six commandments, smoking opium was:

1. breaking the law
2. not being filial
3. breaking up the family
4. harming individual health
5. damaging custom
6. imprisoning the soul.

This rhetoric generally corresponded to the Chinese anti-opium discourse at that time, except the Chinese rhetoric lacked the religious implication of the last commandment. Based on their firsthand encounters with Chinese opium addicts, missionaries' narratives exposed to audiences of their home countries the harmfulness of the drug to the human body and to morality, thus rebutting the argument by the opium trade supporters that opium was no more harmful than alcoholism to the Westerners (Lodwick 1996, 25).[7]

The missionaries' anti-opium propaganda and activities intensified after 1890, manifested in the fact that the *Chinese Recorder*, the main publication of Protestant missionaries in China, devoted more attention to the opium issue. According to Kathleen Lodwick, "Opium was a subject much discussed in the *Chinese Recorder* in the last years of the nineteenth century. Editorially, the periodical took a strong stand against the use of opium" under the two editors in charge from 1890 to 1907 (Lodwick 1996, 32). At various missionary conferences, the opium issue was raised and suppression methods were discussed. At the 1890 Shanghai missionary conference, an agreement was reached to set up the Permanent Committee for the Promotion of Anti-Opium Societies. The Anti-Opium League, a nationwide missionary anti-opium organization, was first proposed by missionaries in Suzhou in 1896, and the first meeting was held in Shanghai the next year. The League's first action was to conduct a survey of views of missionary doctors on the effects of opium use by the Chinese. According to Dr. William Park, organizer of the survey, questions were sent to every foreign doctor in China. In response to the first question asked—What have you observed to be the effects of opium, moral, physical, and social, on its consumers?—the answers were overwhelmingly assertive of the adverse effect opium had on its users, represented by one doctor's answer as "moral—thoroughly demoralizing, physical—most injurious, social—bad every way" (Park 1899, 1). The results of the survey were published in both Chinese and English in a pamphlet in 1899 under the title *Opinions of Over 100 Physicians on the Use of Opium in China*, and every missionary was given a free copy. Since the survey was conducted among professionally trained missionary doctors who had firsthand experience, the findings of the pamphlet had an authority that greatly publicized the harmful effects of opium to both Chinese and Westerners.

During 1905 and 1906, several events pushed the emotional charge of nationalism and opium suppression to a new peak. The first was Japan's spectacular victory during the Russo-Japanese War, which made the Chinese reformists believe China could be on equal footing with the Western powers through adopting constitutional monarchy. The rise of nationalism also provoked a nationwide campaign to boycott American goods in protest of America's discriminatory immigration regulations against the Chinese, especially Chinese laborers. This movement was led by newly established Chambers of Commerce in big cities, especially the Shanghai General Chamber of Commerce. When the Americans tried to renew the existing discriminatory regulations with China in 1905, Shanghai capitalists used newspapers and publicly circulated telegraphs to appeal the Qing Court to ask America to revise the regulations, proclaiming that it was a matter of protecting national rights and economic interests (Xu and Qian 1991, 67–68). This movement signaled the rise of the Chinese bourgeoisie and its increasing role in mobilizing social forces under the rubric of nationalism.

In the same year, the publication of the Report of United States Philippine Commission on Opium also stirred strong Chinese responses. The Report claimed that "there seems to be in China neither a public opinion which controls nor a national life which welds and consolidates a people. There is no Chinese nation, there is merely a Chinese race." It went on to accuse the Chinese government of not making "any earnest effort to diminish the use of opium." The report was translated into Chinese and was widely circulated in China, further fueling the nationalism at the time (Lodwick 1996, 113–15). Amid increasing pressure, the Qing Court received encouraging news that Tang Shaoyi, a senior Chinese diplomat, was informed while he was in India in 1905 that Britain might agree to stop its China opium trade. Tang reported the information to Empress Dowager Cixi in September the same year (Reins 1991, 107–108).

A change in British domestic politics also helped the Qing government. In 1906, the Liberal Party, many members of which opposed the government's involvement in the opium trade, won an overwhelming majority in the House of Commons; a resolution denouncing the opium trade was finally passed on May 30. It proclaimed "that this House reaffirms its conviction that the Indo-Chinese opium trade is morally indefensible, and requests His Majesty's Government to take such steps as may be necessary for bring it to a speedy close" (Cameron 1931, 141). In response to the anti-opium momentum in England, missionaries intensified their efforts to promote opium suppression in China. In May, Rev. Hampden Du Bose, the President of the Anti-Opium League who was based in Suzhou, raised the opium suppression issue to the governor-general of Jiangsu and Jiangxi and secured a promise to transfer the missionary's anti-opium petition to the Qing Court. Du Bose sent out the petition letter to missionaries all over China and within three months had 1,333 signatures. On August 19, Du Bose presented the signed petition letter to the governor-general, who forwarded it to the Court (Jiang and Zhu 1996, 181). The cumulative effects of the above several events finally prompted the Qing Court to launch a nationwide campaign to eradicate opium.

REFORM, DIPLOMACY, AND POLICY ENFORCEMENT: THE ANTI-OPIUM CAMPAIGN OF 1906–1911

Although the emphasis here is on the importance of Chinese nationalism in the making of anti-opium discourse in the last Qing years and in pushing the Chinese government to conduct an anti-opium campaign, it is also important to bear in mind that the rising nationalism was a double-edged sword to the Qing rulers. They had to walk a fine line between using nationalism to promote reforms and, at the same time, preventing the Manchus from becoming the target of the nationalism. It is time here to examine further the different motivations behind the actions taken by both the Qing Court and the Chinese society. Though nationalism was undoubtedly a primary mobilizing force for public participation in the campaign, to the Qing Court, opium suppression was a part of the reform movement initiated after the Boxer Rebellion—the last attempt to transform China into a modern nation-state while preserving Manchu's rule. This reform was broad and far-reaching: old bureaucracies were streamlined, and Ministries of Commerce, Police, Foreign Affairs, and Education were established; constitutional monarchy was set to be experienced; a modern army was planned; the civil service examination and "eight-legged essay" were abolished; students were sent to study abroad; foot-binding of women was denounced; and Chambers of Commerce were organized.

The opium suppression campaign was one of the last major reform programs initiated, but it has been acknowledged as "the most successful of all the Manchu reforms" (Cameron 1931, 136). Although generally speaking the whole reform was too little and too late to save the Qing Court from falling in the revolution of 1911, it is useful to focus on why opium suppression was carried out in such an effective way in the last days of a dying dynasty. The answer may be revealed in the fact that the opium suppression campaign witnessed a mass mobilization by both the government and the society to achieve a common aim. This common aim was forged through the rising of Chinese nationalism, which provided a new dimension to anti-opium discourse, as well as through the general reform efforts of the government, which struggled to convert the Qing dynasty into a modern state. Unlike other reform initiatives, which tended to provoke resistance because of conflicting interests, opium suppression provided a public domain in which the majority of Chinese society was on common ground, thereby provoking minimal resistance. The mobilization campaign was a case of successful synergy between government and society.

On September 20, 1906, the Qing Court issued an edict of opium suppression, which formally inaugurated the campaign. The decree pointed out that the legal-

ization of opium in the past several decades had brought harmful consequences
to individuals, families, and the country as a whole, and expressed the intent of
the Court to use opium suppression as a way to regenerate China. It declared that
within a period of ten years, opium, whether foreign or native, was to be entirely
abolished. Following the edict, specific measures were stipulated in the *Regulations of Opium Suppression* by the Superintendency of Political Affairs. The regulations had ten articles, which adopted the principle of gradual elimination and
focused on suppressing opium supply and consumption. To curb opium supply,
it demanded that local officials conduct surveys on existing poppy planting
acreage, and then issue licenses to poppy planters based on survey data. The
planters had to decrease their planting acreage by one-ninth every year until there
was a complete stop within nine years. The issue of foreign opium importation
was to be solved through negotiations with the British government, with the aim
of eliminating foreign opium. As for opium consumption, measures taken
included shutting down all opium dens within six months, registering addicts,
issuing purchasing licenses, asking addicts under sixty years old to rehabilitate
within a limited time period, and demanding strict compliance from officials, students, and soldiers to quit opium smoking.

During 1907, the Qing Court issued a number of other decrees pressuring government officials to carry on the campaign. Signs of general progress were
recorded, especially in Zhili and Yunnan, which were under the governance of
Yuan Shikai and Xi Liang (Cameron 1931, 143–44; Reins 1991, 128–29). In
1908, the signing of the Anglo-Chinese Ten-Year Opium Suppression Agreement
gave the campaign momentum. The agreement, the details of which will be taken
up later, promised to reduce Indian opium exports to China by one-tenth annually for a period of ten years—provided the Chinese reduced domestic production correspondingly. Derived from a deep-rooted suspicion that doubted the real
resolve of the Chinese to suppress opium, and, from a desire to safeguard their
interests, the British added an article that made the first three years a "trial
period," starting in 1908. Having been long bothered by the treaty obligations to
allow opium imports, the Qing Court did not want to miss this opportunity to
solve the opium problem. The opium issue became an important symbol of
nationalism and reform. This mentality was so strong that it was even echoed in
the edict proclaiming the reaching of the agreement with the British on March
22, 1908:

> Since the spread of the opium epidemic, its poisonous effects have reached an
> extreme degree. Once a person becomes an addict, he will squander his fortune,
> shorten his life, become sluggish, and abandon his profession. . . . The epidemic is
> weakening the race and spirit of our divine land of a long glorious history, making
> our self-strengthening efforts a hopeless wish. . . . If we are unable to get rid of this
> lingering illness, there will be no basis on which this country can exist. . . . It is a
> matter that affects the national strength and the people's longevity. It is hereby com-

manded that all officials shall carry out opium suppression with all their efforts. No matter how difficult it is, the task has to be done within the time limit. Any postponement will be dealt with severe punishment. (Yu Ende 1934, 128)

The Qing dynasty did conduct an effective opium suppression campaign thereafter. According to Cameron, who sketched out opium suppression in each province from 1907 to 1909, enormous progress was made in many places around China. In 1909, opium smoking had been reduced by about one-third in Manchuria and had almost disappeared in Beijing. Shanxi province closed all of its opium shops and wholesale establishments in 1909, and Shandong reported a reduction of 50 to 75 percent in cultivation in 1908 and 1909. After initial ineffectiveness, Sichuan province, the largest opium-producing province, started more stringent suppression in 1907, when Zhao Erfeng became governor-general (Cameron 1931, 147–50). Hampden Du Bose, the President of the Anti-Opium League, in his annual report of 1909 exclaimed, "During three years the rapidity of the prohibition movement has exceeded our highest expectations" (Du Bose 1910, 3). So much progress was made in such a short period of time that the British were finally convinced that the Chinese had the resolve to prohibit opium. This progress also relieved British concern that China would replace foreign opium with native opium after the former was cut off. Not surprisingly, the Anglo-Chinese Agreement was renewed in 1911 after the three-year trial period had expired.

To go back to the question why the Qing Court had so much success in this particular campaign after so many failed attempts at opium suppression, one should put the campaign in the big picture of the reform movement undertaken by the Qing Court. The success of opium suppression was related to, even a consequence of, the government mobilization that pulled diplomatic, financial, and political resources together, and of a new emphasis on policy enforcement.

The negotiation of the Anglo-Chinese Agreement was a rare bright spot in Qing diplomacy in the beginning of the twentieth century. On January 25, 1907, the Qing Court opened the negotiations with six proposals to the British. The first and foremost one was to ask Britain to reduce opium import from India by one-tenth annually in ten years, based on the annual average amount between 1901 and 1905. The others included permitting a Chinese official in Calcutta to inspect the quantity of opium shipped to China, a doubling of the duty on Indian opium from 110 to 220 *taels*, curtailing opium smuggling through Hong Kong, suppressing opium in foreign concessions, and forbidding morphia from entering China. After a year of negotiation, the British government essentially accepted China's proposals, except for the increase of duty on Indian opium, with the qualification of the three-year trial period (Cameron 1931, 144–45).

In retrospect, it was a huge diplomatic victory for the Qing Court to receive British consent to allow a Chinese official to inspect opium shipments from a station in Calcutta, even though he did not have the power of interference, as stipulated by the agreement. The Qing Court had examined the domestic and international environment concerning opium issues and used it to its own advantage. There were several factors contributing to the British government's change in stance. First and foremost, the Indian opium revenue had decreased substantially due to the impact of dominance of native opium in China, as shown in Table 2.2.

Imported opium peaked in 1879 and then, except for several years in the late 1880s, declined gradually until 1908. The quantity of imported opium was outweighed by native opium, however, for some time. The 1906 figure of 54,117 *piculs* seems miniscule next to the International Opium Commission estimate of 584,800 *piculs* of native opium. Foreign opium constituted only about 7.8 percent of the Chinese market that year. Plus, between 1880 and 1906, the importance of opium profits in India decreased, from the equivalent of 14 percent of government revenue to only 7 percent (Reins 1991, 121).

The decline of opium trade to China was the most important factor affecting the shift of British opium policy toward China. To the British government, the continuation of an opium trade might have become a moral liability too heavy to carry in a changed world. For instance, in 1874, the Society for the Suppression of the Opium Trade was founded and had been a leading anti-opium institution in Britain. Leaders of the Society were mostly Quakers and members of other nonconformist churches, and its members included politicians, industrialists, and clergy. The Society published numerous books, pamphlets, and, most importantly, its monthly magazine, *Friend of China,* on subjects of opium. Some industrialists took an anti-opium stance because of a worry that the opium trade hindered their ability to sell other goods in China. Others were opposed to opium for moral reasons, after having observed the horrific effect of opium on China. Sir Joseph Pease, a member of Parliament and the president of the Society, brought up a motion against the opium trade in the House

Table 2.2. Legal Foreign Opium Imports into China, 1867–1908 (in *piculs**)

Year	Amount	Year	Amount	Year	Amount	Year	Amount
1867	60,948	1878	71,492	1889	76,052	1900	49,279
1868	53,915	1879	82,927	1890	76,616	1901	49,484
1869	53,310	1880	75,308	1891	77,445	1902	50,574
1870	58,817	1881	74,005	1892	70,782	1903	58,457
1871	59,670	1882	66,908	1893	68,108	1904	54,752
1872	61,193	1883	68,168	1894	68,819	1905	51,920
1873	65,797	1884	68,819	1895	51,306	1906	54,117
1874	67,468	1885	65,259	1896	48,994	1907	54,584
1875	66,461	1886	67,801	1897	49,309	1908	48,397
1876	68,042	1887	73,877	1898	49,752		
1877	69,297	1888	82,612	1899	59,161		

*1 *picul* = 133.3 lbs.
Source: Reins 1991, 115.

of Commons on April 10, 1891. Though supported by majority, the motion failed to become a resolution because of an amendment calling for the compensation of the Indian government for any financial losses attributed to the suppression of the trade. The anti-opium movement developed more momentum in 1900, when many supporters of the Society won that year's general elections. The momentum culminated in 1906, when the Liberal Party controlled the House of Commons and passed a resolution calling for the end of the Indo-Chinese opium trade (Lodwick 1996, 55–57, 63–68).

Cognizant of attitude changes in the British government, the Chinese government was resolute not to let the opportunity slip away. Their sincerity and insistence enabled China to negotiate an agreement with the British quite distinct from many "unequal treaties" that China had signed at the turn of the century. As a result of obvious progress made during previous years, China was able to negotiate to renew the Anglo-Chinese Agreement in the latter half of 1910. During the negotiations, Chinese, missionary, and British anti-opium forces pressed for a speedier elimination of opium. The British initially asked for another three-year probationary period, but were refused by the Chinese. The two sides eventually reached an agreement on May 8, 1911, in which the Chinese took an upper hand. The British agreed that the full seven-year period would be observed. The Chinese secured that the British would decrease opium exports in the same proportion as the reduction achieved by the Chinese. If China were to eradicate poppy cultivation in less than seven years, the British would stop Indian opium export at the same time. In addition, if any Chinese province suppressed poppy cultivation, Indian opium would cease to enter that province (Cameron 1931, 156–58).

China's success with the diplomacy of opium in that period culminated in its participation in the meeting of the International Opium Commission in Shanghai in 1909. Proposed by the United States, the meeting was attended by thirteen countries: Austria-Hungary, China, France, Germany, Great Britain, Italy, Japan, the Netherlands, Persia, Portugal, Russia, Siam, and the United States. The participants were authorized to investigate the opium problem though their recommendation had no binding force. Nevertheless, it was the first cooperative international effort to tackle the problem, and China's participation was viewed as essential. At the meeting, China was treated as an equal partner among international powers, illustrated by the fact that resolutions passed in the meeting included a recognition of the sincerity and progress of China in her opium suppression campaign (Cameron 1931, 153–55; Lodwick 1996, 137–42).

In addition to diplomatic efforts, the Qing government's resolution to sacrifice fiscal revenue and the subsequent measures it took to make up the loss kept the campaign from derailing. Though the Qing government had been ambivalent toward opium suppression since 1858, with the consideration of revenue advantages often outweighing their anti-opium stance, its desire for reform and to save the falling empire made the difference this time, and the price was not light. After the Sino-Japanese War and the Boxer Rebellion, the huge indemnity inflicted by Japan (230 million *taels*) and Western powers (450 million *taels*) effectively put the Qing Court on the verge of bankruptcy. Opium duties and transit taxes were important revenues for the government. During the period of 1885–1905, the duty and transit taxes on foreign opium amounted to at least 5.5 million *taels* per year, or about 6–7 percent of the central government's total revenue (Reins 1991, 120). After the government levied a consolidated tax on native opium nationwide in 1906, the revenue on both foreign and native opium totaled 14 million taels, which was 14 percent of the annual central government income of about 100 million taels (Jiang and Zhu 1996, 202–203). It took a strong will for the Qing government to implement the opium suppression policy in those years of huge deficit.

Following the signing of the Anglo-Chinese Agreement, the Court solicited suggestions from officials to make up the loss of opium duties. A four-penny increase in the salt tax was implemented in July 1908, but it turned out to be insufficient. So the government raised taxes on purchasing opium at the end of the year. The next year, taxes on field and house transactions were increased. Though local officials proposed many ways to increase taxes, ranging from government monopoly on tobacco to taxes on slaughtering oxen, some provincial governors complained loudly about the fiscal difficulties brought on by the dramatic drop of opium revenue. The Court insisted that the opium suppression be carried on no matter how difficult it was (Yu Ende 1934, 140–41; Jiang and Zhu 1996, 202–205).

Such resolution on the part of the central government did not necessarily guarantee the success of the campaign, however, which to a great degree depended on whether the local officials implemented the regulations. Local officials were often the beneficiaries of opium transactions, and in some cases were directly involved in the business. This made them indifferent to the central government's initiative; as a result, the Court specified severe punishments for those who failed to carry out instructions fully. Furthermore, realizing the inefficiency of the old imperial bureaucracy and the fact that officials at various levels were themselves opium addicts, the Qing Court used the opium suppression as a part of its effort to shake up the old bureaucracy—one of the first priorities of the whole reform program in the early twentieth century. A decree dated January 8, 1901, fully elaborated the Court's reform intention:

> The first essential, however, more important even than the devising of new systems, is to secure men of administrative ability. Without talent no system can be made to succeed. If the letter of our projected reforms be not illuminated and guided by this spirit of efficiency in our officials then must all our hopes of reforming the State disappear into the limbo of lost ideas. We fully recognize that foolish adherence to the system of promotion by seniority has been one of the main factors in bringing about a condition of affairs that is almost incurable. If we would now be rid of it, our first

step evidently is to think no more of selfish interests, but to consider the common-wealth only and to secure efficiency by some new and definite method, so that competent persons only may be in charge of public affairs. But if you, our officials, continue to cling to your ancient ways, following the ruts of procrastination and slothful ease; should you persist in evading responsibility, serving the State with empty catchwords while you batten on the fruits of your misdeeds, assuredly the punishment which the law provides stands ready and no mercy will be shown you! Let this Decree be promulgated throughout the land. (Cameron 1931, 58)

From the beginning, the Qing Court designated officials to be the first ones to quit the habit. *The Regulations of Opium Suppression* stipulated that all officials were to be given six months to be rehabilitated or face dismissal from their positions. Since this kind of policy had been proclaimed before and never vigorously enforced, initially it was not strictly followed. To show the public that it really meant what it said this time, the Court dismissed two princes and several high-ranking officials in the fall of 1907 while extending the deadline for another three months. In the spring of 1908, the Court appointed four commissioners for opium suppression and set up a test center in Beijing to determine whether the rehabilitated officials were in fact cured (Yu Ende 1934, 145). Detailed regulations on this matter were drawn up and vigorously carried out. By 1910, there were 3,229 Beijing officials and 5,399 local officials who passed the test. It was also recorded that 271 officials who failed the test were dismissed or forced to retire, and 136 died in the process of rehabilitation (Jiang and Zhu 1996, 200). In 1911, the government launched a new round of tests that targeted the highest ranking officials in Beijing, since those were the ones who could more easily escape the check (Yu Ende 1934, 131).

Officials were rendered promotions or punishments according to their enforcement results. According to regulations, those officials who accomplished the task of suppression within certain time limits would be promoted in rank, but those who failed would see reduction of their salaries and decrease of their rank (Yu Ende 1934, 132). Under the pressure, the local officials were in no position to muddle their work. To curtail opium cultivation meant to destroy the livelihood of poppy planters. The initiative often met strong resistance, and was as a result hard to handle. There were many instances in which troops had to be used to enforce poppy uprooting.

By 1911, startling progress had been made by the vigorous policy enforcement. During the winter of 1910–1911, in preparation for the upcoming renewal of the Anglo-Chinese Agreement, Alexander Hosie, Commercial Attaché of the British Legation, conducted an investigation trip to the six provinces that were major poppy cultivation places. According to Hosie's report, between 1907 and 1910, poppy cultivation was reduced 25 percent in Gansu, 30 percent in Shaanxi, 70 percent in Guizhou, and 75 percent in Yunnan. More astonishingly, he reported that poppy cultivation had been eradicated in Shanxi and ceased in Sichuan, the largest poppy-producing area in China (Lodwick 1996, 160; for details see 150–63). These accomplishments reflected the great efforts by provincial officials. In the case of Sichuan, even John Jordan, British ambassador to China, acknowledged that Zhao Erxun, governor-general of Sichuan, "had done more than any other man to rid his country of opium." Zhao replied by saying that the "watching eyes of the British" stimulated his efforts (Lodwick 1996, 161); what he did not mention were the watchful eyes of the Qing Court. In early 1910, the Court ordered an investigation of its own to find out whether the reduction of poppy cultivation was as true as reported. The investigation ended in the fall of 1911, having found many discrepancies. The angry Court reiterated its resolution of opium suppression by immediately reprimanding several provincial governors (Yu Ende 1934, 143–44). As far as opium suppression was concerned, the bureaucracy of the Qing dynasty showed a greater degree of efficiency than it did with many other reforms concurrently undertaken. This efficiency was essential for the success of the campaign in 1906–1911.

ANTI-OPIUM SOCIETIES AND THE PUBLIC MOBILIZATION IN LATE QING

The anti-opium mobilization of Chinese society was an important factor in the suppression of opium. The nongovernmental sectors of the society participated and played a key role in the campaign, and the rising of anti-opium rhetoric echoed the rising of nationalism among the general public. The public became involved mainly through Anti-Opium Societies, which were set up in many cities by the opium suppression edict of 1906. It has been pointed out that the initiative was aimed at mobilizing the gentry class to assume a leadership role in the fight against opium, but the term "elite" is perhaps more apt and is used in this book. By the early twentieth century, the components of the ruling class in Chinese society had become more diverse and complex than previously. Though the number of traditional gentry class outnumbered other rival groups, the emerging groups, such as modern intellectuals (those educated in Western-style schools or abroad), professionals (lawyers, engineers, doctors), Chinese Christians, industrialists, and compradores had become more and more influential in the society, especially in big cities and trade ports. All of these new groups seem to have participated in the campaign. In fact, returned students who had studied abroad were among the strongest advocates of the anti-opium course.

Anti-Opium Societies, in existence before 1906, provided a direct venue for the elite to participate in the anti-opium campaign. In 1879, Guo Shongtao, the first Chinese ambassador to Britain, set up the first one in his hometown in Hunan. Guo was one of few Chinese advocates of opium suppression during the years following the legalization of opium. Influenced by the anti-opium activities of the Society for the Suppression of the Opium Trade when he was in England, he presented the Court with two memorials urging the suppression of opium in 1877. His appeal received little response, so he decided to pursue his cause himself after he retired from official service. The Opium Prohibiting Commune members were drawn largely from Guo's own lineage and his fellow villagers. Promising not to smoke opium themselves, members also engaged in anti-opium propaganda in the surrounding areas (Ma Mozhen 1993, 62–64, Wang Jinxiang 1996, 47–50). In other places, more Anti-Opium Societies were set up in the early twentieth century before the government's campaign started.

Foreign missionaries were also active in organizing various Anti-Opium Societies, though many of them "were too casually organized" to have a tangible effect before the mid-1890s (Lodwick 1996, 38). The Anti-Opium League, formally established in 1897, had a period of dormancy in the wake of the Boxer Rebellion, but it became active again around 1906. In fact, it was its president, Rev. Hampden Du Bose who organized the missionary petition to the Emperor in 1906 just before the issuance of the edict of opium suppression. From 1871 on, missionaries also set up many opium refuges in China. By the end of the Qing, the China Inland Mission alone had 101 opium refuges in Chengdu and 71 in Taiyuan. The total number of opium refuges run by all missionaries was estimated around one thousand (Jiang and Zhu 1996, 180–81).

These Anti-Opium Societies, organized by both the Chinese and missionaries, were anti-opium parties of the nongovernmental sectors in China. Yet, during the campaign of 1906–1911, Anti-Opium Societies were set up under the terms of the Court edict and were subject to strict government regulation. Supervised by the governor-generals in each province, it was stipulated that Anti-Opium Societies "shall be purely for prohibiting opium smoking, and shall not discuss any other matters, such as current political affairs or local administration issues or other matters unrelated to opium suppression" (Ma Mozhen 1998, 400). The purpose of the Qing Court was obvious. It wanted to use the power of local elite to mobilize social resources and to extend the control, that, under normal circumstances, it was not able to reach or exercise. Strictly speaking, these Anti-Opium Societies could not be totally independent from the government, but their positive effects on the campaign were crucial. Joyce Madancy has done a detailed study on activities of the Fuzhou Anti-Opium Society, which can serve as a good example of its kind in the campaign of the late Qing.

Fuzhou was a major port city on China's southeast coast, and the seat of the governor-general of Fujian and Zhejiang. The port was opened to Western trade after the First Opium War, and since then had been an important base of the Self-Strengthening Movement. The famous Fuzhou Dockyard was founded in 1866, and a naval school was also established to train China's first navy officers and naval engineers, among whom was the famous Chinese thinker, Yan Fu. It was understandable that the local elite included not only the traditional gentry class but also a new, more powerful class strongly affected by Western influences.

The enthusiasm of the Fuzhou elite for opium suppression was illustrated by the fact that, even before the issuance of the anti-opium edict of the Qing Court in September of 1906, they had formed Anti-Opium Societies. The Fuzhou Anti-Opium Society was established by ten local elites in 1905, and many branches were subsequently organized. From its start, the society was quite influential. During its first anniversary, it held a large-scale anti-opium parade and public burning of confiscated opium (Wu 1983, 15–17). In early 1906, the newly established Fujian General Chamber of Commerce, which was the product of another government reform initiative, also organized an Anti-Opium Society. It urged schools not to accept opium smokers and prohibited business establishments from employing any addicts, from renting out land to plant poppy, or properties for operating opium dens (Eastern Miscellany 3 [8]: Interior Affairs Section, 185). And the Chinese Christians, with strong support of foreign missionaries, were also very active in organizing Anti-Opium Societies. Together, these initiatives reflected the changing components of China's new urban elite.

In the midst of all this, the traditional gentry class was experiencing changes itself and was inseparable from the newly emerged members of the urban elite. Opium suppression provided an issue that the new urban elite and the traditional gentry class could work together on under the banner of reform and nationalism. The enhancement of nationalist sentiment in anti-opium discourse was mainly achieved by the historical interpretation of the Opium Wars, especially by making Lin Zexu a national hero. After the breakout of the First Opium War, Lin was reprimanded by Emperor Daoguang for his role in provoking the British military reaction and sent to a faraway northwest border town as punishment. But in subsequent narratives of the history of the Opium Wars, Lin began to be portrayed as a person who dared to challenge foreign powers, and his subsequent sufferings were interpreted as a sacrifice for the whole nation. This interpretation has since been passed down throughout the twentieth century. Anti-opium advocates have memorialized not only his birthday but also June 3, the day he ordered the destruction of thousands of chests of confiscated opium; June 3 was later designated as China's opium suppression day under the Nationalists. After the establishment of the People's Republic in 1949, a scene depicting the destruction of opium in Humen was engraved on the Monument of the People's Martyrs in the middle of Tiananmen Square. And right up to today, Lin's offspring are still given honorable treatment in events directly connected to the history of the Opium Wars, such as the return of Hong Kong to China in 1997.

Opium opponents in Fuzhou knew well how to use nationalistic history-telling to advance their cause, and no one else was in a better position than them to deploy the symbolic meaning of the Opium Wars to the Chinese. They built on the appeal of Lin Zexu, a native son of Fuzhou, by electing his grandson, Lin Bingzhang, as the president of the Anti-Opium Society. At the time the Anti-Opium Society was formed, Lin was the president of the Fuzhou Provincial College, reflecting the multifaceted status of elite in the late Qing. As Madancy has pointed out, "Lin Bingzhang's leadership brought a sense of inherited mission, and his active participation served as both model and inspiration for the province's reformist elite and officials" (Madancy 1997). As another symbolic tactic, the Anti-Opium Society headquarters were located in a memorial shrine to Lin, and Lin Zexu's image would continue to be featured in mass anti-opium gatherings and parades in the years to come.

After the issuance of the edict of opium suppression of 1906, the Fuzhou Anti-Opium Society took on a leadership role because of a temporary vacancy in the governor-general position at that time. It was said that the Society printed copies of the edict to publicize the newly launched campaign. When the new governor-general assumed his duties in early 1907, the Society seemed to revert to functioning in accordance with the *Regulations of Opium Suppression*. Article seven of the *Regulations* encouraged local gentry to form Anti-Opium Societies to help the campaign, but it did not stipulate the limit of the societies' activities except that they could not be involved in discussing politics. In reality, the local officials often had ties to the Anti-Opium Society, as it was a good way to connect to the local elite. In this case, the Fuzhou prefect attended and spoke at the inaugural meeting of the Society.

The Society's activities focused on several aspects, such as disseminating anti-opium propaganda, organizing anti-opium mass demonstrations, and participating in the implementation of opium suppression. The Society published its own magazine, *Fujian Anti-Opium Society Quarterly,* to facilitate its propaganda drive. Mass anti-opium demonstrations were often accompanied by the public burning of opium and smoking instruments. What really differentiated the Society from its predecessors and its previous activities was that, sanctioned by the government, the society gained unprecedented power in opium suppression actions:

> It [the Society] became involved in everything from the investigation of illegal smokers and opium dens to participation in the official census of smokers and the allocation of opium smoking licenses. Society members also ran addiction treatment centers, and were even known to have physically uprooted poppy plants in areas around Fuzhou. . . . Each of Fuzhou's police wards was to be patrolled by teams of police and Society inspectors, searching for violations of opium restrictions. The inspectors claimed the right to enter any premises in the city, be they business, private residences, religious establishments or administrative offices. This apparent state sanction of the coercive enforcement of state policy by urban elite was extraordinary in its implication that extensive extrabureaucratic involvement would complement, and not impede the official arm of the campaign. (Madancy 1997)

But the power of the Society was not limitless. Its influence was mainly in the urban centers and in the aspect of suppression of opium smoking. It had virtually no say in opium suppression among Fuzhou's Manchu banner troops, where 60–70 percent of soldiers were said to be smokers. It was the sole responsibility of the Manchu General of Fuzhou to carry out the campaign within his military quarter. The Society was also less involved in the suppression of poppy cultivation, which often met with strong resistance and had to be carried out by military forces. Even though by 1911 the Society had established 112 branches throughout the whole province, its main influence was concentrated in major urban centers and towns. Although the local officials encouraged the participation of the

Opium pipes confiscated by the Fuzhou Anti-Opium Society

Public burning of the confiscated opium pipes by the Fuzhou Anti-Opium Society

Society in the campaign, they also always kept watchful eyes on it. The governor-general reported to the Court that he had sent officials to attend every meeting of the Society as an effort to monitor its activities (Madancy 1997).

Generally speaking, in the anti-opium campaign, a degree of synergy was reached between the government and the elite. In this mutually beneficial relationship, the government granted power to the Anti-Opium Societies, allowing them to extend the control of society where the state had difficulty in doing so before. At the same time, the government kept an eye on the Societies. In turn, the urban elites used the Societies in anti-opium campaigns to exercise their power and influences. The luster of reform and nationalism gave special symbolic meaning to opium suppression, which provided a conjuncture where both the government and the elite could work together, no matter how great their differences might be on other reform issues. In fact, the close working relationship between the government apparatus and Anti-Opium Societies resulted in the interchange of leadership between the two, making the synergy more ostensible. Lin Bingzhang was given an appointment in Beijing. Chen Peikun, Lin's successor as the head of the Fuzhou Anti-Opium Society in 1910, was appointed as director of the Fujian Provincial Opium Prohibition Office. In 1913, Chen Peikun was replaced by Chen Nengguang, a Chinese Christian and an officer of the Fuzhou Anti-Opium Society before 1911 (Madancy 1997). The Society's role was diminished, however, following the fall of the Qing dynasty and the subsequent deterioration of government's efforts on opium suppression. After years of de facto nonfunctioning, the Society was finally dissolved in 1921 (Wu 1983, 18), but only three years later China would witness another wave of active mobilization of urban elite against opium (see chapter 3).

In summary, though many factors contributed to the success of the anti-opium campaign of 1906–1911, the rise of nationalism and the desire for reform at the turn of the century were among the most important ones. As a result of the Opium Wars and financial crisis during the internal upheavals, the Qing Court legalized the opium for more than four decades, only to see opium consumption become an epidemic. Nationalism not only made the anti-opium discourse hegemonic in the society, but also made opium an issue of public domain, which in turn mobilized members of the social elite to participate in the government campaign. The Qing Court seized on favorable domestic and international attitudes against opium to launch the campaign and implemented a wide array of diplomatic, financial, and political tactics to carry it out. Unlike other government reform initiatives, which often met strong resistance from the public and state bureaucracy, the anti-opium campaign enjoyed a great degree of public support. Nationalism and reform helped the government and social elite gain consensus on this particular issue. As a part of the broad reform movement, the anti-opium crusade witnessed the mass mobilization of the social and governmental forces on a large scale for the first time at the end of the Qing dynasty. It took a synergy of state and society to accomplish a common goal—an element that would be missing in China's anti-drug campaigns for years to come.

3

Nationalism and the Anti-Drug Mobilization of the Shanghai Elite, 1924–1927

The Qing dynasty fell to the forces of revolution in the end of 1911, and the Republic of China was established in the following year. After only a few months, the revolutionaries, represented by Sun Zhongshan, handed the power to military strongman Yuan Shikai, hoping that he would uphold the Provisional Constitution and the new Republic, only to find out later that Yuan's ambition was to be an emperor himself. Yuan died in 1916 after his imperial restoration failed miserably, leaving behind a power vacuum. China entered a so-called northern warlord period, when power struggles between several major warlord alliances often left the central government up for grabs by sheer force. No matter which of the warlords was in charge of Beijing at one given time, the central government was not in control of areas that belonged to other warlord alliances. The political fragmentation would not change until the Nationalists completed the Northern Expedition and reunited China, at least nominally, in 1928. It was in this context that China's anti-opium efforts experienced a sharp downturn. The failure of the state to exercise the anti-opium campaign prompted the Chinese elite to assume a leadership role.

RHETORIC VERSUS REALITY: OPIUM RESURGENCE IN THE EARLY REPUBLIC

The 1911 revolution disrupted the anti-opium campaign that began in 1906. Opium suppression continued in the newly established Republic, but its momentum deteriorated between 1912 and 1916. On March 2, 1912, President Sun Zhongshan issued a general order demanding that local officials renew their efforts to suppress opium, an order repeated by Yuan Shikai when he took power the same year. A national anti-opium conference was held in 1913, and a National Union Association of Opium Suppression was established. In 1914, a more stringent *Regulations on Prohibiting Poppy Planting* was proclaimed, but the credibility of government anti-opium policies was jeopardized by grim reality. Opium revenue was a priority for many officials, and diverse methods were adopted to circumvent the regulations. For example, local officials in the Gansu province set up an Opium Suppression Bureau in 1914 that prohibited poppy planting. It did not, however, enforce the prohibitions on opium smoking, retailing, and trafficking, thus making Gansu an opium business center and enabling the local government to get revenue it desperately needed. In 1915, to raise money for his monarchical dream, Yuan Shikai approved a government-managed opium monopoly in the Jiangsu, Guangdong, and Jiangxi provinces, effectively acknowledging the legalization of opium again (Su 1997, 240–41).

After Yuan Shikai's death in 1916, the country quickly fell into chaos amid the struggle for control by different warlords. The rise of warlordism is illustrated by two sets of statistics. In 1914, the Chinese army numbered 457,000, increased to 850,000 in 1918, and to 1,380,000 in the early 1919. Correspondingly, the military expense increased from 152,910,000 *yuan* in 1916, to 203,000,000 *yuan* in 1918, and to 600,000,000 *yuan* in 1925 (Su 1997, 260–61). Opium revenue became a major financial resource for many warlords, mainly through "fines" on cultivation, trafficking, selling, and smoking. Ironically, the policy of "suppression through fine" actually made opium more common in many parts of the country, especially the southwestern and northwestern regions of China, which were major opium-producing areas and under local warlords' control following the fall of the Qing.

One of the most startling phenomena in the early Republic era was the way in which the strengthening of the existing anti-opium discourse coincided with the dramatic deterioration of opium control. Generally speaking, there have been three different strategies in the government's approach to the opium problem—absolute suppression, gradual suppression, and relaxation of suppression—all of which can be associated with three different phases in the opium-suppression history of the Qing dynasty. The so-called relaxation of suppression or legalization of opium was adopted from 1858 to 1906, when the Qing faced internal uprisings and foreign pressures. Since 1906, faced with a hegemonic anti-opium discourse, no regimes have dared openly to promote opium legalization again, and the different parties involved in opium-suppression policy have vacillated mainly between strategies of gradual and absolute suppression.

Gradual suppression, started in 1906, involved a state monopoly on the sale of opium and government control of opium production and trafficking. The first part made the state the only supplier of opium to registered addicts, who were required to kick their habits within a fixed period of time. The second part aimed to cut off the sources of illicit opium. But the policy of gradual suppression lost its appeal and legitimacy after 1917, the year that the Ten-Year Agreement expired. According to the Agreement, by the end of 1917 both imported and domestic opium were to be phased out in China, leaving no ground for the continuation of gradual suppression. Absolute suppression makes every aspect of opium illegal, including planting, trafficking, retailing, and consuming. The expiration of the Ten-Year Agreement helped the advocates of absolute suppression gain overwhelming support from society, and, from 1918 on, the overall task of government and the whole society was to prevent opium from coming back and to keep China opium free.

As it witnessed the continuing deterioration of opium control, the private sector of Chinese society was anxious to regroup and exert more pressure on the government. An unsolved issue of the Ten-Year Agreement provided a good opportunity for it in 1918. According to the Agreement, by the end of 1917 no more foreign opium should enter China. But in fact there was a huge stock of foreign opium in Shanghai. With the deadline approaching, national attention focused on how to handle these existing opium stocks. In 1917, rumors circulated that Vice President Feng Guozhang had proposed to purchase 20 million *yuan* worth of opium for "medical use." When the news came out in 1918 that a conglomerate of businessmen and government officials wanted to buy all opium stocks and then to resell them in Jiangsu and Jiangxi provinces for profit, the whole country's public opinion turned against this plan. According to reports in *Shenbao*, the most subscribed-to newspaper in Shanghai, three Anti-Opium Associations were formed in Shanghai to fight against the government's proposal (*Shenbao* 10/08, 1918). Under pressure, President Xu Shichang ordered that the stock of opium be purchased by the Chinese government and publicly burned in Shanghai in early 1919 (Yu Ende 1934, 164).

The public burning of opium stock was held in Shanghai from January 9 to January 16. According to reports, 1,207 chests of opium worth 13,397,940 *yuan* were destroyed (Yu Ende 1934, 164). It was an event that caught national media attention, in general, and Shanghai media, in particular. *Shenbao* gave detailed, daily reports of the event. Several of Shanghai's anti-opium organizations actively participated, and the public burning was held under the watch of representatives from many organizations, including the General Chamber of Commerce, Jiangsu Provincial Council, Jiangsu Education Association, International Anti-Opium Association, YMCA, China Health Association, World Chinese Student's Federation, Bank of China, and Shanghai Bank of Trade and Savings. After the event, some of the representatives, such as Li Denghui, Chen Guangfu, and Wu Liande, became the most active anti-opium advocates in the 1920s and 1930s (*Shenbao* 01/09–01/16, 1919).

The issue of how to handle opium stock became a catalyst that prompted the establishment of the Beijing International Anti-Opium Association in 1918

(IAOA thereafter) and that propelled the Shanghai anti-opium forces to set up a national anti-opium association (*Shenbao* 08/26, 1918). (The Shanghai International Anti-Opium Association was formed in January 17, 1919, just after the public opium burning.) Though members of the Beijing IAOA included many influential political figures, among them President Xu Shichang and former President Li Yuanhong, the organization was actually run by the British General Secretary W. H. Graham Aspland. Within a short period of time, branches were established in a number of provinces (Yu Ende 1934, 183). Beijing IAOA sent representatives to observe the burning of stock opium in Shanghai and was a noticeable presence in China's anti-opium activities before its role was replaced by the NAOA in 1924.

Looking at the history of opium suppression in modern China, especially in the period of warlordism, one cannot help marveling at the discrepancy between anti-opium discourse and the government's revenue-extracting actions. When taken out of the context of modern Chinese history, many government anti-opium regulations and discourses appear to be staunchly anti-opium at first glance. However, when put into historical context, it becomes clear that these regulations could be used for exactly opposite purposes. The flexibility of the Chinese language was exploited to such an extreme degree that both opium-suppression crusaders and profiteers could speak in much the same discourse to achieve their totally different aims.

The idea that opium *should be suppressed* had a consensus in China, but *how it was to be suppressed* was a question open to different answers, providing maneuvering room to those with different aims. Nonetheless, the anti-opium discourse was strong enough to restrain officials from extracting opium revenue without making efforts to claim legitimacy or at least cover up the disgrace attached to opium transactions. In trying to reduce the conflict between strong anti-opium discourse and the actual profiting from opium, various interpretations of opium "suppression" were created. A special phrase, "suppression through taxation," was insistently used to cover the revenue-collecting activities of the authorities. "Suppression" was emphasized in the phrase, but those profiting from opium knew the key word was "taxation," not suppression.

In addition to the multiple interpretations of how to "suppress" opium, the definition of opium itself was as malleable as anti-opium discourse, manifesting in multiple meanings and subtle differences when various terms were referenced. Opium was alternately called *yan* (smokable opium), *yao* (drug or medicine), *tu* (dirt or earth), and *du* (poison) in Chinese.[8] To crusaders against opium, opium was simply called "opium poison," often extending the implication of poison to every aspect of the addict's life. When opium was used for medical purposes, which has a long history in China, nobody related it to the notion of poison. To make opium sound more neutral, imported opium was often called "foreign medicine" and an opium retailer called a "drug store." Morphine and other opium derivatives were made into pills and branded as medicine that could help people give up their addiction to opium. Government opium revenue-collecting organs were named "opium suppression bureaus," and different opium taxes were called "opium prohibition fines." It was this flexibility of interpretation that enabled different parties to maneuver themselves within hegemonic anti-opium discourse and make the opium-suppression issue extremely complex in modern China.

The stock opium issue made Shanghai the center of opium suppression after 1918, but the political situation in the early 1920s made it extremely difficult to enforce opium control in China, and public mobilization against opium waned at that time. The NAOA was organized essentially by the Shanghai elite in 1924 to address the issue both domestically and internationally. Almost immediately after its inception, the NAOA not only enjoyed broad support from the society, becoming the representative of China's voice on the opium issue, but also was able to exert enormous pressure on different Chinese governments to adopt a more aggressive opium-suppression policy. How did the NAOA gain such a uniquely prominent status in little more than a decade of its existence (1924–1937), in modern China in general, and under the Nationalist regime, in particular? In answer to this question, the NAOA can serve as an example to shed some light on issues of nationalism, history, and the relationship between society and state in modern China's anti-opium crusades, issues outlined in the Introduction and to be explored throughout this book.

ANTI-OPIUM MOBILIZATION OF THE SHANGHAI ELITES IN 1924

With the expiration of the Ten-Year Agreement, the opium-control situation deteriorated rapidly. In some places opium cultivation and consumption became open, after paying a so-called poppy cultivation fine, peasants were allowed to plant poppy, and opium transactions became legalized in the form of government taxation and monopoly. In 1919, the British government protested to the Chinese for the alleged widespread poppy cultivation in several provinces (Ma Mozhen 1993, 71–73). British concerns were echoed by other Western powers, and the reality made the Chinese elites lose their faith in the government's willingness and resolution to deal with the opium issue. When the League of Nations decided to hold an International Opium Conference in November of 1924, the Chinese elite saw it as a good opportunity to exercise more pressure on the government, on the one hand, and to defend China's image in the international community, on the other. The formation of the NAOA was a direct result of the Shanghai elite's mobilization.

The NAOA originated from the attention given to the opium issue by various organizations during the summer of 1924, driven by the approaching opening date of the International Opium Conference. In July, the Chinese Association of Higher Education held its annual meeting in Nanjing, and it adopted an anti-opium resolution, urging educational institutions nationwide to advocate opium suppression. It also sent representatives to contact other organizations, seeking cooperation and coordinated actions (Yu Ende 1934, 185). During the process, the most active group was the National Christian Council, which had established an anti-opium committee a year earlier to promote public awareness of the opium epidemic. Finally, coordinated by the Shanghai General Chamber of Commerce and cosponsored by about forty organizations, the NAOA was formed on August 5, 1924, in Shanghai.

From its inception, the NAOA distinguished itself from numerous earlier anti-opium organizations by its broad base and rich social resources. Generally speaking, it represented two types of people: one was educated professionals and the Chinese business class, the other was the Chinese Christians. The NAOA's involvement in anti-opium activities symbolized a genuine mobilization of the Shanghai elite responding to an issue that, from their perspective, had both national and international importance. Following is an incomplete list of constituent members of the NAOA:

Shanghai General Chamber of Commerce	Council on Health Education of China
National Christian Council	Overseas Chinese Union
Jiangsu Education Association	Welfare Association for Chinese Abroad
Red Cross Society of China	Shanghai Students Union
National Association for the Advancement of Education	Union of Daily Newspapers
	Chinese Rate-Payers Union of the International Settlement
Chinese Medical Association	Libraries Union of China
National Women's Federation of China	National Road Construction Association
World Chinese Student's Federation	Wenzhou Association of China
Women's Christian Temperance Union	Shanghai Preachers' Union
National Medical and Pharmaceutical Association	Shanghai Merchants Union
	All-Zhejiang Association
Vocational Educational Association of China	Streets Union of Shanghai
	Shanghai YMCA
China Christian Educational Association	Shanghai YWCA
	Shanghai Women's Union
National Committee YMCA	Shanghai Farmers Union
National Committee YWCA	Chinese Lawyers Association
Boy Scouts Union	Shanghai Medical Practitioners Union[9]

The degree of mobilization of the Shanghai elite can also be measured by the leaders of the fight against the opium epidemic. The first president of the NAOA, Xu Qian, was then a very influential figure in political and legal circles. Starting his bureaucratic career in the last days of the Qing dynasty, Xu was well versed in both Confucian classics and Western politics and law. As attorney general of Beijing, he was one of the Chinese representatives attending the Eighth International Conference on Prison Reform held in Washington, D.C., in 1910. After the Qing dynasty was overthrown, he became an important figure of the newly established Nationalist Party and was a confidant of Sun Zhongshan. He was general secretary of Sun's government in Guangzhou in 1917 and was sent to attend the Paris Peace Conference by Sun as one of the representatives from the South. In 1921, Sun was elected president of the national government by the Special Congress in Guangzhou, and Xu Qian was appointed head of the Justice Council. After Sun was expelled from his position by the warlord Chen Jiongming in August 1922, Xu accompanied Sun to Shanghai. During 1923 and 1924, Xu served as Sun's personal envoy, keeping in alignment different political and military factions. He was especially important as a liaison between Feng Yuxiang and Sun Zhongshan. All these activities earned him a prominent status among the circle of Sun's followers (Wang Yongjun 1989).

A look at Xu Qian's background will explain why he was elected as the first president of the NAOA. His reputation among broad strata of the Chinese elite made him an ideal candidate. Having been a Jinshi (one who had passed the highest level of imperial civic service examination), a Qing official, a lawyer, a professor, an editor, a political party founder, a convert to Christianity, a diplomat, a justice minister, and a politician, Xu could link a variety of constituent sponsors of the NAOA. But in reality Xu was foremost an active politician, and he could devote only limited time and energy to the cause of anti-opium activities. Not surprisingly, after serving a brief term as ceremonial president, he was succeeded by Li Denghui, who had long been active in anti-opium crusades.

Though Li's career path was very different from that of his predecessor, he represented the main force behind the NAOA's initiative. Born and raised in Java, he attended a school affiliated with the Methodist Episcopal Church in today's Singapore and became a devoted Christian. He went on to attend college in the United States and received a bachelor's degree from Yale in 1899 (Fudan University 1985, 247). Foremost an educator, he served as president of the prestigious Fudan (Fuh Tan) University from 1912 to 1936. He was also a social activist. In 1909, he founded the World Chinese Student's Federation, an organization that advocated opium suppression long before 1924; Tang Luyuan, a key figure of the Federation, served as president of the Shanghai International Anti-Opium Association (*Shenbao* 01/18, 1919). As a Protestant, Li was well connected to missionaries. With solid support from anti-opium activists, Li remained in his position until he was succeeded by Luo Yunyan in 1928 and continued to be very active in the NAOA until its final dismantling in 1937.

Chen Guangfu, treasurer of the NAOA, signaled the participation of Shanghai capitalists in the crusade. A Wharton School graduate, Chen founded the Shanghai Bank of Trade and Savings in 1915. Under his management, business grew rapidly, and the bank became a major nationwide bank in China within twenty years. He was a typical product of what Marie-Claire Bergere has called "the golden age of the Chinese bourgeoisie," which blossomed between 1911 and 1937 (Bergere 1986). A self-made, successful banker, Chen had not only a clear consciousness of social responsibility but also a sensitivity to foreign dominance of the Chinese economy. Following his motto, the bank's purpose became: "serve the society, assist industry and commerce, and resist foreign economic aggression"—he even ordered the motto to appear on deposit slips (Zhao Yinglin 1995, 294–95). Before he joined the NAOA, he served as treasurer of the Shanghai International Anti-Opium Association (*Shenbao* 01/18, 1919).

Advocating the elimination of opium had been high on the Chinese bourgeoisie's social agenda for quite some time. Among the leadership of the Shanghai International Anti-Opium Association were Mu Ouchu, a famous textile tycoon; Zhu Baosan, then president of the Shanghai General Chamber of Commerce; and Nie Yuntai, the next president of the Chamber of Commerce (*Shenbao* 01/18, 1919). Nie, who was only forty-one years old, was a leader of a new generation of Chinese capitalists. He was reform-minded and advocated greater participation of capitalists in politics and social work. He led one of three anti-opium associations in Shanghai in 1918 and became president of the Shanghai International Anti-Opium Association in 1921 (*Shenbao* 05/20, 1921). Chen Guangfu's continuous participation in the NAOA was an example of this new generation of Chinese bourgeoisie, who wanted to express its opinion on broad social and political issues.

The secretary-general of the NAOA, Zhong Ketuo (Rev. K. T. Chung), underscored the presence of the Chinese Christian establishment. He was from the National Christian Council and was himself a priest. Though the NAOA had an Executive Committee, it was the Secretariat that was responsible for day-to-day activities. Zhong played a key role in the first four years of the NAOA. He remained very active in the NAOA even after he stepped down as secretary-general in 1929. In fact, his successor, Huang Jiahui, was also a member of the National Christian Council. Among the above four leaders of the NAOA, Xu Qian, Li Denghui, and Zhong Ketuo were devoted Christians. Xu Qian even founded the Christian National Salvation Society in 1918, advocating that Christianity be the basis of the Republic and a Christian anarchist government (Lin Ronghong 1980, 196–97). It is not an exaggeration to say that the Chinese Christian force played a pivotal role within the NAOA.

Even before the formation of the NAOA, however, anti-opium organizations with national influence had been dominated by a missionary connection. Besides the Anti-Opium League, there were the International Reform Bureau, founded in 1908 and led by American Presbyterian Edward White Thwing, and the Beijing IAOA, set up in 1918 and led by British doctor W. H. Graham Aspland. Before the NAOA, there was no Chinese leadership in the Anti-Opium League, the IAOA, or the International Reform Bureau. By sharp contrast, there was not a single foreigner in the Executive Committee of the NAOA. It was the first time that the Chinese had achieved control of an anti-opium organization with Christian connections.

The timing was not accidental, for 1924 was the heyday of the anti-Christian movement then prevalent in China, which was a powerful expression of nationalism in the mid-1920s. After the establishment of the Republic, modern Chinese nationalism continued to influence Chinese politics and society, contributing to the launching of the far-reaching New Culture Movement in the mid-1910s. The nationalist and anti-imperialist movements culminated in the May Fourth Movement in 1919. The May Fourth intellectuals embraced "Mr. Democracy" and "Mr. Science" as two modern sages to save China, rather than the Christian God. Their iconoclastic cultural radicalism went beyond a rejection of Chinese traditions to include Christianity as the enemy of science (Lian 1997, 12). It was in this context that an anti-Christian movement was launched in 1922, which lasted until the end of the decade.

The catalyst of the movement was the decision of the World's Student Christian Federation to hold their first meeting after World War I at Qinghua (Tsinghua) University in Beijing in April of 1922. This news upset a group of anti-Christian students in Shanghai, who viewed the conference as another attempt by foreigners to harm China. Insisting that a government institution should not be used by religious bodies, Shanghai students organized an Anti-Christian Federation on March 9 and asked that the conference be moved out of the Qinghua campus. The anti-Christian declaration of Shanghai students was echoed by Beijing students, who broadened the former's organization into a Great Anti-Religion Federation. Though the planned meeting was held at the Qinghua campus April 4–9, on the last day of the conference more than one thousand students held an anti-religion gathering in Beijing University, denouncing the function of religion in modern society (Lin Ronghong 1980, 130–33). The anti-Christian movement ebbed by the end of the year but was reinvigorated in 1924, at which time mission schools became the main target. In the name of "Education Rights Recovery," Chinese students demanded that mission schools hand over controls to Chinese government and abolish compulsory attendance of religious courses.

It is beyond the scope of this study to go into details of the movement. As Yip Ka-che has pointed out:

> The anti-Christian movement was, in fact, an important manifestation of modern Chinese student nationalism. . . . By the early twenties most intellectuals viewed Christianity as incompatible with modernity. Indeed, by 1924 they viewed Christianity as not only unscientific and outdated, but also as a major obstacle to China's attainment of national independence. Many alleged that it was the vanguard of Western imperialism. These views were, to a large extent, shaped by the nationalist and anti-imperialist campaigns of that decade. (Yip 1980, 2)

The issue that interests us here is one of why, in the midst of a strong anti-Christian movement, the Chinese Christians actively involved themselves in the establishment of the NAOA.

The answer lies in two intertwined aspects of Christianity in China. On the one hand, the choice to tackle the opium issue was a Chinese reaction to the continuing shift in American missionary policy and thought in the early twentieth century. During the first two decades of the century, American Protestant missions gained a dominant role in China. Paralleling the rise of liberalism in American Protestantism, many American missionaries not only "developed appreciative understanding of Chinese religions and of the culture they had set to displace" (Lian 1997, 11), but also "found in humanitarian social programs an answer to the questions of their religious conscience" (Lian 1997, 15). As Lian Xi further points out: "In China, the traditional missionary impulse to save the heathen through the preaching of the Gospel became submerged in institutional programs dedicated to social, educational, and health reforms" (Lian 1997, 10). Backed by a dominant anti-opium discourse and influenced by the liberalism within the mission, Chinese Christians had no difficulty in taking the initiative against opium.

On the other hand, the Chinese Christians' assumption of the leadership role in the NAOA was a nationalistic response framed by the emerging anti-Christian movement, and represented a new phase of the gradual naturalization of Christianity in China. From the very beginning, Western missionaries had held a tight grip on churches in China. But since the turn of the century, the rise of Chinese nationalism—as well as the liberalism in the body of mission itself—propelled more and more missionaries to realize that the future of Christianity in China rested on its indigenization. Analogously, Chinese Christians were also asking for a greater degree of independence. This fact was acknowledged in the Centenary Missionary Conference held in Shanghai in 1907: "The Chinese national spirit has awakened both within and without the Church to an amazing degree. . . . One of its features is a restless impatience of foreign control, or even influence, which makes itself felt in the Church as well as outside" (Centenary Conference Committee 1907, 5). Though the Conference proclaimed that "independence of foreign control is the inherent right of the Chinese Church," there was not a single Chinese among the delegates. The situation changed rapidly. By the 1913 Conference, Chinese delegates accounted for one-third of all the attendees, and a proposal was made for joint control of the church by Chinese and foreign missionaries. In 1922, at the National Christian Conference, the National Christian Council was formed. The organization's constitution required that the majority of its one hundred members be Chinese. Chinese Christian groups finally began to play a more assertive role in and outside churches (Centenary Conference Committee 1907, 6; Lian 1997, 135–36, 158–59).

The NAOA was more than closely associated with the National Christian Council; its president, Li Denghui, had been advocating the independence from foreign control of Chinese Christian organizations for some time. Dissatisfied by the fact that the Shanghai YMCA was controlled by Americans, Li organized the World Chinese Student's Federation in 1905, whose members actively participated in the boycott of American goods in the same year (Fudan University 1985, 248) and urged the government to burn the Shanghai stock opium in 1918. The Chinese Christians' national consciousness made them respond to the anti-Christian movement in a unique way. When the movement broke out in 1922, the foreign missionaries and Chinese Christians responded quite differently. According to Yip, "On the whole, the response was surprisingly optimistic as many Chinese Christians seemed to welcome the movement as an indication of a growing interest in Christianity. Some Christians also thought that the anti-Christian movement might help stimulate church reforms" (Yip 1980, 28–29). One reform the Chinese Christians sought was the continuation of the indigenization of church and the right of self-determination, as an effort to "demonstrate the compatibility of Christianity and Chinese nationalism" (Yip 1980, 84). The formation of the NAOA is a good example of the complexity of modern Chinese nationalism.

The leadership of the NAOA clearly was characterized by highly influential figures from political, business, cultural, and religious circles in Shanghai. Since advocating opium suppression was a no-risk proposition within the context of the hegemonic anti-opium discourse in modern China, it was not difficult to get the names of prominent elites on the list of NAOA's Honorary Directorate, including Presidents Li Yuanhong and Xu Shichang, and former Prime Minister Tang Shaoyi. But the NAOA was keen to realize that what was really important was how to exercise these resources to influence and mobilize the public to the anti-opium cause. By doing so, the NAOA distinguished itself from other similar organizations that existed before or after it.

PROPAGANDA INITIATIVES AND MASS MOBILIZATION

The Shanghai elite enjoyed many advantages. Shanghai was the economic and media capital of China and also an international port city. The advocates of the anti-opium movement were by and large well educated, and many of them had studied abroad. They were well connected to the political, financial, and cultural elite as well as to foreign missionaries, and their position and training enabled them to use their various resources skillfully.

The first propaganda initiative by the NAOA was to designate September 27, 1924, as "Anti-Opium Day." The date was chosen for no specific reason other than it was in advance of the upcoming International Opium Conference. Various anti-opium activities were held in Shanghai and nationwide more than 900 cities and towns in 24 provinces responded to NAOA's call (*Judu* 26: 9). It was a huge success, especially considering the NAOA was established only a month before. The second "Anti-Opium Day" was held in the following year, with the same nationwide response. In Beijing, activities were sponsored by the Beijing branch of the NAOA and attended by prominent figures such as Xiong Xiling, Tao Zhixing, and Fan Yuanlian.[10] Even the ruler of the Beijing government, Duan Qirui, issued an opium-suppression order in response to the petition by the Beijing branch (NAOA 1931, 148–49).

The initial success encouraged the NAOA to extend the "Anti-Opium Day" to "Anti-Opium Week" in 1926. Since most schools started new terms in September, the date was postponed one week to October 3–9 in order to give schools more time to prepare for the event. Each day of the week was assigned a specific focus. October 3 was designated as "propaganda day," in which local newspapers added pages to cover anti-opium activities, and local organizations and churches held public anti-opium lectures. October 4 was "education day," which focused on schools. Activities included public speaking by teachers or social dignitaries and adding anti-opium contents to the school's curriculum. October 5 was "legal day," in which the NAOA and other public associations petitioned the authorities to carry out existing opium-suppression laws and to burn opium publicly to show their resolution. October 6 was "rehabilitation day," when local hospitals and philanthropic institutions convened and discussed ways to set up rehabilitation centers. "Family day" on October 7 was sponsored by women's associations to allow family members of addicts to advocate them quitting opium smoking. October 8 was "branch day," for setting up new branches of the NAOA or giving already existing, local branches an opportunity to make future plans. The last day, October 9, was "convention day," on which a mass anti-drug gathering was held, supplemented by public speaking and popular anti-opium drama, to culminate the activities of the whole week (*Judu* 26: 7, 18–19).

Submitting a petition to the International Opium Conference was another initiative taken by the NAOA. The petition asked the Conference to limit world production of opium and other narcotics to the quantity that met only scientific and medical needs. It was cosigned by more than 4,200 organizations from 24 provinces, which represented about 4,660,000 members nationwide. The NAOA nominated three "people's representatives"—Cai Yuanpei, a widely respected educator; Wu Liande, a famous doctor; and Gu Ziren, a Christian—to attend the conference in Geneva.

In a very short period of time, the NAOA established itself as the authoritative representative of China's anti-opium movement. The positive publicity generated by the NAOA helped it gain a leadership role nationwide. Before its inception, there were many grassroots anti-opium associations in many places, but the lack of strong headquarters and coordination with each other limited their influence. For anti-opium advocates, the emergence of the NAOA encouraged them to set up branches of, or simply attached existing organizations to, the NAOA. Within two years, there were 261 NAOA branches all over China (*Judu* 26: 20). Even the government delegate to the International Opium Conference asked the NAOA to investigate the amount of opium and other narcotics China needed for scientific and medical purposes. The NAOA provided an estimated figure through the

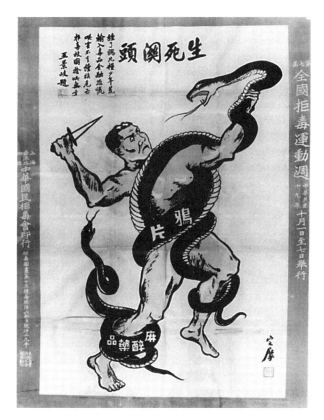

National Anti-Opium Association propaganda

National Medical Association and the National Medical and Pharmaceutical Association, two of its constituent members (NAOA 1931, 146–47).

It is hardly an exaggeration to say that the NAOA was a master of conducting propaganda in modern society. The NAOA took advantage of its rich connection to the Shanghai press to publicize its activities. From its very inception, major newspapers such as *Shenbao* devoted much attention to covering its activities. During the annual Anti-Opium Week sponsored by the NAOA, many newspapers published special editions or editorials to show their support. The NAOA had no difficulty voicing its concerns through Shanghai's general press.

Yet the NAOA wanted more people to hear its agenda and made enormous efforts to build its own propaganda apparatus. *Judu*, a monthly magazine with an English title, *Opium A National Issue*, started publishing in May 1926. It served as the main propaganda means of the NAOA for over a decade. And in order to reach more foreign audiences, an English quarterly entitled *Opium A World Problem* was published in July 1927 (NAOA 1931, 158). The NAOA also published its own annual report on the opium epidemic in China, and a number of other books and pamphlets, including the *Directory of the Anti-Opium Movement*, addressed every aspect of conducting opium prohibition activities during that period. A more ambitious move was the establishment of the Anti-Opium News Agency by the NAOA in April 1927. The agency devoted itself exclusively to opium-related news and sent it to newspapers all over China for publication every week (NAOA 1931, 157).

Supported by the general press and backed by its own publishing instruments, the NAOA was well positioned to launch propaganda initiatives. For example, to prepare for the Anti-Opium Week of 1926, the NAOA issued an open letter to public organizations and newspapers nationwide, asking them to participate. The letter was carried by *Judu* as well as by a number of newspapers. Fifty thousand copies of a brochure detailing step-by-step organizational plans were printed and sent out to potential participants, along with the same number of anti-opium posters. During Anti-Opium Week, activities were reported by *Shenbao* daily. Immediately following Anti-Opium Week, the NAOA asked *Shenbao* to publish a special anti-opium issue on October 10, which numbered 200,000 copies (NAOA 1931, 154).

The NAOA was also very active in exploring other channels and forms to advance its agenda. Students were one of its targeted groups. Its aim was twofold. First, since students were among the very few Chinese who could get an education then, they were the future leaders of society and therefore should be the first ones to avoid opium smoking. Second, as an educated and well-organized group, students could be an important force in the opium-suppression movement. The NAOA made strong efforts to put anti-opium content into school curricula at different levels. For example, it sponsored an anti-opium speech contest every year in colleges and middle schools for which prominent figures were honored as judges, and the award-winning speeches were published in *Judu* in full text.

But the efficacy of written propaganda was limited, since the majority of the population and opium addicts was illiterate. To reach a large audience, the NAOA was very creative at mixing education with entertainment. It held anti-opium gatherings and parades, organized drama companies to play anti-opium dramas, aired anti-drug speeches on radio, even pioneered using film to advance the cause of opium suppression. Financed by the Chinese community in New York, the NAOA solicited a number of novels and playwrights and tried to make films with an anti-opium focus in 1926. During Anti-Opium Week, anti-opium slides were screened before the start of films in theaters. The week's activities were documented by the film company, and the documentary show was well received in New York as well as in Shanghai, Jiangsu, and Zhejiang (NAOA 1931, 153, 172).

Such spreading of propaganda to an international audience was another important task of the NAOA. In addition to participating and attending the International Opium Conference and publishing *Opium A World Problem,* the NAOA also took advantage of various international gatherings to publicize its efforts. In 1925, Dr. Luo Yunyan, a key member of the NAOA and the successor to president Li Denghui, was sent to Japan and Southeast Asia to promote the anti-opium cause. He made contacts with similar organizations in Japan to forge cooperative action prohibiting Japanese drugs from entering China (NAOA 1931, 149). In the same year, Dr. Wu Liande, president of the Harbin branch of the NAOA, presented a paper entitled "Public Health and Narcotics" at the Far East Conference on Tropical Medicine. In response to the NAOA's request, he also presented a proposal for narcotics suppression, which was approved at the conference. After the meeting, Dr. Wu went to Southeast Asia, continuing to advocate opium suppression (*Judu* 4: 20–26). The activities of the third Anti-Opium Week were reported to the League of Nations' Opium Advisory Committee by Chinese representative Zhu Zhaoxin. The NAOA was recognized by the Advisory Committee for its cooperation in the task of fighting the opium evil in the Far East and was granted the privilege to audit meetings as a representative of the Chinese people (NAOA 1931, 156).

NATIONALISM AND THE NAOA

Due to the mobilization of the Shanghai elite, it took only a short period of time for the NAOA to establish itself as the most influential anti-opium organization in China. Its initial success was inseparable from its efforts to present the opium epidemic to the Chinese people as well as to the international community. What was the integrating force behind the Shanghai elite's enthusiasm? By examining the origin of the NAOA and its activities, it was not difficult to recognize that nationalism played an important role in mobilizing the Shanghai elite.

The International Opium Conference of 1924 was the third major international conference on narcotics during the period. The first one was held in Shanghai in 1909; the second, the Hague Convention of 1912, was the first concrete result of international narcotics control and contained "a number of general principles which remain the foundation and mainspring of all drug control subsequently developed" (Renborg 1947, 15). China was one of the three countries that ratified the convention in 1915 (Renborg 1947, 16); but the following years did not see much improvement in world narcotics control, especially the control of opium. The League of Nations decided to hold a conference to deal with this issue. Naturally, China was perceived as one of several key countries needed to address the problem.

The Chinese elite, represented by those in Shanghai, had high expectations of the coming conference. Their optimism derived from the fact that during the first conference held in Shanghai, for the first time since the First Opium War, China was treated equally with other participants, most of which were Western powers

(Reins 1991, 141). This memory kept the hope alive for the Chinese elite that they could use the conference to pressure the government to adopt a stricter opium-suppression policy, and at the same time to request cooperation from international communities to cut off the inflow of narcotics from foreign countries into China.

According to resolutions passed by the Fourth Assembly of the League of Nations on September 27, 1923, the Council proclaimed that two international conferences should be held in Geneva: the First Opium Conference from November 3, 1924, to February 11, 1925, and the Second Opium Conference from November 17, 1924, to February 19, 1925. The former was specifically designated to discuss opium consumption in the Western powers' Far Eastern territories and the current situation in China. Unlike the Second Opium Conference, in which all members of the League of Nations and parties to the Hague Convention of 1912 participated, the First Opium Conference consisted of only eight delegations: British Empire, China, France, India, Japan, the Netherlands, Portugal, and Siam. The Chinese government took this conference quite seriously and sent the largest of all delegations to the conference.

Yet from the beginning of the conference, China became the primary target of attacks from Britain and other participants. Citing a figure given in a pamphlet issued by the International Anti-Opium Association of Peking, during the opening days of the conference, the British colony of India (then a main source of raw opium production) accused China of producing 15,000 tons of opium or nine-tenths of the total world production. The accusation, echoed by the British as well as a number of other delegations, produced repeated exchanges between Chinese and Indian delegates during several meetings (League of Nations 1925a, 77). This episode set a tone that was different from what both the official Chinese delegates and the representative of the NAOA had expected.

Nonetheless, the main differences between Western powers and China focused on two major questions: (1) Should a definite timetable be set up for Western powers to bring on effective suppression and end then-legalized use of prepared opium in their Far Eastern territories? (2) Should effective measures be taken by producing countries to restrict the production of opium and prevent its illicit export as a precondition for Western powers to carry out the first task? Strongly opposed by Portugal, which had not yet adopted government monopoly to control opium consumption and trafficking in its colony, Macao, no specific timetable was ever set up to apply to the first issue. From the Chinese viewpoint, financial considerations played an important role in the matter, since many Far Eastern territories obtained large public revenues from the trafficking and consumption of opium. As for the second issue, if the precondition was adopted, the Western powers could easily blame all drug problems on their Far Eastern territories as long as China or some other country had not totally solved the opium problem—a stance that was unacceptable to the Chinese delegation.[11]

The irreconcilable differences over these two issues between the Chinese and other delegations resulted in the withdrawal of the Chinese delegation from the First Opium Conference on February 10, 1925. In its Memorandum to the President of the First Opium Conference, the Chinese delegation declared:

> It was the expectation of the world, and certainly that of the Chinese people, that the Powers signatory to the Hague Convention which continued to legalize the use of opium would take prompt and decisive steps to introduce systems of control which would, by their operation, necessarily bring the temporarily legalized smoking of opium to an end within a few years, or at the termination of a specified period. . . . No such effective action is made obligatory upon the Powers by the draft Agreement that resulted from the labors of the Conference. . . . The obligation to make the manufacture of prepared opium a Government monopoly is qualified by the phrase "as soon as circumstances permit." . . . Retail shops for the sale of opium and divans for the smoking of opium are to be limited in number "as much as possible"; there is not even an obligation not to increase the number of retail shops and smoking-dens now existing. Educational and other efforts to discourage the use of prepared opium are to be exerted by only those Governments which consider such measures desirable under conditions existing in their several territories. (League of Nations 1925a, 168–69)

China also withdrew from the Second Opium Conference, along with the United States of America, and did not sign the 1925 Convention because of a similar reason in defining the starting date for opium suppression by Western powers in their colonies. As Renborg has pointed out, "The 1925 Convention failed, however, to devise any special international methods of 'bringing about a more effective limitation of the production and manufacture' of narcotic substances, although this was stated in the preamble as one of the aims of the convention. Limitation of production of raw opium is not referred to at all in the text of convention itself" (Renborg 1947, 19).

The Geneva Conferences disappointed the NAOA, which followed the proceedings closely and sent its own representative. The NAOA made itself known in the First Conference by sending a cable message to the Chinese delegation, claiming that the activities of the NAOA had been extended to 24 provinces and had 300,000 supporters in 600 cities. The message was presented to the president of the Conference in a letter by the Chinese delegate, who asked him to have it circulated (League of Nations 1925a, 151). Witnessing the lack of commitment of Western powers and angered by their blaming China, the NAOA supported the withdrawal of the Chinese delegation from the conferences. Based on its diminished expectations and unpleasant experience, in the following years, the NAOA became noncooperative toward the League of Nations and its drug control organs. This was illustrated by its open opposition to the Far Eastern Opium Investigation Commission.

In 1928, according to a proposal by the British delegate, a special Far Eastern Opium Investigation Commission was to be set up by the Advisory Committee on Traffic in Opium and Other Dangerous Drugs. Its mission was to investigate the opium situation in the Far East. The Chinese delegate asked that the investigation area be enlarged to include other opium-producing countries and that a Chinese member be appointed to the Commission. Neither request was granted (*Judu* 25: 8). The NAOA saw it as a conspiracy aimed at singling out China's opium epidemic and claimed it was the same excuse that was used in 1925 to indefinitely postpone the Western powers' obligation to suppress narcotic drugs in their colonies. In its declaration against the Far Eastern Investigation Commission, the NAOA called opium a ready weapon of economic invasion and foreplay of military aggression of imperialism, and saw the Commission as an attempt to intervene in China's internal affairs (*Judu* 25: 7–8). A few years had made a big difference. Gone was the enthusiasm and expectations for the International Opium Conferences from four years earlier, replaced by deep suspicion and antagonism toward the Advisory Committee on Traffic in Opium and Other Dangerous Drugs of the League of Nations.

According to the NAOA, if the League of Nations was sincere in its attempt to wipe out the drug epidemic in the world, it would be fair to China only if the Far Eastern Commission (1) enlarged its investigation area to the whole world, (2) investigated not only opium but also other narcotics, and (3) included a Chinese representative in the Commission. When Deputy Secretary-General Joseph Avenol of the League visited China in February 1929, the NAOA held a reception in his honor and reiterated its requirements in a petition to the League of Nations. Emphasizing the fact that more and more foreign-made narcotic drugs, especially morphine and heroin, were being smuggled into China and had become a serious threat to the success of China's anti-drug efforts, the NAOA asked the League of Nations why it limited the Commission's task only to the opium issue (*Judu* 29: 10–12). Its petition fell on deaf ears. When the Commission arrived in Shanghai in May 1930, the NAOA issued another declaration refusing to recognize the legitimacy of the Commission (*Judu* 39: 29–30).

The NAOA exerted a large effort to show its independence from foreign influence. One way was by replacing the IAOA as the spokesman for and the leader of China's anti-drug crusade. Before the establishment of the NAOA, foreign missionaries played the spokesman role through anti-opium associations under their control, such as the International Reform Bureau and the IAOA. The leader of the International Reform Bureau, Edward White Thwing had the reputation of being the staunchest figure of opium suppression in the 1910s. His role was taken over by the IAOA, which was established in 1918 in Beijing after the expiration of the Ten-Year Agreement. In a short time, branches were established in Shanghai, Tianjin, Shandong, Hubei, Jiangsu, and other places. In July of 1919, the IAOA of Beijing, Shanghai, and Tianjin reached an agreement to acknowledge Beijing's association as the national headquarters in charge of dealing with international and diplomatic issues and collecting information provided by various branches. Each branch, however, made its own plan and raised its own operation funds. In other words, each branch was to operate independently from Beijing headquarters, while letting it represent them collectively to the world.

As the collective representative for the IAOA, the IAOA in Beijing became China's authoritative voice on the opium issue. Because the reports provided to the League of Nations by Chinese Government Opium Investigating Commissioners were often incomplete and sometimes not totally true, the League of Nations recognized the IAOA as a more reliable alternative source of information on opium. As John Jordan, assessor to the Advisory Committee, pointed out, the IAOA, "though not an official body, was undoubtedly the best body to form an opinion on the whole situation in China" (League of Nations 1924, 42).

To deal with the incomplete report on the opium situation in China, before the First Opium Conference, the League of Nations asked the Chinese government to make more thorough inquiries about the cultivation of the poppy in China so as to be able to supply the League with a reliable report; to include in the Commission of Investigation representatives of organizations such as Chambers of Commerce and Educational Associations; and to attach to the Commission of Investigation a representative of the International Anti-Opium Association in Beijing and to authorize this representative to transmit through the Chinese government a report to the League as a supplement to the general report of the Commission of Investigation (League of Nations 1924, 44).

But the Chinese government never formally endorsed the IAOA's report as official and complete, and made little effort to honor the request by the League that the representatives of the IAOA be included (League of Nations 1924, 45). Therefore, when other League members cited the IAOA's report to point out the failure of the Chinese to suppress opium, it made many Chinese anti-opium activists, especially those in Shanghai, uneasy toward the IAOA. The fact that the IAOA was run by the British made it more susceptible to Chinese anti-opium activists in the nationalist zeal of the 1920s. As mentioned above, China was accused by other delegates of producing 90 percent of the world's opium, based on figures provided in an IAOA pamphlet at the First Opium Conference. The Chinese delegate responded angrily and pointed out that the figure was inaccurate due to the way the information was collected, which was through missionaries in various parts of China. In China, the opium trafficking route from its major interior producing areas to its coastal consumption market was very long, and therefore—according to the delegate—every missionary who saw the opium pass by would report it to the IAOA as a separate case; thus the IAOA's figure was actually many times greater than the real (League of Nations 1925a, 77).

It was not a coincidence that the Chinese delegate made a special announcement about the activities of the NAOA, an organization they viewed as representative of China's unofficial anti-opium organizations. From its inception, the NAOA consciously tried to position itself as the leader of China's anti-drug force. Actually, the NAOA was one of eight private associations from the world that was allowed to address the Second Opium Conference on November 20,

1924. Gu Ziren, the representative of the NAOA delivered the speech. After a brief introduction of the NAOA, Gu outlined four tasks it would undertake: (1) to suppress the planting of opium in China; (2) to prevent opium smoking and the abuse of morphine, cocaine, and other narcotics; (3) to stop illicit trade in narcotics; (4) to solve the problem of opium smoking by overseas Chinese. It is worth pointing out that Gu spoke very confidently and emphasized the NAOA would "wage a war against opium" in China. He claimed that the Chinese "have seen the growth in recent years of the consciousness and power of people, and this consciousness and power have in recent years been expressed on more than one occasion of national crisis. It is because of this knowledge that I can speak to you to-day with the confidence and assurance that I have on this subject" (League of Nations 1925b, 445–46).

In the meantime, the NAOA deliberately distanced itself from the IAOA. Many people who were active in the IAOA's Shanghai branch simply joined the NAOA, such as Chen Guangfu and Wu Liande (*Shenbao* 01/18, 1919). The IAOA was rarely mentioned in publications of the NAOA. Nevertheless it was not until 1927 that the NAOA openly denounced the IAOA the first time, when the latter's report on the quantity of illicit opium seized by Chinese customs was once again used by the Advisory Committee in its report to the Council of the League of Nations. The Chinese representative pointed out that the report of the IAOA, as a private organization, could not be accepted as official by the Chinese government. This episode was reported by Ge Gongzhen, a famous journalist of that time, to the NAOA. From Ge's point of view, the report exaggerated not only the opium situation in China but also questioned the intention of IAOA's General Secretary Aspland. Ge viewed Aspland as a conspirator with British and Indian representatives on the Advisory Committee, providing them materials to attack China's opium policy. Noticing that Aspland issued the report in the name of "by the order of Board of Directors," which consisted mostly of prominent Chinese, including Li Yuanhong, Yan Huiqing, Wang Chonghui, and Xong Xiling, Ge opined that they might have been manipulated and misused by Aspland (*Judu* 11: 3–4).

In reality, after the establishment of the NAOA, many branches of the IAOA continued to exist, at least in name. It caused some people to mistake the two organizations as a single one. After 1927, Mr. Aspland continued to publish articles that the NAOA viewed as offensive. His report in the *China Annual Book of 1928* was seen as depicting a too gloomy picture of China's anti-opium future. In 1928, the NAOA finally called for the dismantling of all branches of the IAOA and replacing them with ones of the NAOA. The NAOA declared that the IAOA was only a private organization of the English and had nothing to do with the NAOA. While acknowledging that it had done some works for the anti-opium cause before, the NAOA pointed out that in fact the IAOA had ceased its activities after the formation of the NAOA. In addition, though Li Yuanhong, Wang Chonghui, and Yan Huiqing had withdrawn from the IAOA, the IAOA continued to list their names on its letterhead, thus raising the question of its credibility. The

NAOA further claimed that it had received a letter from the IAOA that expressed its willingness to hand over all its local branches to the NAOA, making the continuing existence of the IAOA neither necessary nor possible (*Judu* 20: 25–26). Over the next few years, the influence of the NAOA continued to grow to such a degree that even the League of Nations asked to have its publications as references in 1928 (NAOA 1931, 176).

In summary, opium suppression efforts deteriorated rapidly after the fall of the Qing dynasty, exposing the vast gap between anti-opium rhetoric and reality in the early years of the Republic. The formation of the NAOA was an attempt by the growing Chinese private sector, represented by the Shanghai elite, to exercise its power on social issues of national concern, during a time when the central government in Beijing had no actual authority over the whole country. The rich resources the NAOA possessed enabled it to mobilize the public to an unprecedented degree and made itself an instant, dominant, anti-opium organization in China. Though the origins of the NAOA sprang partly from a vague internationalism that sought to solve the opium problem through a cooperative international community, the experiences of the First and Second Opium Conferences made the NAOA abolish its hopes and turn to nationalism to get the public mobilized. With its close ties to the Chinese Christian forces, the NAOA, on the one hand, was an adoption of the Social Gospel trend at the time, which focused on promoting social reform by targeting concrete social issues. On the other hand, it was also a result of Chinese Christians' continuing effort to take leadership away from foreign missionaries. Amid a nationwide anti-Christian movement, the participation of Chinese Christian forces in the NAOA was a response to, as well as a unique manifestation of, modern Chinese nationalism. The NAOA replaced previous foreign-related anti-opium organizations with its "Chineseness"— namely it was run by Chinese people and used them as its main power base. Its mastery of modern techniques of mobilization and propaganda enabled the NAOA to exercise its influence both in China and internationally. It was under these conditions that the NAOA continued to advocate its goal under the newly established Nationalist regime in Nanjing, a regime that turned out to be even more resistant to the efforts of the NAOA.

4

Society versus State:
NAOA and Opium Policies of
the Nationalists, 1927–1934

The Nationalists initiated the Northern Expedition from Guangdong in July 1926, aiming to overthrow the warlords and unify the whole country. Led by Jiang Jieshi, the Nationalist troops advanced rapidly and seized Shanghai and Nanjing in March 1927. The Northern Expedition concluded triumphantly in the following year, with the takeover of Beijing and the pledged allegiance from Zhang Xueliang, who ruled Manchuria. There were reasons for the NAOA to have high expectations on the opium issue for the newly established Nanjing government. Ideologically, the Nationalists were against both warlords and imperialists, and a strong central government should have helped effective opium-suppression enforcement. But in reality, Jiang Jieshi was challenged by other regional military strongmen, and the Nanjing government was further weakened by factional struggles within the Nationalist Party. All of these factors made the national unification only nominal. From the end of the 1920s to the mid-1930s, in addition to facing the Japanese threat, Jiang conducted a series of military campaigns against his enemies, both regional militarists and the Communists, to consolidate his power. To the Nanjing government, the mounting fiscal shortage once again outweighed the official anti-opium stance, and the government often resorted to the opium revenue to alleviate its financial burden—precipitating the conflict between the NAOA and the government over the opium policy.

THE NATIONALISTS AND THE SHANGHAI ELITE

Many scholars have argued that China has not had a fully developed civil society like Western countries. Others have pointed out that the weakness of central government during the ten years preceding the establishment of the Nationalist regime in 1927 led Chinese local elites, represented by the Chinese bourgeoisie, to play major roles in governance in places like Shanghai where they had a dominant presence. For instance, Bergere has pointed out "the modalities through which the bourgeois groups were moved to take such steps, namely (a) the part played by professional organizations in bringing about this transition from action of hitherto essentially corporatist and local nature to political commitment and activism, and (b) the accession to maturity of an autonomous society that had been left to its own devices by the collapse of State power and now discovered within itself prodigious powers of adaptation and initiative" (Bergere 1986, 213). The NAOA, as we have seen, was a product of this trend, though it had a broader popular base than did a pure bourgeois organization such as the Shanghai General Chamber of Commerce.

Among various organizations in Shanghai, the Shanghai General Chamber of Commerce was the most important, simply because its members represented the most powerful business class and enjoyed a reputation as China's strongest Chamber of Commerce. Shanghai capitalists actively participated in national politics. During 1922–1923, their three main demands on the then Beijing government were reducing army size, establishing a constitution, and consolidating finances. Disappointed at the Beijing government's failure to adhere to parliamentary politics, they looked for alternatives. It was during the same period that the theory of direct rule by the people became popular. The ultimate experiment with this doctrine was the establishment of the People's Government Council by the Shanghai General Chamber of Commerce in July 1923, in reaction to the coup by the warlord Cao Kun in Beijing. The aim of the Council was to set up a government ruled directly by the people, but the Chamber made the Council a subcommittee of its own in order to gain total control. This act narrowed its base and doomed its chance of success from the outset. The Council was short-lived and did not produce any results (Xu and Qian 1991, 316–24).

The failure of the Council reveals a problem in the relationship between society and state in that time. Citing Bergere again:

> This upsurge of the bourgeoisie during its golden age was the most audacious move made by Chinese autonomous society during the modern period. But what can a society achieve when abandoned to itself? How could its actions possibly be effective at a national level without the intervention of a government capable of converting its many proposals into a plan of most general application? Left without a partner, in the shape of the State, the Chinese bourgeoisie exhausted itself in a sterile monologue; the moves that it initiated collapsed and became bogged down in a nar-

row corporatism, a corporatism that sought to change the board of directors of the Shanghai Chamber of Commerce into the national government! (Bergere 1986, 226)

Bergere's discussion of the Shanghai capitalists can be used to describe the dilemma faced by all the Shanghai elite, of which the bourgeoisie was an important component. It was in the context of opium prohibition that members of the NAOA had high expectations for the Nationalists, who at least appeared to have gained control of the country by 1927. They hoped that a strong central government could carry out opium suppression effectively, clearing up an excuse often cited during the warlord period; and they wanted to have more say in the government's opium policy based on their established reputation and some members' close relation to the highest rank of the Nationalist leadership. In fact, Chen Guangfu, treasurer of the NAOA, was among the first Shanghai bankers to whom Jiang Jieshi looked for financial help (Xu and Qian 1991, 371).

The optimistic sentiment of NAOA toward the new Nationalist government was brief. It soon became clear that the Nationalist regime had no interest in sharing political power with other groups. As Parks M. Coble pointed out, to the Nationalists,

the landlords, the capitalists, labor, the peasants, students and intellectuals—all could potentially challenge the government. Nanking systematically suppressed all organizations representing these elements and sought to bring them under government supervision. Political repression was essential in achieving these ends. The independent press was curtailed; student groups were crushed and reorganized as government-dominated bodies; labor unions were emasculated; and landlord control of local government agencies was gradually challenged. By weakening these social forces, the government could pursue politics without reference to any sector but itself. (Coble 1980, 268)

The Shanghai General Chamber of Commerce was one of the first casualties of the Nanjing government. From April 1927 to May 1929, the struggles between the Chamber and the government ended in the victory of the government. The new Shanghai Chamber of Commerce was set up on June 21, 1930, under direct control of the Nationalists (Xu and Qian 1991, 361–401).

Much of the work that has been done on the fate of Shanghai capitalists has challenged the old assumption that the Nationalist government was based on an alliance with Shanghai capitalists (Bergere 1986; Coble 1980; Eastman 1974). Bergere has pointed out that the Chinese bourgeoisie contributed to the reestablishment of the state authority but at the same time became the victim of this process when it gave up its political autonomy (Bergere 1986, 239–40). Coble describes the process by which the Nationalist regime succeeded in controlling the Shanghai capitalists not only politically but also economically by using both cooperation and coercion. In sum, the Nanjing government ended the golden age of the Chinese bourgeoisie and the development of Chinese civil society.

This chapter demonstrates that even though the Shanghai elite and the capitalists retreated from political and economical fronts under pressure from the Nationalist government, they did not do so without fighting and did stand as firmly as they could. The process of eroding the political and economic power of the Shanghai capitalists was composed of attacks and counterattacks, overt coercion, and behind-closed-doors negotiations. The attempts by the government to limit the Shanghai elite's influence on the social front were met with the greatest resistance, since this was the area where the entire elite group had common ground and got the most support from the society. The issue of opium suppression provided a domain for the public sphere in which to challenge the government. The NAOA was one of the few organizations that for quite a long period of time not only dared to confront the Nanjing regime's opium policy openly but also exerted pressure on the latter by mobilizing public opinion. This was the same technique the Shanghai capitalists had used to express their political views before. The complexity of the relationship between the NAOA and the Nationalist government demonstrates that the Nationalists never developed total control of society. The private sector had not been totally destroyed, as it would be later by the Communist regime.

INITIAL CONTACTS: THE NAOA
AND NANJING GOVERNMENT BEFORE 1928

With the crackdown against Communist-dominated labor unions in Shanghai on April 12, 1927, by the right-wing Nationalists, and the subsequent establishment of the Nanjing government, the Shanghai urban elite had very high expectations that the new regime would do the same for opium, which had become the worst of this city's modern vices (Wakeman 1995, 24). The high hopes arose from the Nationalists' revolutionary and nationalist ideology, which targeted both warlords and imperialists—the two main culprits for the failure of opium suppression in China, according to the then-hegemonic, anti-opium discourse.

Within two months of the Nationalists' entry into Shanghai, however, no concrete opium-suppression measure had yet been implemented by Shanghai authorities. The NAOA felt the need to push the opium issue to the new ruler. On May 16, a joint conference on the opium issue by major Shanghai civic organizations was held by the request of the NAOA. It passed a letter to the Central Political Council's Shanghai Branch, then the highest authority in the city, suggesting the formation of an Opium Suppression Committee and the enforcement of a prohibition plan (*Judu* 12: 10–11). Two elements should be distinguished here. The first was that in the joint meeting, the perennially participating organizations like the Shanghai General Chamber of Commerce, YMCA, and the Red Cross Society of China were joined by new groups such as Shanghai Party Headquarters, Shanghai United Labor Union, Shanghai Suburb Peasant Association, and Nationalist Youth League. This reflected a bid by the Nationalists to influence social issues like opium suppression. The second was the way the NAOA viewed itself as the leader of the opium-suppression movement; in particular, they requested that three members of their organization be included in the proposed Opium Suppression Committee, for which only one member was to come from each of the Public Security Bureau, Public Health Bureau, Municipal Party Headquarters, Maritime Customs, and Postal Bureau.

The NAOA also petitioned the Central Political Council of Nationalist Party in Nanjing and conducted intensive anti-opium lobbying. Benefiting from its rich social resources, the NAOA first secured support from several important political figures, such as Cai Yuanpei, Niu Yongjian, and Wu Chaoshu. Among the economic policy makers of the new Nationalist government, Qian Xinzhi and Chen Guangfu were on the NAOA's Honorary Directorate, where they played a mediating role between the Nationalist government and the NAOA. As a result of anti-opium lobby, the 105th meeting of the Central Political Council of Nationalist Party passed a resolution that demanded the total suppression of opium in three years (*Judu* 25: 41).

But the NAOA had little time to celebrate before it found out the true intentions of the Nanjing government on opium suppression. Ironically, the newly established Opium Suppression Bureau was put under the jurisdiction of the Ministry of Finance, not the Ministry of Interior Affairs or Ministry of Civic Affairs. The suspicions this raised were confirmed when, in September, the Ministry of Finance revealed the *Temporary Regulations of Opium Suppression*, which included articles permitting addicts over age 25 to continue their habits and, to make things worse, legalizing opium sales as long as the retailers applied for special permits (Yu Ende 1934, 284–85).

The obvious aim of the regulations was to extract revenue from opium in the name of "suppression through taxation." This drew an immediate outcry from various sectors of society. In an angry response to this new policy, the NAOA issued a declaration denouncing the legalization of the sale of opium:

> Opium has been an instrument of imperialist aggression and a blood pipeline of warlords and bureaucrats. It is a dangerous enemy of the Three People's Doctrine and a cause of demise of the Chinese nation and state. . . . This association has had trust in policies of Nationalist government and restrained itself from voicing disagreement, hoping a fruitful result on the opium issue would come by allowing more time. But the current opium suppression plan is not only completely contrary to the policy of the abolition of opium in three years, but also irreconcilable to the teaching of Sun Zhongshan. It only encourages local tyrants and evil gentry to run amuck and sordid merchants to take the opportunity to speculate. How can this plan be explained and vindicated according to the original aim of revolution? The revolution is said to be beneficial to the country and people, actually it delivers the exact opposite! According to teaching on opium suppression by Sun Zhongshan, this kind of plan is exactly what he called the public enemy of people's opinion and an action of betraying the motherland. (*Judu* 15: 10–11)

This excerpt is a good example of the basic strategy the NAOA adopted in the propaganda war against the opium policy of Nanjing government—that is, to reiterate anti-imperialist, anti-warlord, and anti-opium stands the Nationalists had proclaimed to counterattack their current deeds. By emphasizing the differences between "reactionary" warlord regimes and the "revolutionary" Nationalist government, the NAOA effectively put the Nationalists on the defensive. Invoking the teaching of Sun Zhongshan on opium suppression to a certain degree safeguarded the NAOA from possible political retaliations when it launched sharp criticisms against the regime. Reciting Sun Zhongshan's will was one routine of many Nationalist gatherings; the NAOA adopted the ritual and added the recitation of Sun Zhongshan's teaching on opium suppression before its meetings. The teaching was also printed on front pages of *Judu* magazine. An embarrassment to the Nationalist opium policymakers, this gave the NAOA the upper hand in the fight for public opinion.

The opium policymakers not only faced harsh public criticism from outside the party, but also met with criticisms from within the Nationalist Party. The authorities of Zhejiang province were some of the most ardent opponents to the new opium-suppression regulations. The provincial party headquarters and most of its municipal and county branches were against the policy of suppression through taxation. A Committee Against Legalizing Opium Sale was formed and a telegram was sent to the Nanjing government asking for the rescission of the *Temporary Regulations* by the Ministry of Finance. The province went on to declare that it would conduct opium suppression by itself and would deprive the Ministry of Finance the right to handle the opium issue in the province. Faced with tremendous pressures, the Nanjing government revised the *Temporary Regulations* in November 1927, and again in April 1928. Though the scope of regulations was enlarged and punishments of offenses in some cases became more severe, the key issue of taxation did not change (Yu Ende 1934, 192–96). In the meantime, the Ministry of Finance reached a compromise with Zhejiang province in February 1928, and thus put an end to the dispute between the central and local governments.

The setbacks of the anti-opium crusade propelled the NAOA to fight more vigorously and to take more initiatives. In September and November of 1927, two more joint opium-suppression meetings of various Shanghai civic organizations were held to advocate the revision of the *Temporary Regulations*. In the first meeting, Li Jihong, director of the Opium Suppression Bureau of the Ministry of Finance, gave explanations of the current policy and presented a new version of the *Regulations*. But to many representatives at the meeting, there was no essential distinction between the two. Li became the target of discontent and left in the middle of the meeting. At the second meeting, the NAOA suggested the formation of a National Opium Suppression Commission (NOSC hereafter), which would be the highest authority in charge of the opium issue (Yu Ende 1934, 192–96). Though the NAOA could only express its stand by holding numerous anti-opium meetings, giving public speeches, publishing articles, and passing and sending petition letters to the Nationalist government, they did contribute to the mobilization of anti-opium sentiment during the first several months of the Nanjing government.

Both anti-opium sentiment, in general, and the efforts by the NAOA, in particular, were manifested by the magnitude of public mobilization during the fourth Anti-Opium Week during October 2 to 8, 1927, in Shanghai. According to NAOA statistics, institutions and organizations involved in the Anti-Opium Week included 10 party headquarters; 24 general unions of workers, peasants, merchants, and students; 114 schools; 71 churches; more than 600 worker unions; 42 Chambers of Commerce; 15 newspapers; and 21 film and drama theaters, plus several entertainment centers. Thirteen mass anti-opium gatherings and 54 public speakings were held during the week. The merchants' anti-opium gathering was held at Shanghai General Chamber of Commerce, with attendance of more than 1,000, and six petition articles and a circular telegram were passed to the Nanjing government, asking merchants all over China to oppose opium. All activities culminated at the Shanghai Citizens Anti-Opium Gathering in the Public Sports Field on the last day of the week, which was attended by more than 30,000 people. A declaration and a telegram to the Nanjing government were passed, asking for real action on opium prohibition.

The total number of participants was recorded as 1,763,600 for the week (*Judu* 15: 27–36). Considering Shanghai's population was about 3 million at that time, this number, if not exaggerated, was very impressive. Even though the Nationalists were trying to bring the Shanghai elite under their control, the success of the Anti-Opium Week was a manifestation of the mobilizing power that the elite still possessed.

A SHORT-LIVED PARTNERSHIP:
THE NAOA AND NANJING GOVERNMENT IN 1928

Realizing that the NAOA was the de facto leader of the anti-opium crusade in China, Nanjing became more receptive to the organization. At the same time, the NAOA intensified its lobby in Nanjing, targeting the removal of the Ministry of Finance in charge of opium "suppression," and modification of the government's regulations. In response to NAOA's request, Sun Ke (Sun Fo), Minister of Finance, agreed to meet with representatives of the NAOA to discuss the issue in late 1927. The actual meeting was attended by an assistant minister instead, who cited again the urgent military monetary need as an excuse for policy lapses; some progress, however, was made at the meeting. Both sides agreed that the existing regulations needed to be revised, and an outline of organizational procedures for a National Opium Suppression Commission was drafted (*Judu* 16: 9–12).

Despite this, the practice of opium revenue collection was business as usual in the late 1927 and early 1928. The NAOA continued its public opinion war against the authorities. The turning point came in March 1928, when the 46th meeting of the Nationalist government decided to set up a National Opium Suppression Commission (NOSC hereafter) and called for a National Opium Suppression Conference. The meeting sent two senior government advisers to Shanghai to investigate the opium issue and consult with the NAOA. Sensing the opportunity, the NAOA called two joint anti-opium meetings of Shanghai civic organizations on March 25 and 29 and invited the two government advisers to attend. Members of the NAOA also accompanied them to visit opium shops to collect firsthand evidence (*Judu* 24: 52–53). Upon their return to Nanjing, these two advisers subsequently submitted a report very favorable to the NAOA.

At the same meeting, General Zhang Zhijiang was appointed to set up the proposed NOSC. Zhang, a subordinate to Jiang Jieshi's rival General Feng Yuxiang, was not a member of the inner circle around Jiang. After the appointment, one of the first things he did was to send a telegram to Li Denghui and Zhong Ketuo asking for the NAOA's participation and cooperation (*Judu* 24: 53). It was likely that Zhang Zhijiang wanted to use the NAOA to consolidate his newly appointed position, but to the NAOA, this gesture signified the acknowledgment by the Nanjing government of the NAOA's legitimacy and importance to opium suppression. In the following several months, a partnership between the NAOA and the government's opium-suppression policy-making organ was forged.

In June 1928, the Nationalist Army captured Beijing, concluding the Northern Expedition. The formal unification of China under the Nanjing government and the end of large-scale military action took away the Ministry of Finance's excuse for collecting opium revenue. The NAOA was quick to use this opportunity to press the Ministry to transfer its jurisdiction over opium suppression to the Ministry of Civic Affairs, as had been promised (*Judu* 22: 5). In late June, the Minister of Finance T. V. Soong convened the National Economic Conference. Among nearly seventy representatives were Chen Guangfu and Zhong Ketu, the Treasurer and General Secretary of the NAOA. Zhong lobbied for opium suppression at the Conference, even though the main theme of the Conference was rebuilding China's economy (Coble 1980, 49; *Judu* 24: 53).

Continuing pressure by the NAOA prompted Nanjing to accelerate the formation of the NOSC in the 74th meeting of the Nationalist government on June 26. In August, the NAOA again petitioned the fifth plenary meeting of the Second Congress of the Nationalist Party on the issue of opium suppression. The proposed NOSC was finally set up on August 20, and Li Denghui and Zhong Ketuo were appointed members of the fourteen-member commission by the Nationalist government (*Judu* 24: 53). The NAOA's presence in the NOSC was by no means a small achievement, as evidenced by the status of the other twelve members. The NOSC included Jiang Jieshi himself, as well as his three main military rivals: Feng Yuxiang, Yan Xishan, and Li Zongren. Other members like He Yingqin, Li

Jishen, Li Liejun, Chen Shaokuan, Zhang Zhijiang were all senior military and political figures. In addition it had three natural members: Minister of Interior Affairs, Minister of Justice, and Minister of Foreign Affairs. The only noticeable absence was the Minister of Finance. Zhong Ketuo also sat on the two-member Standing Committee, along with the Minister of Interior Affairs (Lai 1986, 16). It symbolized not only the official recognition of the NAOA by the Nanjing government, but also its allowing the NAOA to play an active role in suppressing opium.

The involvement of NAOA in the making of opium policy for the Nanjing government culminated in the convening of the National Opium Suppression Conference, which was held from November 1–10, 1928, in Nanjing. The Conference's goal was to solve the opium problem through implementing laws and regulations at every link in the chain, including planting, trafficking, manufacturing, sale, and consumption. Representatives came from provincial governments, provincial Chambers of Commerce, military high commanders, people's anti-opium organizations, as well as experts on narcotic drugs. The opening of the Conference gave some hope to the NAOA that Nanjing would really change its existing taxation policy. Zhong Ketuo praised the formation of the NOSC and declared that the participation of the NAOA signaled the coming of a "cooperation era between government and people to suppress opium." But he also reminded the representatives of the disappointing government policy adopted earlier and challenged them not only to be opium-suppression representatives in name, but also to get involved actively in the crusade (NOSC 1929, Annex 16–17).

The unprecedented influence of the NAOA was visible at the Conference. Li and Zhong were among eighteen people who served as council members; including Jiang Jieshi, Feng Yuxiang, Li Zongren, T. V. Soong, Zhang Zhijiang, and several cabinet members and social dignitaries. The Minister of Public Health acknowledged that the Conference was the direct result of the efforts and insistence by the NAOA. Zhang Zhijiang praised the NAOA as one of the most noble and valuable people's organizations in Chinese history (NOSC 1929, Annex, 15–17). Not only did Zhong Ketuo serve as the general secretary of the conference, but also the NAOA acted as its secretariat and even hosted a banquet for all representatives.

Jiang Jieshi attended the Conference and gave an empty and ambiguous speech. He claimed that the central government had not got a penny from the opium tax in 1928—a statement that troubled the NAOA. Citing statistics provided by the Ministry of Finance, according to the NAOA, income from the opium tax amounted to 633,958 *yuan* and 648,044.34 *yuan* for October and November 1927 respectively. The numbers were not significant in terms of the total revenue of the government, which prompted the NAOA to argue that government would be foolish to sacrifice moral standards and government credibility for such a small financial gain (*Judu* 18: 11–12). Whether these numbers were accurate is impossible to say, yet interestingly enough, Jiang also complained in the speech that though the central government did not get a penny, many local rulers had made money by conducting opium-related businesses. He did proclaim that the national government would absolutely not receive a penny from opium, otherwise this government should be recognized as morally bankrupt and untrustworthy (NOSC 1929, speeches section, 40).

The honeymoon between the NAOA and the Nanjing government was short-lived. Immediately after the National Opium Suppression Conference, on November 22, a boat named *Jiangan* carrying a large quantity of opium arrived in Shanghai. An army unit that was unloading the opium clashed with a police unit that arrived later. Both claimed they were seizing the opium following the order to "suppress opium." In the conflict, several policemen were beaten up by the army soldiers. This incident provoked another public outcry on the opium issue in Chinese media. The NAOA telegraphed the Nanjing government on November 27, asking for a thorough investigation. Three days later, the NAOA convened representatives from twenty-six public organizations to make coordinated plans for dealing with this incident. Under pressure, Nanjing sent Zhang Zhijiang and Minister of Justice Wei Daoming to Shanghai. But the investigation dragged on for a long time without concrete conclusion (NAOA 1931, 176).

The result of the *Jiangan* opium case reminded the NAOA of what had happened earlier with the Nanjing regime on the issue of opium—their words seldom matched their deeds. None of the forty-four resolutions presented at the National Opium Suppression Conference was implemented, revealing that the NOSC was an organization that could not exercise even the power it was supposed to possess. Since Zhang Zhijiang, its chairman, was not a member of Jiang Jieshi's inner circle, he was never trusted and given full power to handle the Commission's mission. Realizing his nominal position, Zhang threatened to resign in early 1929, citing poor health, which put the NOSC in a state of limbo (NAOA 1931, 178).

A LONE FIGHTER: THE NAOA AFTER 1928

One year after the establishment of the NOSC, the NAOA issued a sharply worded declaration, denouncing the Commission on these counts: (1) it had done little in a year; (2) it faced a worse opium situation in many provinces; (3) it had no plans to deal with the Far Eastern Opium Investigation Commission or the International Opium Conference that would be held in 1930 (*Judu* 33: 13–14). The declaration expressed the frustration of the NAOA toward the Nanjing government, which, in the years to come, continued to use opium as a source of revenue. Coble analyzed the relationship between the Nanjing government and Shanghai capitalists; "Chiang's [Jiang] paramount concern was income for his military, and he seemed to care little how it was raised" (Coble 1980, 262).

In this situation, the relationship between the NAOA and the Nanjing government sank to a level lower than before their short-lived partnership. The NAOA's hope in the Nationalists quickly disappeared after the NOSC became paralyzed soon after the National Opium Suppression Conference. Having witnessed the Nationalists' efforts to bring previously independent organizations under their supervision, the NAOA had to insist on its nonpolitical nature to protect itself. Though the NAOA did not alter its ardent anti-opium stance, the changing relationship with the Nationalists prompted it to emphasize that it was a "people's organization." It claimed that the NAOA "consisted of people's organizations aimed solely at an anti-opium crusade. It had neither a political function nor any other purposes" (*Judu* 22: 5). Its principle was to "follow the anti-opium teaching of Sun Zhongshan and enhance the people's anti-opium wish" (*Judu* 22: 5).

The NAOA's main weapon to advocate an anti-opium crusade remained the mobilization of public opinion in these years. The annual, national, Anti-Opium Week continued to be the showcase of the NAOA. In 1929, in an attempt to enhance its influence nationwide, the NAOA organized a National Circuit Anti-Opium Movement, with dispatches sent into four main areas: the Northeast, the Yangzi Delta, South China, and the Yangzi Corridor. Big cities covered in the movement included Shanghai, Hangzhou, Shengyang, Jilin, Changchun, Harbin, Guangzhoo, Xiamen, Fuzhou, Wuhan, Changsha, and Nanchang (NAOA 1931, 179). Its mouthpiece *Judu* continued to publish articles criticizing the government's opium policy, even though "it became a crime in 1931 to criticize the Nationalist Party in the press" (Wakeman 1995, 29). The hegemonic anti-opium discourse forced the Nationalists to be more tolerant of the criticisms of the NAOA.

In the years following 1928, the most notable achievement of the NAOA was its forging of a public opinion campaign to ward off the government's plan in 1931 to legalize opium sales. The rumor of the change in Nanjing's policy circulated at the end of 1930, so on New Year's Day of 1931, the NAOA issued a declaration asking the Nanjing government to carry out opium suppression thoroughly. The NAOA again wrote to the NOSC asking for clarification of the rumor, and was told there was no truth to it (*Judu* 48: 13–14).

Yet in January, the Ministry of Finance sent Li Jihong, who had been in charge of collecting the "special tax" for years, on a tour of investigation to Taiwan. He was sent there to examine the opium monopoly in Japanese-occupied Taiwan in advance of the preparation of a similar policy that was under consideration. Li's activities were reported to the NAOA by local Chinese, which enhanced the public's suspicion of the government's real intention. Ironically, the monopoly plan was echoed by an eminent member of the NAOA, Dr. Wu Liande. On February 6, Wu published an article promoting the idea of abolishing opium through government monopoly in fifteen years, which prompted an angry denunciation by the NAOA. Wu was a well-respected doctor at times and very influential in the anti-opium circle, but the NAOA saw Wu's argument as no accident but an action in collusion with the government. Because Wu Liande, as well as Li Jihong, had been appointed new members of the reorganized NOSC, it was put under the jurisdiction of the Executive Council (*Judu* 48: 14).

On February 13, the NAOA called a meeting of its Standing Executive Committee to discuss strategies to fight back. A strongly worded statement was issued that declared that adopting the monopoly policy would signal the total bankruptcy of political morality of China. The NAOA pointed out that the proposed plan would be against the teachings of the late Sun Zhongshan, and that it could cause a loss of government credibility with foreigners abroad as well as with the people of China. It was also against the Constitution of the Nationalist Party and the law of Nanjing government. If implemented, a dramatic increase in the number of opium addicts was predictable (*Judu* 48: 7). On February 19, a joint conference against opium monopoly was held by Shanghai civic organizations that was attended by more than 200 representatives. The conference adopted twelve anti-opium resolutions and issued a circular telegraph to the whole country protesting the government's proposal.

Protests were organized by local branches of the NAOA and the Chinese press participated in the protest. The proposed monopoly plan not only became the target of public opinion, but also met criticisms from members of the Nationalist Party. Jiangsu Party Reform Committee asked the Central Committee to clarify the rumor. So did some local party branches in Shanghai and Zhejiang (*Judu* 48: 18–21). In the Citizen's Conference held in May, under pressure from 130 representatives, Jiang Jieshi gave an explanation of the government's opium policy. Attributing the difficulties of opium suppression to the existence of foreign concessions in China, Jiang emphasized the need of adopting "scientific methods" to achieve the goal (Lai 1986, 33–34).

Jiang did not elaborate what "scientific method" he meant, but to the NAOA, this was revealed by government's action. In June, the National Opium Investigation and Seizure Bureau was set up and was put into jurisdiction under the Ministry of Finance. Li Jihong was appointed its chief. Under the plan, local branches were to be set up in provinces, which would be in charge of issuing licenses to opium retailers. Obviously it was another version of legalizing opium, and it drew another wave of protest from the public. In response to public opinion, in late June, the Ministry of Finance denied the Opium Investigation and Seizure Bureau was one of its organs, claiming it belonged to the NOSC. Nevertheless, the Opium Investigation and Seizure Bureau, along with its local branches, was formally set up on July 1, 1931, but to everyone's surprise, only one week later the Executive Council ordered it to be dismantled, for it had become clear the bureau would always be a target of public contempt and a catalyst of struggle between different interest groups within the Nanjing government (*Judu* 50: 7–10).

The NAOA did not get this hard-fought victory without cost. It was the first time the differences among its leadership surfaced in public. The first general secretary of the NAOA, Zhong Ketuo, resigned in 1929 and took a government post. Though he continued to participate in the activities of the NAOA in the following years, he served mostly in the capacity of a government official supervising the opium suppression; at the same time, he often acted as a mediator between the

NAOA and NOSC (Lai 1986, 126). Another former president of the NAOA, Luo Yunyan, along with Dr. Wu Liande, was appointed to the reorganized NOSC. In the wake of Wu's support for an opium monopoly by the government, the NAOA passed a resolution, forbidding members of its Executive Committee from serving on the NOSC. This measure was obviously aimed at cutting Wu's ties with the NAOA (*Judu* 48: 14).

The most dramatic attempt to damage the reputation of the NAOA was made at the height of its struggle against legalizing opium. In March 1931, the NAOA sent Huang Jiahui, its general secretary, to Taiwan, to investigate what Li Jihong had done on the island (*Judu* 48: 13–21). On March 15, a Shanghai newspaper reported that Bai Zhiying, Huang's wife, was arrested by Hong Kong customs for trafficking in morphine. The news was spread rapidly in and outside Shanghai, because of Bai's special social status. At the time the news broke, the Huang couple was still in Taiwan. They were asked by the NAOA to come back immediately to Shanghai to explain things. After the Huangs came back, it became clear that the incident was a total fabrication. According to the investigation conducted by the NAOA, it was set up by the same person who advocated an opium monopoly by the government. Though the investigation did not specify names, it implicated Wu Liande as a conspirator (NAOA 1931, 40, 193).

On another front, the relationship between the NAOA and Nanjing government deteriorated further in the same time period. In November 1931, the Huairou county branch of the Hebei Anti-Opium Association was vandalized by local officials, who, according to the Hebei Association, were all opium addicts. The local branch petitioned the Provincial Party Headquarters for a settlement. Calling the Anti-Opium Association "an illegal organization," the Provincial Party Headquarters ordered the Association banned. Interestingly, there was a difference between the Provincial government and the Provincial Party Headquarters as to how to handle the incident. The former asked local governments to give the Association "help and supervision," but the latter ordered local party branches to ban all anti-opium associations. It prompted the Hebei Anti-Opium Association to telegraph the Central Executive Committee of the Nationalist Party, accusing the Provincial Party Headquarters of illegally destroying anti-opium organizations and requesting withdrawal of the order (*Judu* 52: 7–11).

After the failure of the opium monopoly plan in 1931, the Nanjing government attempted to resurrect the plan in other names, but eventually succumbed to the pressure of public opinion. In August 1932, the NAOA called a National Anti-Drug Representative Conference, which was a big embarrassment to the Nanjing government. According to the organizational article of the 1928 National Opium Suppression Conference, the Conference should be convened one to two times each year; in fact, the second meeting was postponed several times and eventually it became clear that the government had no intention of holding another one. By convening a National Anti-Drug Representative Conference, the NAOA reaffirmed its leadership role in China's anti-opium crusade. In the Conference's final declaration, the representatives recognized that "the people's anti-drug movement should be the main force to achieve opium suppression in China" (*Judu* 59: 14), which could also be read as an expression of total disappointment with the role of Nanjing government.

The activities of the NAOA had become such an obstacle to the monopoly plan of the Nationalists that the Nanjing government implemented more aggressive measures against the organization. First Nanjing tried to weaken the NAOA financially. Under the influence of government committee members of the American Boxer Indemnity Fund, it terminated support to the NAOA in 1931. Perennial advertisers in *Judu* monthly, such as the Bank of China and the Bank of Communications, withdrew in fear of alienating officials in the Ministry of Finance, who were also in charge of collecting opium taxes. Since the Indemnity Fund and the advertisement income supplied more than two-thirds of the NAOA's total budget, the decreasing budget effectively forced the NAOA to operate on a much reduced scale.

In addition, articles and advertisements from the NAOA opposing the monopoly plan of the government were banned from Shanghai Chinese newspapers, and monopoly advocates such as Wu Liande spread defamatory letters and circulars about the NAOA and Huang Jiahui. These actions were designed to weaken public support for the NAOA, thus further reducing its ability to solicit public contributions. Huang Jiahui even became a target of personal attack; in late 1932, a bomb was sent to his residence that fortunately did not explode. Following that incident, suspicious persons continued to appear at both the office and residence of Huang Jiahui, and he was forced to keep his whereabouts secret. The activities of the NAOA were very much affected by this intimidation and harassment (U.S.D.S. 1985, Narcotics/1992, Narcotics/625).[12]

These actions were taken amid the Sino-Japanese conflicts in the early 1930s. The timing was deliberately chosen because at the time the public's attention was occupied by the national crisis. It was not until the NAOA was very much weakened and public criticism had lessened that the government declared the Six-Year Opium Suppression Plan in 1935, which included a government opium monopoly. The response of the NAOA was as negative as usual, since it saw this kind of anti-opium plan as nothing new. As a response, the NAOA published the entire text of the speech given by Jiang Jieshi at the National Opium Suppression Conference, which had promised the government would not get one penny from opium (*Judu* 99: 2–3).

To take control of public opinion, the Shanghai Party Headquarters organized its own anti-opium propaganda week in April of 1936. Though the NAOA was listed as a constituent member and the week was an obvious imitation of NAOA's annual Anti-Opium Week, the NAOA was marginalized and had little say in the plans (*Judu* 99: 5–8). Not surprisingly, the event drew sarcastic reports from the NAOA (*Judu* 100: 39–41). Bruised and weakened, under the leadership of Huang Jiahui, the NAOA continued its fight against the proposed government opium monopoly without compromise.

Two final attempts were made by forces in and outside of the NAOA to align the NAOA more toward the opium policy of the Nanjing government. First, Christian forces represented by Shanghai missionaries tried to deprive Huang Jiahui of his position in the late spring of 1937, but with backup from members of the Executive Committee, Huang was able to uphold both his position and the policy of advocating absolute suppression. In the second case, in late May or early June 1937, representatives of the government offered Huang the option of continuing to lead the NAOA in exchange for him refraining from criticizing the Six-Year Plan until its expiration in 1940. Participating in the meeting were Yan Baohang (Paul Yen), Executive Secretary of the New Life Movement and Huang Renlin (J. L. Huang), General Secretary of the Officers Moral Endeavor Association—both government officials with close ties to Jiang Jieshi. They even promised to provide enough funding for the NAOA and to clear up Jiang's "misunderstandings" regarding Huang's strong anti-government and anti-monopoly activities in the past (U.S.D.S. 1985, 893.114, Narcotics/1992).

The second offer would have effectively changed the NAOA into an organ serving the government's opium policy. Once again the proposal was rejected by Huang Jiahui. Faced with increasing government hostility and financial difficulties, yet not willing to compromise its stand against an opium monopoly, the Executive Committee of the NAOA decided to dissolve the Association in a meeting on June 28, 1937, just days before the outbreak of the Sino-Japanese War (*Chinese Recorder* 1937, 533–34).

To sum up, the weakness of the Chinese government in Beijing prompted the Shanghai elite to form the NAOA in the hope that a civil organization against opium could better represent China on the international stage. But without support from a strong state, it was almost impossible to overcome its primary obstacles—namely, warlordism inside China and imperialism outside. With the advance of the Nationalists, the Shanghai elite hoped the establishment of the Nanjing regime would change the picture. Especially at the beginning, Jiang Jieshi and the right-wing Nationalists seemed to treat the Shanghai elite as an ally in the struggle against the Communists and left-wing Nationalists; the Nationalists' official discourse on opium was not very different from that of the NAOA.

It soon became clear, however, that the real purpose of opium "suppression" by the Nanjing government was to collect revenue to subsidize Jiang's military operation. The disappointed NAOA voiced its discontent with Nanjing. Surprisingly, soon it was the Nationalists who felt pressure from the hegemony of anti-opium discourse, mobilized and represented by the NAOA, with which they dared not disagree publicly. Although the Nationalists were successful in putting the Shanghai elite under their control politically and economically, they were less effective on social issues such as opium suppression. In fact, the pressure from the anti-opium discourse was so immense that, for a while, the Nationalists were forced to cooperate with the NAOA on opium-suppression issues.

The honeymoon between the NAOA and the Nanjing government was short-lived, however. After the National Opium Suppression Conference, Jiang Jieshi adopted a policy similar to that of the previous warlords, that is, extracting opium revenue in the name of opium suppression without regard to public opinion. The relationship between the NAOA and Nanjing became estranged and even hostile. But in a time when the Nationalists had greatly consolidated their power and become more and more authoritarian, the NAOA stood out as one of few private organizations that dared openly to voice sharp criticisms toward the government. Since opium was made a domain of public sphere by the hegemonic anti-opium discourse, the NAOA had a strong protective umbrella against the assault from political power of the state. But along with the consolidation of power by the Nationalists and Jiang Jieshi, the state gradually narrowed the room for the survival of organizations and finally wore down the NAOA in 1937. The Six-Year Opium Suppression Plan sponsored by the Nationalist government was carried out in a much different context.

5

The Six-Year Opium
Suppression Plan and the
New Life Movement

In the early 1930s, Jiang Jieshi had become a dominant figure in Nanjing, but his power was by no means unchallengeable, and he was forced constantly to struggle to consolidate his authority. Opium, as a vital financial resource, was an integral part of Jiang's political efforts, which resulted in his increased personal involvement in the making of opium policy. In the beginning, the Nanjing government's policy toward opium suppression was very ambiguous. On the one hand, the government issued anti-drug laws and regulations, with little effort or intent to enforce them. On the other hand, the government collected opium revenue in the name of a "special tax" or even "opium suppression tax." The opium issue became such a focus of public opinion that even members of the Nationalist Party demanded the government adopt a more rigorous and sincere approach to drug suppression. Responding to the mounting pressure, in the mid-1930s the Nationalists finally launched a nationwide anti-drug campaign under the title of the Six-Year Opium Suppression Plan (1935–1940). This chapter examines how the crusade was not only a campaign to solve a social vice but also an integral part of a larger political initiative to consolidate the power of the central government nationwide by cutting off the revenue sources of regional powers. Equally important, it enhanced the authority of Jiang Jieshi by bringing the everyday lives of Chinese people under rigid, ideological control. Nevertheless, the government's half-hearted policy concerning opium revenue, the resistance from regional powers, and the Sino-Japanese War conspired to doom the campaign from the outset.

JIANG JIESHI AND OPIUM SUPPRESSION

The issue of opium suppression became highly visible in the early 1930s, particularly because of Jiang Jieshi's involvement. Before 1930, he had adopted an anti-drug position in public yet given tacit consent to the practice of taxing opium for state revenue. In 1931, at the Citizens' Conference, in response to representatives' proposal of eliminating the special tax on opium, Jiang Jieshi blamed the existence of foreign concessions as the main obstacle of achieving this goal:

> The opium epidemic has been an evil for a long time. If we hope to eradicate it in a short time by adopting draconian law without cutting off its sources from the foreign concessions, according to previous experience, the results will only make prisons crowded with drug offenders and give traffickers and smugglers opportunities to fleece the people. So in order to eliminate the problem, we have to take back all foreign concessions that have been the bases of opium trafficking for the imperialists. The Conference should trust the resolution of the government to suppress opium, and believe that within the six-year tutelage period, the government will definitely nullify all unequal treaties and regain all concessions to foreigners. At the same time the government will accomplish the task of opium suppression through scientific methods. (Lai 1986, 33–34)

As mentioned above, Jiang did not elaborate what the "scientific methods" were, and his ambiguous position drew a sarcastic response from the NAOA. The plan to follow "scientific methods" by adopting a government opium monopoly was aborted under public pressure.

Only one year later, Jiang adopted draconian opium-suppression policies, which signaled a 180-degree shift from his earlier stance. In 1932, while conducting a campaign to suppress the Communists in Er-Yu-Wan area (Hubei, Henan, and Anhui provinces), Jiang issued a number of anti-opium regulations through the General Headquarters of Bandits Suppression. According to *Matters Needing Attention on Prohibiting Poppy Cultivation*, special opium-suppression dispatches and county magistrates were instructed to paste slogans and notices on the walls of all villages, declaring that capital punishment would apply to opium offenders. Not only would those poppy cultivators caught by special dispatches be executed, but also the county magistrates and district heads where poppy cultivators were found would be disciplined. The severity of punishment also applied to opium addicts. The *Rehabilitation Methods for Party, Administration, and Military Personnel and Students within a Limited Time* ordered that addicts had to register with the party or the government's supervisory bureau within two weeks and be rehabilitated within 30 to 45 days. Those who did not register and were found using opium, morphine, or other substitutes beyond the time limit would be executed (Lai 1986, 43–46).

It was not these policies, but rather the institution named to be in charge of opium suppression that revealed the inconsistencies and contradictions in Jiang's ostensible efforts to combat opium. The institution was the notorious Special Tax Liquidation Bureau of Hubei. Its predecessor, the Special Tax Liquidation Bureau of Hubei and Hunan, was set up by the Ministry of Finance in Wuhan in 1929. Its task was to gather unpaid taxes of stock opium, to extract taxes on opium on the way to market, and finally to destroy opium. Initially, the Bureau was supposed to exist at most for six months, but it became a permanent institute and served mainly as a revenue-generation arm of the government. In 1931, the original Bureau broke up into two separate bureaus responsible for Hubei and Hunan, respectively. The reputation of the Bureau as an opium taxation institute was so notorious that even the Hubei Party Committee appealed for its dismantling at the fourth plenary meeting of the Third Congress of the Nationalist Party (Lai 1986, 42). But for obvious reasons, this appeal made little impression on the policymakers Nanjing.

The main tasks of the Special Tax Liquidation Bureau were to regulate opium traffic and trade. No matter how harsh the opium-suppression regulations seemed to be, the strategy Jiang adopted was so-called *jianjin* (suppression by stages). A grace period of up to six years was given to old and infirm opium addicts to quit the habit, resulting in a "legitimate" demand for opium consumption before the expiration of the grace period. It was in this context that the Special Tax Liquidation Bureau of Hubei was given authority to control almost every step of opium transactions.

The transaction process was clearly outlined. Anyone who wanted to purchase opium from poppy-growing border provinces had to get a purchasing certificate from the Bureau. Transportation without the certificate would be considered smuggling and the opium subject to confiscation. The Bureau set up a number of warehouses along the main traffic routes. The opium-purchasing merchants had to transport their opium along these designated routes and hand it over to the Bureau as soon as they reached a place where there was an authorized warehouse or a transportation unit. Therefore it was the warehouse that was responsible for the storage and distribution of opium. The distribution of opium was through opium wholesale shops that held transit certificates issued by the Bureau. The opium retail outlet (*tugao dian*) could purchase opium from the wholesale shop (*tugao hang*) but not from the warehouse directly. The retail outlet could then sell its product to opium addicts, who had to buy opium with their time-limited rehabilitation certificates—also issued by the Bureau (Lai 1986, 49–50).

Obviously the Bureau's task was to enforce the opium monopoly under Jiang's military authorities. At that time, Jiang's military campaigns were operating under a huge deficit, and were complicated by his policy dispute with the Minister of Finance, T. V. Soong, over the fact that Jiang put the Communists as enemy number one, although Soong saw the Japanese as more threatening. In the fiscal year beginning July 1932, the monthly military expenditures averaged 26.7 million *yuan*, but Soong had agreed to raise only 15 million *yuan* for Jiang (Coble 1980, 121). The 10 million *yuan* monthly deficit the government was running pushed Jiang to seek alternative sources of revenue. He found them in the Special Tax Liquidation Bureau, which in 1931, handed in 14 million *yuan* to the Ministry of Finance (Zhu, Jiang, and Zhang 1995, 229).

In the following years, opium suppression was closely linked to Jiang's military operations. For example, in May 1933, Jiang moved his field headquarters to Nanchang in the midst of his efforts to suppress the Communists. In April 1934, Jiang dismantled the Special Tax Liquidation Bureau of Hubei and established a Supervisory Bureau of Opium Suppression instead; its headquarters was in Hankou and it was under the direct command of the Military Committee headed by Jiang. The Supervisory Bureau's authority included control of opium transportation and trade in ten provinces,[13] though its main function remained the same as its predecessor (Lai 1986, 52–53).

Jiang's action deprived the NOSC, the official government organ in charge of opium suppression nationwide, of any real authority. In June 1934, the NOSC voluntarily appealed to the Executive Council to hand NOSC's opium-suppression responsibility in the ten provinces to Jiang's Military Committee. This appeal was promptly granted and made public on July 12, 1934. Admitting that the drug problem had become worse, the NOSC claimed that only by following Jiang's practice of using military law could the problem be solved (Lai 1986, 57–58).

Aside from the increasing involvement of Jiang and his Military Committee, there was virtually no difference in the opium-suppression practice of the Nationalists before and after 1932. It is very hard to believe Jiang's anti-drug campaign had any real effect besides its revenue-generation function. As Lai Shuqing points out, the campaign had limited effects in the Er-Yu-Wan area, and was never coordinated in the ten provinces under the jurisdiction of the Military Committee (Lai 1986, 50, 59). But Jiang's involvement in the opium issue continued and culminated when he became the General Supervisor of Opium Prohibition in 1935 to carry out the Six-Year Opium Suppression Plan, which was the most detailed blueprint of a nationwide anti-drug campaign the Nationalists ever undertook following their takeover of Nanjing in 1927.

THE SIX-YEAR OPIUM SUPPRESSION
PLAN AND ITS IMPLEMENTATION

Initiated in April 1935, the plan by all accounts was the most comprehensive and far-reaching opium-suppression campaign conducted by the Nationalists. On April 1, 1935, Jiang issued a general order of opium suppression and made public the *Implementation Methods of Opium Prohibition* and the *Implementation Methods of Dangerous Drugs Prohibition*.[14] The outline of the campaign was set by these two regulations, which were drafted by Jiang's field headquarters. The campaign's timetable was defined from 1935 to 1940. The content of the campaign consisted of the Six-Year Opium Prohibition Plan and the Two-Year Dangerous Drugs Prohibition Plan. The campaign was to regulate all four aspects of the drug problem, namely drug making (poppy planting), trafficking, distribution, and consumption (Lai 1986, 63–64).

Jiang did not hesitate to take control of the campaign. On April 4, he asked the Nanjing government to add another nine provinces and three cities to the jurisdiction of the Military Committee over opium prohibition.[15] His request was granted by the Executive Council on April 18. According to the *Implementation Methods of Opium Prohibition,* a general committee of opium suppression should be set up in the field headquarters of the Military Committee, and committees and branch committees should be established at provincial, municipal, and county levels. On June 5, 1935, the Nanjing government dismantled the already emasculated NOSC and named Jiang as the General Supervisor of Opium Prohibition (Lai 1986, 64–65, 78–79).

The campaign's implementation strategy was to eradicate opium and dangerous drugs step by step, but only two years were given to solve the problem of using morphine and other dangerous drugs. All addicts were ordered to be rehabilitated before the end of 1935, otherwise they would go through compulsory rehabilitation plus a prison term of five years or more. Beginning in 1937, addicts found using morphine intravenously or smoking other drugs would be sentenced to life in prison or suffer the death penalty (Lai 1986, 76). Compared to opium offenders, drug makers and traffickers were subjected to harsher punishment. In 1936, among a total of 18,523 arrested drug offenders, 1,294 were sentenced to death and 469 to life in prison, but only 14 opium offenders got the death penalty and 392 life in prison (Second National Historical Archives, 1937–1938).

The six years given to eradicate the opium problem included poppy cultivating, opium transportation, opium selling, and consumption. As far as poppy cultiva-

A drug rehabilitation center in Tianjin run by the Nationalist government

tion was concerned, most provinces were ordered to stop planting opium poppy immediately, except for seven provinces that were allowed to phase out poppy planting within five years. The timetable for those seven provinces varied according to different situations. The time each province took to come into compliance with the requirement also varied significantly, as illustrated in Table 5.1.

According to the original plan, Yunnan was to eliminate poppy planting in thirty-eight counties (districts) in 1935, another forty-seven in 1936, and finally forty-four more in 1937. But in 1937, in eighteen of forty-four districts, most of them in remote border areas, the plan was delayed one year or more due to the difficulty of enforcement, mainly caused by the resistance of the local poppy cultivators. After the Sino-Japanese War broke out in 1937, some provinces carried out the plan earlier in order to enlarge grain cultivation to supply provisions for the troops. Examples of this were Gansu and Suiyuan, as demonstrated in Table 5.1 (Lai 1986, 105, 107).

Suppression of opium consumption was planned to follow the general timetable. In 1936, the registration of opium addicts was to be carried out and those registered would be given rehabilitation certificates, with which they could buy opium through opium retailers. Addicts were to rehabilitate themselves at home or in rehabilitation hospitals and centers. One-fifth of the total number of addicts would be rehabilitated in the centers every year until 1940, beginning with addicts under forty. Accordingly, one-fifth of the total addicts would revoke their rehabilitation certificates each year and lose their privilege to buy and consume opium legally. Their opium-smoking instruments were also subject to confiscation, and their effectiveness of rehabilitation could be re-examined by designated hospitals (Lai 1986, 96–97).

Table 5.1. Timetable (by Year) of Eradication of Poppy Planting in Seven Provinces

Province		*1933*	*1934*	*1935*	*1936*	*1937*	*1938*	*1939*
Sichuan	Planned				xxx	xxx	xxx	xxx
	Carried out				xxx	xxx	xxx	
Yunnan	Planned			xxx	xxx	xxx		
	Carried out			xxx	xxx	xxx	xxx	xxx
Guizhou	Planned			xxx	xxx	xxx	xxx	xxx
	Carried out			xxx	xxx	xxx	xxx	
Shanxi	Planned	xxx	xxx	xxx	xxx	xxx		
	Carried out	xxx	xxx	xxx	xxx	xxx		
Gansu	Planned		xxx	xxx	xxx	xxx	xxx	
	Carried out		xxx	xxx	xxx	xxx		
Suiyuan	Planned			xxx	xxx	xxx	xxx	xxx
	Carried out			xxx	xxx	xxx	xxx	
Ningxia	Planned			xxx	xxx			
	Carried out			xxx	xxx	xxx		

Source: Lai Shuqing 1986, 106.

As long as there were addicts with rehabilitation certificates in their hands, opium would be legally available. Opium purchasing, transportation, distribution, and retail were put under government monopoly. From 1937 on, the old system that depended on private merchants to purchase and transport opium was to be demolished and would be replaced by opium-suppression organs that were granted the right to purchase raw opium from the remaining seven poppy-planting provinces. Crude opium would be transported to the planned government refineries to make *gonggao* (official or public opium). A certain amount of *gonggao*, to correspond to four-fifths of the amount needed for the addicts in 1936, would be sent out from the government opium refineries to the whole country. In the meantime, existing opium wholesale shops and retail outlets would be closed and the *gonggao* sold to addicts by individual contractors. Interestingly, contractors were to be chosen from among those old wholesale shops and retail outlets. The price of *gonggao* was to be set by the Opium Suppression Bureau. The amount of *gonggao* produced would decrease by one-fifth every year until 1940, when, according to the plan, all addicts would have been rehabilitated; thus there would be no poppy cultivation allowed and no need for government opium refineries (Lai 1986, 90–95).

In fact, the government-controlled opium monopoly never materialized as originally planned. The main obstacle was that the government found it impossible to purchase all crude opium held by the public. Consequently, the government-run opium refineries were never established. Opium was distributed as before—by those wholesale shops and retail outlets, whose number increased rather than decreased during 1936–1938 (Lai 1986, 318). In an attempt to renew the plan of the opium monopoly, in August 1938 the Ministry of Interior proposed phasing out wholesale and retail shops by lottery before the end of 1940. The Ministry of Finance ordered all of them replaced by Opium Administrative Institutions, run by county or city governments, in the spring of 1939. These Institutions got their opium supply from warehouses run by the Supervisory Bureau of Opium Suppression and then sold to addicts. With the deadline of the Six-Year Plan approaching, the Ministry ordered most of these Institutions dismantled before June, with extraordinary cases getting an extension until September (Lai 1986, 111–12).

Jiang Jieshi's resignation as the General Supervisor of Opium Prohibition on March 1, 1938, was the watershed event of the whole campaign. Before his resignation, all aspects of opium suppression were under Jiang's direct control, which guaranteed some degree of coordination in policy implementation. The outbreak of the Sino-Japanese War, however, changed Jiang's priorities. After his resignation, the General Committee on Opium Suppression became a subordinate of the Ministry of Interior. Because the Supervisory Bureau of Opium Suppression, in charge of opium transportation and distribution, was put under the jurisdiction of the Ministry of Finance, the Ministry of Interior was actually only in charge of preventing poppy cultivation and opium consumption. From 1938 to 1940, the remaining period of the campaign witnessed overlapping opium-suppression organs set up by different ministries and with a lesser degree of coordination, which to a great extent jeopardized the effectiveness of their anti-drug efforts (Lai 1986, 165).

It would be unfair not to acknowledge the great efforts the Nationalists made in making detailed plans, issuing laws and regulations, setting up institutions, and carrying out the Six-Year Plan. Though there are many statistics illustrating progress made in the campaign, however, it is very hard to convince anyone that the campaign was a success simply because of the fact that the opium was not eradicated, and an opium problem continued to exist after 1940. The importance of this campaign comes when it is put into the broader context of modern China. The following sections demonstrate how the reason and timing for conducting the Six-Year Opium Plan was deeply connected with Jiang's desire to consolidate his personal authority as well as the power of the central government. The anti-opium campaign and the New Life Movement (NLM hereafter) were attempts by Jiang to enhance the legitimacy of the Nationalist government and to deprive his regional rivals of financial support and moral credibility.

THE NEW LIFE MOVEMENT AND ANTI-DRUG CRUSADE

The timing of Jiang's involvement in anti-opium initiatives coincided with his efforts to consolidate his power. Following the establishment of the Nanjing government in 1927, Jiang's position was challenged constantly by both his intra-party rivals and several major militarists. He was briefly ousted from power twice, mainly by his rivals in the Nationalist Party—once in late 1927 for about five months, and again at the end of 1931 for six weeks. From 1929 to 1931, Jiang engaged in a series of battles against regional military powers like Feng Yuxiang, Yan Xishan, and the Guangxi Clique (including Li Zongren, Bai Chongxi, and Li Jishen). Combining military muscle and political manipulation, Jiang managed to defeat his political and military rivals and emerged as the dominant strong man in China. As Lloyd Eastman has pointed out, after Jiang returned to become head of the newly created Military Committee in January 1932, he remained the "overwhelmingly dominant leader of the Nationalist regime" until 1949 (Eastman 1986, 130).

But this does not mean that Jiang had a firm grip on all weakened major rivals and those small warlords in many regions. Although most of them pledged their loyalty to the Nationalist government after the Northern Expedition, some of the provincial militarists remained de facto independent in the early 1930s, especially those in southwestern parts of China. Since their power bases were often limited to one province or even smaller domains, they did not constitute a direct threat to the central government—though they ardently resisted Jiang's attempts to subordinate them to his control. In other words, as long as the provincial militarists nominally pledged their loyalty to the Nanjing regime, Jiang, who was already tied up by anti-Communist military campaigns and the continued intra-party power struggle, was reluctant or unable to subordinate these regional war-lords through military means. Always backed up by his military force, Jiang instead attempted to consolidate his power by establishing his moral leadership in the whole society. It is this context that prompted him to launch both the New Life Movement and the anti-opium initiative in the mid-1930s.

In a speech at his field headquarters in Nanchang, Jiang launched the NLM on February 19, 1934. The Nanchang NLM Promotion Committee was subsequently established with Jiang as its chairman. Calling for the regeneration of the country and the Chinese nation, Jiang admitted that the only way to achieve the goal was by enhancing citizens' morality and knowledge, not by military force. He used the emergence of fascist Germany as an example, applauding the high degree of morality and the knowledge of the German people as the source of its ascendancy. In contrast, he deplored the low national spirituality of the Chinese as exemplified by their undesirable habits in everyday life. The remedy proposed by Jiang was to ask the people to honor the traditional moral principles called *li, yi, lian, chi* (pro-priety, righteousness, integrity, and sense of shame) and practice them by adopt-ing a "hygienic" and "disciplined" lifestyle (Jiang Jieshi 1944a, 1–8).

Jiang's principles on the NLM were further elaborated in a series of speeches during March. The model citizen's life was depicted as "militarized," "productive," and "artistic." According to Jiang, a militarized life should be characterized by a patriotic spirit, simple lifestyle, swiftness in action, and obedience to authorities. A productive life was one of frugality, and that showed an effective use of time and of Chinese-made products. To be artistic in life required being strict with oneself and lenient toward others, and being honest, upright, and efficient at work. Above all else, according to Jiang, if guided by principles of *li, yi, lian, chi*, the citizens of China would be united, disciplined, and strong (Xie 1982, 282).

Jiang was very enthusiastic in promoting the NLM and was personally involved in its planning and implementation. Only three days after its inception, Jiang called a meeting of directors of the Promotion Committee to discuss plans and regulations. Jiang's initial intention was to have an experiment in Jiangxi province first, but soon the NLM was being followed in many other places around the country. In June, an *Outline of the NLM* was declared to be a standard guideline for conducting the movement. On July 1, a new General Promotion Committee of the NLM replaced the old Nanchang NLM Promotion Committee, signaling that the movement had become a national campaign. Jiang, as the Chairman of the NLM Committee, was in charge of all leadership and promotion responsibilities (Xie 1982, 249).

The spread of the NLM was very impressive. Even in 1934, Promotion Commit-tees of the NLM were set up in Nanjing, Shanghai, and Beiping, as well as in Hubei, Hunan, Shanxi, Henan, Shandong, Fujian, Anhui, Shaanxi, Jiangsu, Zhejiang, Gansu, Cahaer, Suiyuan, Hebei, and Qinghai provinces, excluding only Jiangxi, which was under the direct guidance of the General Committee in Nanchang. In 1935, the Sichuan, Yunnan, Guizhou, and Ningxia provinces, which had not been under the actual control of the central government, also established Promotion Committees. The number of counties that had established the Promotion Committee reached 1,132. Ten Promotion Committees were set up by overseas Chinese in Chinese communities in Japan, Burma, Singapore, Australia, Vietnam and as far away as in Mexico and Peru between February 1934 and February 1937 (Xie 1982, 251, 260–66). The establishment of NLM organizations nationwide gave Jiang the symbolic status as the leader of the spiritual regeneration of Nationalist China.

It was this context that laid the groundwork for conducting the anti-opium campaign. Broadly speaking, opium suppression after 1934 became a part of the NLM. Since the NLM aimed to change Chinese people into "new citizens" through changes in their everyday life, the rampant opium addiction was a natural target of the NLM. Yunnan, Guizhou, Suiyuan, Hunan, and Anhui all listed the suppression of opium as the work of the NLM (Promotion Committee of the NLM 1944, vol. 2, 6–25). From its inception, Jiang put forth the opium issue as an immediate task of the NLM. In a speech on October 16, 1934, entitled *Conducting the NLM and Constructing Shaanxi*, Jiang listed opium suppression as one of the issues that was to be dealt with immediately (Jiang Jieshi 1944b, 40). Less than one month later, in another speech entitled *Objects and Implementation Methods of the NLM*, Jiang singled out foot-binding, opium addiction, gambling, and prostitution as practices in Shanxi that were contrary to the principles of the NLM. According to Jiang, "there is no way to realize a new life as long as opium has not been gotten rid of" (Jiang Jieshi 1944c, 44). Nine years later, in a speech to promote the NLM in Guizhou, Jiang recalled the rampant opium cultivation he had seen in the spring of 1935 and how sad and sorrowful he felt for the Guizhou people, and then praised the progress that Guizhou had made under the NLM (Jiang Jieshi 1944d, 99).

In the name of regenerating China, the principles of the NLM promoted by Jiang achieved, at least nominally, ideological dominance on the issue of opium suppression. This gave Jiang leverage over regional powers to conduct the anti-drug campaign the way he wanted to. His position was further enhanced after the Sino-Japanese War began, since opium-suppression efforts were related to the enhancement of a citizen's health, which was a part of the broader war efforts then under way. Jiang also made it a patriotic issue to resist the Japanese attempts to drug China, which was Japanese policy in the areas under their control. In his speech to commemorate the sixth anniversary of the NLM in 1940 (and the last year of the Six-Year Opium Suppression Plan), Jiang called on all branches of society to get rid of the opium problem, especially those in the Japanese-occupied areas (Jiang Jieshi 1944e, 70). One year later, the anti-drug and anti-Japanese rhetoric was reiterated by Jiang who proclaimed that the central task of the NLM of 1941 was to get rid of the residual opium problem, stressing that "the drug suppression should be seen as important as fighting the enemy in the battle field" (Jiang Jieshi 1944f, 76).

The NLM manifested Jiang's wish that his control permeate every aspect of people's daily lives. To achieve this aim, a mass mobilization drive was launched. In addition to setting up Promotion Committees at provincial, county, and township levels to coordinate the movement, he used mass propaganda as a key strategy for indoctrinating ordinary people. From the beginning, a three-stage plan was established to carry out the movement, and launching propaganda was the task of the first stage. On March 11, 1934, a public gathering of over 100,000 residents promoting the NLM was held and followed by a parade in Nanchang. One week later, a lantern festival attracted even more people. School students were dispatched to advise and show people the proper ways of the New Life from home to home. In every corner of the city, those whose appearance or deeds were not in conformity with the principles of the movement were subjected to inspections by the advocates of the NLM (Promotion Committee of the NLM 1944, vol. 1, 1).

In its heyday from February 1934 to July 1937, propaganda work was very much the backbone of the NLM. Not only were propaganda units dispatched to targeted areas such as entertainment places and the countryside, but also to individual homes. Even priests were asked to recite doctrines of the NLM to their congregations. Hygiene classes in schools promoted the movement. The radio station run by Jiang's field headquarters regularly broadcast news about the NLM. In addition to periodicals published by many Promotion Committees of the NLM, numerous books about the NLM were written, films made, and songs composed. Attempts to introduce the NLM to foreign audiences were also undertaken, in the form of articles and addresses in English by Madame Jiang, as well as through the English edition of the *Outline of the NLM* (Xie 1982, 268–76).

The propaganda initiatives went hand in hand with mass mobilization, the most concrete example of this was the formation of the NLM Labor Corps. In April 1935, Jiang directed that various NLM groups were reorganized into the NLM Labor Corps. Members were required to do at least one hour of volunteer work every day for the cause of the NLM. Their activities ranged from promoting punctuality, literacy, work study, public hygiene, and physical exercise, to helping the police conduct investigations. By the end of 1935, the Labor Corps had 295 units and 69,018 members in 11 provinces. The numbers increased to 2,470 and 395,263, respectively, in 1936, including 39 women units and about 6,600 women members (Xie 1982, 252–56).

ANTI-OPIUM CAMPAIGN AND
JIANG'S EFFORTS TO CONTROL REGIONAL POWERS

If the aim of the NLM were to legitimize Jiang's moral superiority, the Six-Year Opium Suppression Plan was a direct threat to the power of many provincial warlords. Coincidentally, provinces—such as Sichuan, Yunnan, Guizhou, and Guangxi—still controlled by local warlords, were either leading poppy-cultivation areas or along major opium traffic routes. As mentioned earlier, Jiang's anti-opium initiatives began with his campaigns to suppress the "Communist bandits," and they served at least partly as a means of generating revenue in support of his military operation. Opium-related revenue was even more vital, however, to the survival of the provincial warlords. They had no difficulty determining the hidden agenda of the Six-Year Plan, looking behind Jiang's discourse of the NLM and the regeneration of the nation, and they did all they could to resist the Six-Year Plan whenever their interests were threatened.

The case of Sichuan is illustrative. After the collapse of the Qing dynasty, the province was controlled by warlords, mostly by non-Sichuanese before 1926 and by Sichuanese after 1926 till 1935. Before the Nanjing government was finally able to enter Sichuan while pursuing the Communist Red Army on the Long March in 1935, the province was ruled by five warlords divided by their garrison areas; among them, Liu Xiang was the strongest. A warlord in his garrison area had unlimited power over those subjects within the boundary of his rule. Sustaining rule and military expenditure depended on the warlord's ability to extract as many financial resources as possible in his domain. Warlords' practices of taxing virtually every product or commodity had won them a notorious reputation. Not surprisingly, one of the most lucrative taxes was dubbed the tax for opium suppression, because under the rule of warlords, Sichuan led the country in both opium cultivation and production. As Robert Kapp has pointed out, "The rapid spread of opium cultivation, for example, brought huge profits to the militarists who could tax or sell opium, but it cut down the amount of land devoted to food crops and raised food prices, while subjecting millions of Szechwanese to the ravages of opium addiction" (Kapp 1973, 56).

The importance of the opium tax to the financial viability of the warlords is evident in Table 5.2, which reveals the proportion of opium tax to the total tax income of Liu Xiang's Twenty-first Army. Considering that these figures were made public by the Twenty-first Army itself, the actual figures might be much higher. One estimate puts the opium tax revenue in 1933 as high as 33 percent of the gross income. According to other statistics, the opium tax occupied 45.59 and 32.57 percent of the total revenue of Yang Sen's Twentieth Army in 1930 and 1931, respectively (Kuang and Yang 1985, 253–54).

Table 5.2. Opium Tax Revenue of Twenty-first Army

Year	Opium Taxes (yuan)	Opium Taxes/Gross Income (%)
1928	902,478.22	7.52
1929	3,193,410.64	16.65
1930	11,179,279.44	37.10
1931	8,352,144.70	30.44
1932	8,570,892.32	27.06
1933	9,277,876.18	20.55

Source: Kuang and Yang 1985, 254.

Opium-related income also played a great role in other southwestern provinces. Yunnan had relied on opium revenue since the beginning of the warlord era in the early 1910s, and even used opium as currency to pay soldiers' salaries. In 1935, the opium-suppression tax was used to make up a fiscal deficit of 3.71 million *yuan* (Gao 1983, 53). Guizhou's reliance on opium revenue was no lesser than Yunnan's. In 1928, a total of 2.4 million *yuan* in opium-cultivation tax and 3.16 million *yuan* in opium-transit tax were collected, exceeding the approximately 4 million *yuan* collected from all other tax revenue. Subtracting about 9 million *yuan* of government expenditure, the opium income made a half million *yuan* surplus for Zhou Xichen, the warlord who was then in control of the province (Ma Fengcheng 1985, 351). The situation was no different in Guangxi. Though Guangxi was not a principal opium-cultivation area, it was in the middle of the opium transit route from Yunnan and Guizhou to the consumption market of Guangdong and Hong Kong, and the transit tax on opium constituted a large amount of its fiscal revenue. In 1932, opium-related tax was 15.88 million *yuan*, more than half of the total provincial tax income of 31 million *yuan* (Gao 1983, 55).

No one recognized the importance of the opium tax to warlords better than Jiang Jieshi. From his days of conducting anti-Communist military campaigns, Jiang always placed opium-revenue collection organs under his direct control. The Special Tax Liquidation Bureau of Hubei and Hunan, as well as its successive organization, the Supervisory Bureau of Opium Suppression, were all directly subordinate to Jiang's field headquarters. After being appointed the General Supervisor of Opium Prohibition, Jiang made the Bureau report directly to him rather than to the General Committee on Opium Suppression. After his resignation from the post in March 1938, the Bureau was nominally transferred to the Ministry of Finance, but it actually stayed on and was never under the Ministry's control in the remaining period of the Six-Year Plan (Lai 1986, 169).

As discussed earlier, the Supervisory Bureau was in charge of opium transportation and distribution, which generated most of the taxes. By controlling the Bureau, Jiang could achieve his twofold goal. On the one hand, opium taxes collected by the Supervisory Bureau became his personal exchequer, enabling him to finance forces loyal only to him, such as the secret police (Zhu, Jiang, and Zhang 1995, 233). On the other hand, by depriving opium revenue from the hands of regional warlords, Jiang could severely weaken their financial viability, thus making it easier to subject them to the control of the central government. To achieve this aim, the Bureau established a vast net of operations, with numerous branch bureaus, local offices, and special agents in many provinces (Lai 1986, 123).

Sichuan was one of a small number of provinces not affected by the power of the Bureau, and for a period warlords enjoyed autonomy in levying numerous opium-related taxes. At the end of 1934, however, the threat of the Red Army and the economic crisis propelled Sichuan's strongman Liu Xiang to turn to the central government for help. In the name of pursuing the Red Army, Jiang dispatched his forces into Sichuan and forced Liu Xiang to carry out a provincial reform designed to incorporate the province into the governance of the Nanjing. regime. The garrison area system was abolished, troops of warlords were incorporated into the central military structure, and their budgets were appropriated by the national government. The right to collect tax was concentrated in the hands of the provincial and national governments. The campaign to suppress the Communists also provided an opportunity for Jiang to increase his influences on Yunnan and Guizhou to a degree he had not been able to achieve before.

Jiang did not hesitate to capitalize on the situation. He came to Sichuan on March 2, 1935, and stayed there most of the time until October 31. During his stay, the NLM was promoted to such a degree that students at the Omei Training Corps had to endure eight hours of NLM lectures daily. Even Liu Xiang's wife became chairwoman of the local Promotion Committee of the NLM (Kapp 1973, 118, 125). At the same time, the anti-opium campaign was conducted in a highly publicized way. Shortly after Jiang's arrival in Chongqing, 1,300 opium dens were reportedly shut down. Jiang even moved the General Committee on Opium Suppression to Chongqing in November 1935 for three months until it was moved back to Nanjing in January 1936 (Kapp 1973, 118, 126).

Jiang was a master of using opium as a stick-and-carrot issue to achieve his strategic political aims. He used opium revenue to subsidize or bribe warlords into winning their support. When the Supervisory Bureau was handed to the Ministry of Finance, Jiang sent a letter to Minister Kong Xiangxi, asking him to keep those subsidies intact (Lai 1986, 167). Jiang also routinely embarrassed and pressured disobedient warlords by exposing their involvement in illicit opium trafficking.

Jiang's manipulation of opium affairs was sometimes more effective than his military muscle. For example, after being defeated by Jiang in 1930, the Guangxi Clique retreated to their home province and continued to be at odds with Jiang, relying heavily on taxes collected on opium in transit from Guizhou and Yunnan as its main revenue source. In 1935, pursuing and attacking the Communists on the Long March, forces of the central government entered Guizhou. Jiang ordered Guizhou and Yunnan to channel opium through Hunan, not Guangxi, in the name of opium suppression. The result was a drastic decrease of opium-tax income in Guangxi, from more than 10 million *yuan* to only 4 million *yuan* annually. Facing a financial crisis and military threat, the Guangxi Clique had no choice but to succumb to Jiang for a second time (Lary 1974, 190–99, 57–58).

Jiang's success in dealing with the Guangxi Clique does not preclude, however, that there was no resistance to his opium manipulation. The opium revenue was so crucial to their physical existence that regional warlords had no intention of giving it up totally. While claiming that they were following the Six-Year Plan, they developed opium monopolies in areas under their own control. This strategy was very effective for the very reason that it was for Jiang's, though the latter tried to do it at the national level. Yunnan had succeeded in resisting the control of Jiang's Supervisory Bureau before 1935. In response to the Six-Year Plan, Long Yun claimed to phase out poppy cultivation and established his own Yunnan Unified

Opium Transportation Bureau in 1935. Crude opium was purchased by the Bureau, then refined and made into a standard package of opium named Yunnan Common Goods (Yunnan gonghuo), ready for export to the rest of the country. The revenue generated by the opium monopoly went neither to the central government nor to Jiang Jieshi, but to the treasury of Long Yun (Gao 1983, 52).

In Sichuan, as soon as Jiang left the province, the opium-suppression campaign reverted to the hands of Liu Xiang. In return for helping Jiang bring Sichuan under central government control, Liu was appointed Chairman of the provincial government, head of the Pacification Bureau, and Supervisor of Opium Suppression, which enabled him to keep control over Sichuan, though to a reduced degree. According to Kapp, "By 1937, with the financial support of Chungking bankers, provincial authorities and private merchants organized a monopoly company to buy and sell all Szechwanese opium; prices were kept high, and the monopoly brought enormous profit for its creators and backers" (Kapp 1973, 122). According to the official provincial budget, total revenue in 1937 amounted to 86.3 million *yuan*, of which 60 million was from items of provincial tax. The special tax (opium tax) accounted for 24 million *yuan*, or about 40 percent of provincial tax revenue (Gao 1983, 54).

For those provinces in which the Supervisory Bureau was strongly present, the Bureau often became the target of conflicts between regional and central interests. The Bureau's attempts to establish an opium monopoly often provoked discontent, sometimes even direct confrontation from local authorities who also cast greedy eyes on opium. Accusing the Bureau of issuing unlimited certificates of transportation to opium merchants, the Henan provincial government proclaimed new regulations requiring opium wholesale shops and retail outlets to operate within defined areas and to purchase opium with only government certificates beginning August 1937. In spite of strong opposition from the Supervisory Bureau, the provincial government implemented the new plan in February 1938. In another case, since opium wholesale shops and opium dens mostly were set up by the Supervisory Bureau without approval of the provincial authorities in Guizhou, in January 1938, citing the fact that opium dens did not contribute to provincial taxation but were detrimental to the efforts of opium suppression, the provincial government got permission from the Executive Council to shut all of them down. Naturally, this initiative was challenged by the Supervisory Bureau, which collected a great deal of tax revenue from these opium dens. The conflict was finally solved through intervention by the Ministry of Interior, which had just been handed the responsibility of opium suppression after Jiang resigned as the General Supervisor of Opium Prohibition (Lai 1986, 321–23). These incidents were only two episodes in a larger drama of opium politics orchestrated and played out by Jiang and many other characters.

To sum up, Jiang's personal involvement with opium suppression increased after 1932, coinciding with his emergence as the dominant figure of the Nanjing regime. The issue of opium suppression was incorporated into his continuing efforts to consolidate his authority and that of the central government, which he represented. To achieve his aim, he adopted various strategies that enabled him to get the most gain from the opium issue materially and ideologically, at the same time depriving his regional rivals of them both. This purpose, however, meant that his anti-opium policies were half-hearted and doomed to be ineffective.

Before 1934, his opium-suppression initiatives were primarily aimed at generating much needed revenue to support his anti-Communist military campaigns. In 1934 and 1935, the pursuit of Communists on the Long March gave him an opportunity to expand the central government's influence into the southwestern provinces of China, which were the main areas of opium cultivation and which relied heavily on opium revenue. Opium suppression then became even more important in Jiang's efforts to bring the entire country under his control. If the Six-Year Plan had been carried out, the central government would have turned out to be the biggest beneficiary, and regional powers would have lost their financial vitality. Jiang was not hesitant to take personal charge of the campaign, and on different occasions was very effective at achieving political aims by playing the opium card. This, as we have seen, was evident in his dealing with the Guangxi Clique.

The NLM was another attempt to enhance his authority. By promoting a new life for the Chinese people, Jiang tried to become the spiritual leader of China as well. The intensive propaganda drive and mass mobilization gave him a lot of publicity. By making the opium issue a target of the NLM, Jiang further deprived individuals or institutions of any legitimacy to conduct opium business, thus putting his rivals, many of whom were involved in opium transactions, on the defensive.

But Jiang met strong resistance on every side. Strong regional powers like Yunnan and Shanxi succeeded in conducting opium monopolies themselves without allowing Jiang any access, meanwhile, semi-independent powers like the Sichuan warlords acted one way in front of Jiang and another way once his back was turned. Jiang's opium-suppression machine, the Supervisory Bureau, was directly challenged in many places. Compounded by the interruption of the Japanese invasion and rampant corruption, the Six-Year Plan was not a success and Jiang's aim was never fully realized. The reason for this failure is to be found within Jiang's regime itself. In retrospect, using the anti-opium campaign as a means to build a centralized Chinese state was not itself a wrong strategy, but to succeed this strategy required at minimum a central government free from the politics of warlordism, which Jiang's government was not able to achieve. The task of conducting a successful anti-opium campaign and at the same time using it as a means of state building was to be accomplished by the Communists in the early 1950s, which will be discussed in chapter 6.

6

Nationalism, Identity, and State Building: Anti-Drug Crusade in the People's Republic, 1949–1952

The People's Republic of China was established on October 1, 1949. In the so-called consolidation and reconstruction period of 1949 to 1952, the Chinese Communists took many initiatives to consolidate their newly gained power. The most important ones include movements for Land Reform; Resist America and Aid Korea; Suppress Counter-Revolutionaries; and the Three Antis and Five Antis Movements. These mass campaigns, and even the smaller scale campaign to abolish prostitution, have drawn general scholarly attention.[16] But the anti-drug campaign from the same period has remained today a virtually untouched topic. It was a campaign that involved most of China's urban population and successfully eliminated the centuries-long epidemic of opium abuse. It was also a political initiative that witnessed massive mobilization that had dramatic and penetrating effects on Chinese society, yet it was kept invisible to the outside world.

The lack of scholarly works on the anti-drug campaign is mainly due to the fact that, in the campaign's decisive phase in late 1952, the Communists intentionally avoided creating any public records about the campaign, and it remained invisible until very recently. This chapter, using newly available materials, reconstructs a brief history of the campaign.[17] In addition, by focusing on the ways the crusade was carried out in the historical contexts of the consolidation and reconstruction period, it also demonstrates that the crusade was a presentation of the

Communists' desire for a "new China" identity and was an integral part of the state-building process in the early 1950s.

COMMUNISTS' DISCOURSE ON OPIUM BEFORE 1949

The Communists, like the Nationalists and other previous regimes, had taken an anti-drug stand in public well before they took full power in 1949. Going back to the early 1930s, the Soviet governments declared poppy cultivation illegal in those areas that were under their control (Ma Mozhen 1998, 1599–1604). For example, in the Northern Sichuan Soviet established by Xu Xiangqian and Zhang Guotao in 1933, "opium cultivation was prohibited, and a graduated program to eliminate opium smoking was announced" (Kapp 1973, 89). But it was during the Sino-Japanese War that anti-drug discourse focused on Japan as a tangible target to enhance the existing nationalist tone. In response to the "poisonous policy," which promoted an opium monopoly in the territories occupied by the Japanese, the drug issue was tied even more tightly to the very existence of the nation. On February 29, 1939, the Executive Council of the Jin-Cha-Ji Border Region controlled by the Communists issued an order forbidding poppy cultivation. In addition to the claim that opium "sickens the country and harms the people," it warned that disobeying the order would severely affect the anti-Japanese war efforts and thus fall into the Japanese plot (Jinchaji Border Region 1939, 79). In *Opium and Narcotics Suppression Regulations of the Shan-Gan-Ning Border Region*, of which Yanan was the center, one article specifically elaborated that Chinese drug offenders endangered the vitality of the nation and would be subject to a much more severe punishment according to the *Regulations for Punishment of Traitors* (Shanganning Border Region 1942, 76).[18]

This type of anti-drug rhetoric and regulation continued through the period of civil war. Various anti-drug regulations were pronounced in the "liberated areas." With the countrywide victory over the Nationalists imminent, it was finally time for Mao Zedong and the Communists to put forth their idea of a "new China," which they had been envisioning for years:

> For many years we Communists have struggled not only for China's political and economic revolution but also for her cultural revolution; all this aims at building up a new society and a new state for the Chinese nation. In that new society and new state there will be not only new politics and a new economy but also a new culture. That is to say, we want not only to change a politically oppressed and economically exploited China into a politically free and economically prosperous China, but also to change a China which has been ignorant and backward under the rule of the old culture into a China that will be enlightened and progressive under the rule of a new culture. In a word, we want to build up a new China. (Mao 1965, 340)

According to Mao, the new China would get rid of all "capitalist" and "feudal" cultural elements of the old China and instead have a "national, scientific and mass culture" (Mao 1965, 380–82). It is in this broad context of discourse that opium, drugs, gambling, and prostitution became the first targets of Communist state building right after 1949.

THE FIRST PHASE OF THE CRUSADE: 1949–EARLY 1952

Signifying the start of a nationwide anti-drug crusade, on February 24, 1950, the Government Administrative Council issued a *General Order on Elimination of Opium and Narcotics*. In the *General Order*, several arguments were presented to legitimize the initiative, with a clear demarcation of before/after liberation attached. Before liberation, the opium problem was associated with the regimes of compradors, warlords, and feudal bureaucrats—who had forced people to cultivate opium poppy—and with the imperialists, who had forced it upon the Chinese people. The *General Order* begins with:

> It's been more than a century since opium was forcibly imported into China by the imperialists. Due to the reactionary rule and the decadent life style of the feudal bureaucrats, compradors, and warlords, opium not only was not suppressed, but we were forced to cultivate it; especially due to the Japanese systematically carrying out a plot to poison China during their aggression, uncountable people's lives and properties have been lost. Now that the people have been liberated, the following methods of opium and other narcotics suppression are specifically stipulated to protect people's health, to recover, and to accelerate production. (Government Administrative Council 1950, 97)

Though there is not much new in the anti-drug rhetoric, the *General Order* did give specific instructions to local authorities for carrying out the crusade, which were generally followed during the whole process of the campaign. They included:

1. Conduct propaganda to mobilize the masses
2. The People's Congress at various levels should discuss the issue and set up methods to get rid of opium within a limited timetable
3. Wipe out poppy cultivation in the areas where military operations have been ended, followed by other areas immediately after the end of military operations
4. Prohibit production, trafficking, or selling of opium and other narcotics
5. Ask the general public to hand in opium held in their hands
6. Register addicts within a set timetable
7. Make medications and prescriptions available to drug addicts, but under strict control by the Health Department in order to prevent them from becoming addicted to substitutes of drugs
8. Set up rehabilitation centers in cities with severe opium problems

9. Detailed methods and specific time table of opium suppression should be worked out by each Major Administrative Region or Military Control Commission in accordance with the *General Order*. (Government Administrative Council 1950, 97–98)

The last item of the *General Order* was carried out within one year, and many provinces and big cities formulated their own regulations accordingly. For example, Yunnan province, notorious for its high-potency *yuntu* and vast poppy cultivation, issued an Opium Suppression Directive on June 27, 1950, even before the issuance of the Enforcement Regulations by the Southwest Military Control Commission, its direct superior, on July 31 (Yunnan Provincial Government 1950, 3–4). On January 30, 1950, only thirty-five days after the establishment of the provincial government in Guizhou province, the authorities issued an opium-suppression notice and an open letter to the people, asking them to get rid of the evil of opium left over from the Nationalists and to strive to build a "new Guizhou." The notice was reiterated on August 25 with the issuance of the Provincial Opium Suppression Enforcement Regulations (Jin and Liao 1993, 274).

From early 1950 on, the opium-suppression campaign was carried out nationwide for the first time under Communist rule. The actions taken ranged from the registration and rehabilitation of addicts to curtailment of poppy cultivation and drug trafficking. Much progress was made. In Guizhou, opium dens were closed, addicts rehabilitated, poppy plants destroyed, and drug traffickers arrested. Many public trials were held, and a number of big traffickers were executed. In 1951, 49,646 *mu* (3,310 hectares) of poppies were wiped out, 3,000 opium dens were closed, 11,700 opium addicts were rehabilitated, and 6,333 drug offenders were arrested. Among those arrested, two were sentenced to death, 4,163 were sent to prison, and 445 sent to labor camps. But in a province with an estimated more than 3 million addicts out of its 14 million total population, curing 12 thousand of them was not a particularly impressive achievement, even though the authorities seemed to pursue opium suppression quite aggressively compared to other areas (Jin and Liao 1993, 280, 273).

In fact, inconsistency and inefficiency were common during the first phase of the anti-drug campaign. There was no systematic or well-constructed plan to coordinate the crusade with other initiatives taken by the central government. In that period, even though ideologically the government was determined to solve the problem, in reality, the Communists simply lacked the resources necessary to carry out this project completely and were too preoccupied with various other tasks they were facing—among which the most important were to revive the economy devastated by the civil war, to rebuild social order at home, and to fight the Americans in Korea. In Nanjing, the former capital of the Nationalists, the government gave up its efforts to set up rehabilitation centers because of a lack of necessary medical resources (Ning 1993, 365). In Guizhou, the government was preoccupied with the task of suppressing bandits in the first half of 1950, and opium suppression actually was not being aggressively pursued (Jin and Liao 1993, 276).

A related problem is that in the case of drug offenses, the punishments were often lenient or replaced by fines. From May 1949 to December 1949, of the total 472 drug offenders detained in Nanjing, only 26 were sentenced by the court with six-month to two-year prison terms. Of the 2,090 detained in 1950, 345 were sent to prison (Ning 1993, 364). Compared with the percentage of those caught in 1952 (see Table 6.1), these figures are significantly low.

In an effort to intensify the anti-drug crusade, in the fall of 1950 the Interior Ministry of the Government Administrative Council issued a directive asking for more severe punishment to drug offenders. More significantly, the directive abolished the practice of giving bonuses to law enforcement agencies or individuals according to the amount of opium seized. In November 1950, the Supreme People's Court also ordered that drug offenders could no longer be exempted from imprisonment by instead paying fines, and that all offenders should be sentenced to prison or labor camp for terms dependent on the degree of guilt (Ma Weigang 1993, 3).

It was obvious that in the early days of Communist rule, drug suppression was not, and could not be a high priority among the tasks of state building. In the meanwhile, local officials did use their creativity to put the crusade within the contexts of the then-more-important initiatives. In rural areas, the reduction of poppy cultivation was achieved by linking it to Land Reform, which was conducted in the early 1950s. And the discourse on opium suppression was associated with concurrent government campaigns. Quitting opium was interpreted as an action to prove one's newly gained master status, or as a response to the Communists' call to "increase production and practice economy," as well as to resist America and aid Korea when the Korean War broke out. And many anti-drug public trials and gatherings were held in association with the Counter-Revolutionaries Suppression Campaign, during which most drug traffickers executed were identified as counter-revolutionaries. On April 14, 1951, about 40,000 people gathered at Dali, Yunnan, to hold a mass rally to "Resist America, Aid Korea;

Table 6.1. Punishments Given to Arrested Drug Offenders in Nanjing, 1952

Term	Number	Percentage
Death	19	1.6
>10 years	135	11.7
5–10 years	332	29
3–5 years	285	24.7
Surveillance	138	11.9
Released	97	8.4
To-be-tried	146	12.7
Total	1,153	100

Source: Ning 1993, 365.

Oppose Reactionaries and Suppress Opium." Those there witnessed the execution of six so-called counter-revolutionaries and the public burning of more than 43,000 *liang* of opium (*Yunnan Ribao* 05/07, 1951). This issue of political spectacle will be discussed in more detail later in this chapter.

THE SECOND PHASE OF THE CRUSADE IN 1952

After more than two years, it became clear that more assiduous efforts were needed to wipe out China's deeply rooted drug problem. Thus, the Chinese authorities in the second half of 1952 started a campaign that has generally been seen as very successful. If the first phase of the campaign was sporadically and inconsistently carried out without much severity against the offenders, the second phase was the opposite. It was executed with well-formulated plans, intensive propaganda, mass mobilization, and much harsher punishments on a nationwide scale. The leads and information obtained from Three Antis and Five Antis campaigns of 1951–1952 prompted the highest authorities to initiate the decisive drug-suppression action taken in the second half of 1952.

The Three Antis campaign (anti-corruption, anti-waste, and anti-bureaucracy) was launched in November 1951, mainly against corrupt cadres. The Five Antis (anti-bribery, anti-tax evasion, anti-embezzlement of state assets, anti-shoddy work, and anti-pilferage of information about the state economy) launched in January 1952, targeted the national bourgeoisie. It soon appeared that many corruption cases involved drug trafficking, and their handling became a concern to policymakers at various levels. When the Jilin Provincial Committee of the CCP reported the issue to the Northeast Bureau of the CCP in March 1952, the Bureau responded by calling upon local authorities to cease anti-drug actions until a plan could be drawn up. This was in accordance with the instructions from the Central Committee, which stressed that the focus should be on the ongoing Five Antis campaign; the local authorities were told not to arrest drug traffickers in order to avoid frightening the national bourgeoisie, which was already under pressure due to the current campaign and was crucial in keeping the economy stable. Therefore, in the Three and Five Antis period, the task of local authorities was to uncover and collect information on drug trafficking, and make and hold lists of drug offenders until instructed to take action from the Central Committee (Northeast Bureau of the CCP 1952a).

The *Directive on Eradication of Drug Epidemic* came from the Central Committee on April 15, 1952. It called for a mass anti-drug crusade to solve the problem once and for all, based on the information uncovered and leads developed in the Three- and Five-Antis campaigns. According to the Directive's outline, drug trafficking was the main problem to be solved. Large and medium-sized cities, ports, and centers of drug cultivation and distribution were targeted. Punishments were to be focused on drug kingpins and drug lords, especially those who refused to confess their crimes to the authorities (Central Committee of the CCP 1952c).

More than three months were spent preparing for the campaign. The Central Ministry of Public Security was placed in charge of coordinating the campaign nationwide. Peng Zhen, a member of the Politburo, was assigned to preside over the whole range of operations, which involved many ministries and bureaus, including the ministries of the railroads, communications, interior, and public health as well as the postal service, customs, courts, and procuratorate. The need to thoroughly investigate and gather information was once again emphasized, and local bureaus of public security were asked to delay any action against known traffickers until receiving orders from the Ministry (Central Committee of the CCP 1952c).

On July 19, 1952, the *Directive on Anti-Drug Propaganda* was issued jointly by the Central Propaganda Department of the CCP and the Central Ministry of Public Security. In it, the propaganda contents and forms were clearly defined, and any propaganda in written forms was prohibited. In late July, a working conference was held in Beijing to plan the campaign. Xu Zirong, Vice Minister of Public Security, gave a speech on the implementation of the campaign, and claimed that, based on preliminary investigations nationwide, there were more than 165,000 drug offenders already being uncovered, including drug producers, traffickers, and poppy-cultivation promoters. The actual figure was anticipated to reach 250,000. Of the total drug offenders, about 5 percent were drug makers and 95 percent were drug traffickers, and among the total about 10 percent were state employees (Xu Zirong 1952). (See Table 6.2 for a breakdown of the numbers of offenders in each Major Administrative Region.)

The campaign started with the first wave of mass arrests on and around August 10 in different areas, followed by an intensive propaganda campaign and two or three more waves of mass arrests. Apparently the later arrests were based upon new leads and information gathered from the first. The second wave of arrests was carried out in late August or early September, and by October, massive actions against drug offenders were suspended. The focus shifted to putting the arrested on trial and consolidating the results of the preceding work.

For example, in Tianjin, the campaign started at 2:00 A.M. on August 10, when

Table 6.2. Drug Offenders in Each Major Administrative Region

Areas	Number	Percent of total
South central China	38,000	22.8
Northern China	28,000	16.8
Southwestern China	43,000	25.6
Eastern China	23,000	13.8
Northeastern China	23,000	13.8
Northwestern China	12,000	7.2
China Total	167,000	100

Source: Xu Zirong 1952.

145 out of 150 targeted drug offenders were arrested during an eight-hour action. While detainees were intensively interrogated, an intensive propaganda program reached out to the 800,000 people of the city. Following the first round of arrests, the Bureau of Public Security formulated the plan of the second phase of the campaign and programmed the arrests to be made in second and third waves. On September 3, the second wave of arrests was made, with 301 detained. By the end of October, the total number of arrests reached 677, which was in accordance with the original plan (Xiang 1993, 352–62).

Though the campaign targeted mainly drug producers and traffickers, drug addicts were forced to quit their habit. The Central Committee's policy was that addicts should be rehabilitated collectively or individually in programs administered by the government and under surveillance of the masses, with the exceptions of the elderly and the sick, who could have some extension periods. This task was carried out mostly at the end of the campaign. With drug supply channels being cut off and the masses mobilized, drug addicts had no choice but to give up. In Nanjing, there were still 1,120 addicts (711 male and 409 female) by 1952. Two rehabilitation centers were set up, providing necessary medicine to those who required it. Most addicts were affected by the mass mobilization and undertook rehabilitation at home with the help of family members and "under surveillance of the masses." Only fifty addicts had to be put on compulsory rehabilitation under watch of the authority of public security. By the end of the year it was claimed that all addicts were cleared (Ning 1993, 380).

Nationwide, the campaign was carried out decisively and in a coordinated manner. In his summary report on the national anti-drug campaign dated December 14, 1952, Luo Ruiqing, Minister of Public Security, proclaimed that the campaign's concentrated crackdown had "triumphantly finished in the country's 1,202 targeted areas. The campaign had uncovered drug makers and traffickers totaling 369,705, more than the original estimation of 250,000. A total of 82,056, or 22 percent of the uncovered, were arrested. Of those, 51,627 were prosecuted, 34,775 were sentenced to prison (including death penalty and life sentences), 2,138 were sent to labor camps, 6,843 were put under surveillance, 3,534 were released, and 4,337 were uncategorized" (Luo Ruiqing 1952).

Among Luo's long list of campaign achievements—including confiscating instruments used to make and traffic drugs, and weapons used to resist drug suppression—the amount of confiscated drug, the equivalent of 3,996,056 *liang* of opium stood out as well below the official estimation of drugs held by the public, which ranged from 50 to 100 million *liang*. Luo's explanation was that much had been confiscated prior to the campaign and that there were a lot of drugs in rural areas that had not been touched by this campaign (Luo Ruiqing 1952). To resolve the latter problem, the Government Administrative Council issued a directive on December 12, 1952, that called on the people to quit opium smoking, forbade poppy cultivation, and authorized the confiscation of remaining drugs in rural areas. This essentially ended the campaign nationwide.

AN INVISIBLE CAMPAIGN:
ORAL PROPAGANDA AND MASS MOBILIZATION

To today's observers, the most puzzling question is why the Communists did not allow the campaign to leave any public records. Before 1952, newspapers had carried anti-drug news regularly. A review of articles in the *Yunnan Daily* in 1950 and 1951 reveals more than twenty pieces of news reports in relation to drug problems. However, there were no records about the 1952 campaign whatsoever in papers, books, pamphlets, or any other written forms, except in government documentary archives. There was nothing on radio, either. The crusade was deliberately kept invisible to foreigners by the highest authorities in China.

This was partly due to the Chinese government's reaction to the accusation made by the Americans that China was exporting drugs to Japan. It was reported on February 19, 1951, that Japanese narcotics agents seized twenty pounds of heroin in Kobe. Among the nineteen packages seized, four bore the labels Duro-Well Pharmaceutic Laboratory, Luch Street, Tientsin [Tianjin], China (U.S. Government 1952, 3). In the official *Report on Traffic in Opium and Other Dangerous Drugs* of 1951, the U.S. government expressed "considerable concern" about the "reported flow of heroin from Tientsin and points in Manchuria into Japan, via Hong Kong" and claimed some of this heroin found its way into the United States and other countries. The report urged "this traffic should be suppressed by the Communist authorities in China" (U.S. Government 1952, 3). The tone turned more acrimonious one year later. The UN Commission on Narcotic Drugs held its Seventh Session in New York from April 15 to May 9, 1952. According to the official U.S. report in 1952, in the session, "the United States representative reported that investigations, arrests and seizures in Japan during 1951 proved conclusively that Chinese Communists are smuggling heroin from China to Japan and are using the proceeds from the sale thereof to finance party activities and to obtain strategic materials for China" (U.S. Government 1953, 2).

The accusation made by the United States was not groundless but also not as "conclusive" as was claimed. Historically, Tianjin had been a major drug-production and traffic center, especially during the period of the Japanese occupation. It was known that prior to 1952, most of the drug selling in Tianjin originated from "Yuda Company." The company usually transported opium to Hong Kong to make heroin, then resold most of it to interior China via Guangzhou; in 1950 alone, it transferred 400,000 *liang* of opium to Hong Kong. It is not clear whether Duro-Well Pharmaceutics Laboratory was related to Yuda, but the intensity and scale of drug trafficking in Tianjin decreased dramatically after the authorities ordered Yuda Company to cease operation at the end of 1950 (Xiang 1993, 345). In another case, a Chinese drug-trafficking group in Wuhan bought Japanese-manufactured heroin in Hong Kong, then smuggled it into China (Ma

Mozhen 1993, 130). Considering the active role Hong Kong played in drug transit, it was highly possible that some heroin originating from Tianjin ended up in Japan through Hong Kong, as the U.S. representative reported to the United Nations. But there was little evidence that the Communist Party was running the operation or benefited from it financially. The Cold War rhetoric had been attached to the issue and the United States continued to list Communist China as the principal source of heroin for many years.[19]

In a swift response to the American accusation, the Central Committee decided in June 1952 to temporarily suspend publishing drug-suppression news in the newspapers, and extended the ban indefinitely in July (Central Committee of the CCP 1952a). To the Chinese, what was at stake was China's new image in the community of the nations in the world. Assuming that America would use the news and information about drug producing and trafficking in China to prove its accusation, the Central Committee decided the propaganda campaign should be carried out orally among an inner circle of people, and that anything on this topic should be excluded from newspapers, magazines, radios, or the New China News Agency. Jointly issued by the Central Propaganda Department of the CCP and the Central Ministry of Public Security on July 19, 1952, the *Directive on Anti-Drug Propaganda* focused on a counterattack against the Americans. It instructed local authorities that the first priority of propaganda should be to reveal the roles of imperialists and the previous Chinese rulers in using drugs to poison the Chinese people. It blamed the American imperialists and remnants of the Nationalists for the lingering drug activities in China, which posed severe threats to China's public order, the people's health, customs, morality, productivity, and national construction. Thus to the Chinese, the anti-drug campaign became a patriotic movement that would strike out against the aggressive conspiracy of the American imperialists and protect the people's interests. Thus, any case related to producing, smuggling, or trafficking drugs by imperialist countries should be emphasized in propaganda, along with the history of importation of drugs to China in the past. The Directive also stressed the need to disclose those drug offenders who were also counter-revolutionaries or drug kingpins, and to publicize the policy that encouraged confession in exchange for lenient punishment (Central Department of Propaganda 1952b).

The Communists' concerns with image making was also revealed by the list of issues not, or less, subject to propaganda in the Directive. This list included cases related to government organs, to prominent figures of the United Front, to minority peoples, and to drug smuggling to the outside world. The statistics of drug offenders arrested and drugs confiscated were also to be kept secret (Central Department of Propaganda 1952b). The Directive instructed local authorities to refrain from exposing drug cases related to industry and the commercial sector, because by then the Five Antis Movement had caused a decline in production and an increase of unemployment in some big cities. Beijing did not want to distract national capitalists further from the main task of reviving the economy.[20]

To keep the campaign invisible to the outside world, the task was laid on the local officials to mobilize the masses. Such limits did not prevent them from carrying out a massive propaganda campaign that was pivotal to the success of the whole anti-drug crusade. With few exceptions, the first wave of arrests did not make an impact strong enough to be felt by the drug offenders or the rest of society. Many simply saw this as a routine crackdown like those that had happened before, and many doubted the resolution of the government. In Xian, for example, people thought that drug suppression was a good thing to do but were not sure that the epidemic could be eradicated completely this time, given that neither the Qing dynasty nor the Nationalists had succeeded in doing so. The Communists had sometimes been lenient to drug criminals in their first two years in power, and, despite the arrests of 312 drug offenders in a single day on August 11, the masses were not yet motivated to participate actively in the campaign. In the following week, only 917 drug traffickers came to be registered, and the city received only 935 reports by the masses. Faced with this situation, the authorities decided to intensify the propaganda campaign. Within ten days, 5,843 propaganda meetings were held that involved 147,620 people. The campaign turned the corner with this propaganda drive and a second wave of arrests on August 22. During a mass anti-drug rally participated in by 150,000 people on August 23, as many as 721 people asked to make a confession of their crimes, and 19,464 reports were received on the spot (Zhang Chengjun 1993, 306–310).

With the newspaper and radio excluded, the authorities employed various other means, often very creative ones, to get their points heard and seen. The most common method was to use propaganda trucks circling the streets to broadcast the government's policy against drugs through loudspeakers on the top. In Guilin, Guangxi province, arrested drug offenders were put on the circling trucks to demonstrate the government's resolution on drug suppression (Zhao Shikung 1993, 264). To make the message more accessible, the campaign's policy was elaborated through traditional opera, clapper talk, comic dialogue, folk dance, and other popular entertainment forms. Sometimes a closed-circuit radio was set up to reach larger audiences. Yet the propaganda method that reached the most people was group gatherings, which profoundly penetrated every segment of society. There were anti-drug gatherings for people's representatives, party members and activists, members of the military, youth, senior citizens, women, students, and drug addicts and their relatives. In some places, it could be claimed without exaggeration that the campaign was made known to every single person. According to official statistics, the campaign held a total of 764,423 propaganda meetings nationwide, through which 74,595,181 people were educated. The numbers in Shenyang were 21,425 meetings and 1,171,648 people; in Guangzhou, 11,046 gatherings were held and 1,239,283 people participated. In key targeted areas in the southwest, it was said that the average number of anti-drug education meetings attended by each person was two to three (Luo Ruiqing 1952).

In retrospect, two characteristics of the propaganda campaign need to be emphasized. One is that the very reason for keeping the campaign secret also helped to mobilize the popular Nationalist sentiment against the American imperialists, at the time China's number-one enemy. The local authorities were instructed to portray the Americans as the main culprits of China's drug problem, and later as the source of vicious rumors against China's drug suppression campaign. They were also told to explain to the masses that the main reason for conducting the campaign in this invisible way was to avoid providing the Americans with anything that might be used by them to attack China (Central Department of Propaganda 1952a).

The Chinese were so concerned about this secrecy issue that sometimes it reached the level of an obsession. Not only was nothing allowed to appear in newspapers, magazines, or radio, but also reference to the drug campaign was forbidden in any other written form, such as posters, cartoons, billboards, or public exhibitions. Even putting titles like "Committee on Drug Suppression" on envelopes or letterheads was prohibited. On August 8, Lijiang county in Guangxi province held an anti-drug mass rally, in which 150 copies of propaganda texts, 170 slogan posters, 80 pieces of propaganda instructions, and 800 forms were handed out to assist the propaganda drive. This incident, along with the fact that the county had carried out the first wave of arrests several days ahead of the plan, got quick response from its superiors all the way up to the Central Ministry, who ordered a thorough investigation on the incident (Ministry of Public Security 1952).

The second characteristic, related to the first, is that in the daily propaganda practice, it was not the nationalistic anti-drug arguments, but those closely associated with people's real life, that played a more important and persuasive role. At the time of the Korean War, drug suppression was deliberately tied to patriotism. In Xian, propaganda activists were asked to tell the masses that conducting anti-drug crusades was a very concrete patriotic behavior that allowed them to participate in the campaign to "resist America and aid Korea" (Zhang Chengjun 1993, 307). But as some other local authorities acknowledged, invoking the history of the Opium Wars or the drug policy of the imperialists was not, in general, a very effective way of reaching the masses. Rather, the focus was to be on how various crimes committed by imperialists and local drug traffickers—such as seducing people to use drugs, forcing female addicts to become prostitutes, stealing others' property, and supporting bandits—had inflicted so much misery on the lives of ordinary people (Northeast Bureau 1952b). In Beijing, the fact that several heroin-overdose victims could be found in the Tianqiao district every day during the Japanese occupation was used to condemn their "poisonous policy" (Beijing City 1952). Many relatives of drug addicts were encouraged to speak out about the miserable lives drugs had brought to their family members and the addicts themselves. Angry sentiments were directed toward drug traffickers and makers so as to isolate them in society.

MASS RALLY AND PUBLIC TRIAL AS POLITICAL RITUALS

Professor Ma Mozhen, an acknowledged expert on the history of drug suppression in China, once said that her motivation in studying this subject was to refute the impression held among American scholars that China got rid of the drug problem in the 1950s simply by killing drug offenders (Chen Jing 1995, 43). The number of executions in the campaign has been kept secret over the past several decades, which may have misled Western scholars to make exaggerated estimates. The recorded number turns out to be 880 nationwide in the second phase of the campaign in 1952 (Luo Ruiqing 1952). Though this is not a small number, when it is compared with the number of executions in the campaign against counter-revolutionaries, estimates of which ranged from 500,000 to 800,000, it is relatively insignificant.[21] Most of the executions were proclaimed and carried out during mass rallies and public trials, which served as the main propaganda methods for mobilizing the masses and a psychological means of intimidating drug offenders.

The mass rallies and public trials were the culmination of the propaganda drive during the campaign of 1952. In the early days following the first wave of arrests, most areas reported that the action did not seem to have a substantial effect on society as a whole. The propaganda drive was subsequently intensified and various creative publicity forms were adopted. Nevertheless, it was by and large the mass rallies and public trials that gave momentum to the campaign. The situation in Wuhan was typical. After the first wave of arrests, most sectors of society remained untouched. Even a number of arrested offenders appeared not to take the matter seriously. Many of them did not tell the truth about the offenses they had committed and some (and their relatives) even had direct confrontations with the authorities. Having experienced the Five Antis, which was very thorough in investigating offenders but quite lenient with punishments, those arrested thought the authorities could only persuade idiots to confess, because few people were being executed for drug offenses. Of those who had not been arrested, some hid or escaped, some transferred drugs and properties to safe places, some threatened government informants, some circulated rumors that confiscated morphine would be resold in the department stores for fiscal gain by the Communists, some even took advantage of the campaign to hike up the price of drugs (Chen Shouqian 1993, 236–37). At this point, the campaign for drug suppression was a long way from its goal.

To deal with the situation, the authorities used mass rallies to launch an intensive propaganda drive. On August 16, three days after the first arrests were complete, a conference attended by 10,000 was held by the Propaganda Department of the Wuhan Municipal Party Committee. In the session, 300 kilograms of narcotics were burned to show the government's resolution. However, it was not until September 9, when a municipal public trial attended by more than 20,000 people was held, that the whole campaign finally reached its climax, as shown by the dramatic atmosphere of this event. During the session, party and municipal leaders vowed to carry the campaign to a successful conclusion, and representatives from democratic parties and people's organizations offered their support. Among the twenty drug offenders being tried, two were sentenced to death and immediately executed, fourteen were sent to prison—three with terms from seven to fifteen years, five for five to ten years, five for three to five years, and one got less than three years. One was put under the surveillance of the masses, and three were released after education. One of the released drug offenders expressed his appreciation for the leniency from the authorities, using himself as an example to call on others to follow. The public trial seemed to have immediate effects on those drug offenders still holding out. Many rushed to confess in order to avoid the possible death penalty. Those who had not been arrested started to turn themselves in for lenient treatment. In the evening right after the public trial, it was said that 124 people voluntarily confessed, turning over 94 *liang* of morphine, 1,012 *liang* of opium, and 1,315 *liang* of acetic acid. In conjunction with the mass arrests before and after this public trial, the campaign achieved desired results before the middle of October (Chen Shouqian 1993, 236–37).

It is worth mentioning here that mass rallies and public trials had been used by the Communists to mobilize the masses for many other campaigns since the early 1920s, and they were also used in the first phase of the anti-drug campaigns. In Guizhou, numerous mass rallies and public trials were held before 1952. In Guiyang, on June 16, 1950, and November 12, 1950, mass rallies and public trials were held, with 32,000 and 23,000 *liang,* respectively, of opium burned in public, and two drug offenders sentenced to death with immediate execution on the latter occasion. In Zunyi on October 2 and November 17, 1950, two and four drug offenders, respectively, were executed in the anti-drug mass rallies attended by more than 10,000 people; also a significant amount of opium was burned. Similar anti-drug mass rallies and public trials were held in several other cities. Despite all these efforts, however, the drug problem was still pervasive in the province before the start of the second phase of the campaign (Jin and Liao 1993, 277–79).

To explain the effectiveness of the mass rally and public trial in the 1952 campaign, it is necessary to go back to the issue of the number of executions being carried out. As stated previously, the number is not excessive considering the vast scope of the campaign and in comparison to the campaigns against the counter-revolutionaries or for Land Reform. This time, however, the mass rallies and public trials were used because of their psychological effects on society in general, and on drug offenders in particular. This effect was achieved in association with several conditions not existent before. The first condition was that the period of consolidation and reconstruction had almost been completed. With the Land Reform and Counter-Revolutionaries Suppression partially completed, and the Three Antis and Five Antis finished, social order was restored nationwide and Communist control had been strengthened. Second, having completed various urgent tasks to consolidate their newly gained power, the Communists finally could join their resources together and focus on the drug issue. In the pre-1952 period, drug suppression was carried out in connection with central tasks in different major campaigns at different times. This time, local authorities were asked to carry out campaigns that focused on the suppression of drug trafficking and use. Wuhan, for instance, made drug suppression the second priority of government work, right behind the campaign to "increase production and practice economy." The Wuhan Party Committee also asked that the campaign be directed by district leaders, and that 80 percent of the resources of public security and the court system to be put into anti-drug action (Chen Shouqian 1993, 235).

The third, and the most important factor that made the big difference between the first and second phases was that the latter was well planned and systematically and vigorously carried out. With the information accumulated during the Three Antis and Five Antis, and in light of the Directive from the Central Committee, local public security organs spent almost four months preparing for the implementation of the campaign's second phase. The issue of how many executions ought to be carried out was specified in advance and modified during the operation. In the speech given July 28, 1952, by Xu Zirong, Vice Minister of Public Security, on the operation of the national anti-drug campaign, the percentage was temporarily set at 0.5 percent of the total number of drug offenders arrested. He instructed that only those who were guilty of the most heinous crimes should be executed in order to achieve the following three aims: to get rid of drug kingpins, to reform accomplices, and to educate the masses. He did mention that it was not appropriate to execute too many drug offenders, and that only those deserving capital punishment should be killed. In addition, only the provincial-level authority could authorize the executions (Xu Zirong 1952). On August 29, in response to the report by Luo Ruiqing, Minister of Public Security, the Central Committee agreed to hold public trials in those specially targeted areas, and authorized each city to execute "several" to "more than a dozen" drug kingpins, without giving a specific quota. On October 3, the Central Committee instructed local authorities that "it is easier to get people's sympathy by killing drug offenders than killing counter-revolutionaries. So at least 2 percent of those arrested should be killed" (Central Committee of the CCP 1952d). The number of actual executions turned out to represent 1 percent of the total arrests. The reason may be partly due to local differences in implementing the quota, and partly to "*xian jin hou song*" (strict in the beginning and flexible in the end) policies that were adopted in some places, so that those real drug kingpins could be executed without exceeding the quota in the latter part of the campaign (Jin and Liao 1993, 285). The statistics given in Table 6.3 are from mid-December 1952, but not many more executions were carried out in the following months, when the national anti-drug campaign ended.

Table 6.3. Number of Executions versus Arrests in Major Areas

Areas	Executions	Arrests	Executions as percent of arrests
Yunnan	38	6,239	0.61
Guizhou	25	3,915	0.64
Fujian	27	1,659	1.62
Guangxi	24	4,476	0.54
Tianjin	10	667	1.48
Changchun	3	148	2.03
Nanjing	19	1,153	1.65
Xuchang	4	107	3.74

Source: Ma Weigang 1993.

It took all three of these conditions to create an environment no other regime had ever enjoyed, or even envisioned, to give the Communists the leverage to generate their huge political effect with mass rallies and public trials. By accomplishing a task at which no other regime had ever succeeded, the anti-drug campaign in 1952 signified the unprecedented state hegemony the Communists had built in just a few years over the whole society and all its members. Well-designed policy like "yan cha kuan ban" (strict in investigation and flexible in punishment), in addition to public trials, might have enabled the Communists to achieve their aims at minimal cost to human lives and social cohesion.

ANTI-DRUG CAMPAIGN AND THE
ESTABLISHMENT OF URBAN CONTROL

As described by Bin Wong, opium suppression was closely connected with the task of nation building, especially with the state's attempts to establish effective social control in China (Wong 1997). In more than two hundred years, no one had enjoyed substantial success until the Communists did in the early 1950s. Why did the Communists succeed in wiping out opium while others failed? Though this complex question cannot be thoroughly addressed in this chapter, certain conclusions can be drawn. Based on the history of the campaign of 1952 described above, it is vital to emphasize and elaborate on the fact that, before the start of the campaign, the Communists had already built a social control mechanism that was unprecedented in terms of its power and effectiveness. The success of the anti-drug campaign was derived from the existing mechanism and simultaneously contributed to the consolidation of the system.

At the beginning, the Communists connected the moral imperative of opium suppression with a nationalistic interpretation concerning the nationhood of the new People's Republic. The concern for building and maintaining a "new" identity for Communist China had, to a great extent, shaped the way the campaign was carried out. Different from other campaigns conducted during the same period, the rationale for conducting drug suppression was not based solely on the doctrine of class struggle but also on the concern for building up a new national identity. In this process, several contrasts were carefully elaborated: the Old China versus the New; the Nationalists versus the Communists; the imperialists versus the Chinese people. By proving that they could do what other regimes could not, the Communists enhanced the legitimacy of their rule. Not surprisingly, in the second phase of the campaign, the Chinese took American accusations so seriously that they ordered the campaign be carried out invisibly to the outside world. Thus the masses were mobilized through oral propaganda and public trials.

Through mass mobilization, the campaign became a well-orchestrated initiative that tightened social control over the urban public and formed an integral part of the state-building process. Derived directly from the Three Antis and Five Antis, at the end of the consolidation and reconstruction period, the anti-drug campaign contributed to the establishment of a social control system that eventually had "the means of totalitarian rule that preceding authoritarian regimes— the late Qing monarchy, Yuan Shikai's abortive republic, the Nationalists' Nanking regime—could hardly have imagined" (Wakeman 1991, 65). The means of implemeting the anti-drug campaign of 1952 have shown that the state did not achieve social control by merely using state violence; rather, state hegemony was achieved through a combination of coercive force and surveillance together with propaganda and persuasion. This process was completed with the help of institutions of social control the Communists put into China's urban society after 1949.

Franz Schurmann has pointed out that the Communists tried to control the urban population from two directions. One was through the expanded civil-administration functions of the police, by staffing the local police station with so-called household register policeman whose main responsibility was to look at almost everything in the community under his/her jurisdiction. The other was through mass organizations and their grassroots efforts (Schurmann 1968, 373). These included the Communist Youth League, the Women's Association, the Trade Union, and groups of residents. In the anti-drug campaign, they were indispensable in conveying government policies to ordinary urban dwellers, especially to those who did not affiliate with state-controlled institutions or enterprises. The growth of mass organizations in general, and the residents committees in particular, enabled the campaign to be carried out in an invisible way, yet it reached the vast majority of China's urban population.

In fact, by the end of the Five Antis Movement, the Communists had established a vast propaganda network in big cities. In Shanghai, there were more than 16,000 propagandists, many of them from the Communist Youth League and other mass organizations. In August 1952, the Shanghai Party Committee announced that it would recruit 54,000 new propagandists in the second half of the year (Gardner 1969, 532–33). Undoubtedly, these propagandists contributed a great deal to the mobilization efforts in the following anti-drug campaign. The decision to use only oral propaganda might have worked out in favor of the authorities since the illiteracy rate was very high among city residents—the figure in Shanghai alone was 46 percent (Gardner 1969, 499).

The residents committees also played a big role in making the campaign touch the everyday lives of individuals. The neighborhood organization was first set up in big cities, such as Shanghai and Tianjin in 1951, and gradually introduced to other cities in the early 1950s. The main tasks of the residents committees included to make residents aware of government policies; to carry out activities of community concern, such as public sanitation and arbitration of disputes; and to collect and reflect opinions and demands of the residents (Schurmann 1968, 374–76). In Shanghai, there were 2,083 residents committees by December 1951 (Gardner 1969, 496). If we accept the estimate by Franz Schurmann that a residential unit consisted of from 150 to 500 households, and if we assume that the average size of a residents committee was 300 households with four members, the number of people who belonged to residents committees was around two and a half million—about half of the total population in Shanghai at that time.

The role played by the residents committees in the anti-drug campaign was prominent. In Jianghan district of Wuhan, more than 4,700 residential cadres and activists were mobilized to hold propaganda meetings with residents (Chen Shouqian 1993, 237). In Tianjin, cadres were dispatched to organize residents meetings to publicize the anti-drug campaign. Individual propagandists even held meetings at household complexes or conducted propaganda from door to door. Police stations used the residential literacy classes to explain the government policy on drugs. In Tianjin, more than 800,000 were educated through these various forms of propaganda (Xiang 1993, 356). In Qingdao, the propaganda was carried out by the public-security section of the residents committees, the newspaper reading groups, and women's groups—not only on streets, but often within individual families. A total of 3,420 meetings were convened in the city (Lan 1993, 395).

The unprecedented degree of mobilization generated by the anti-drug campaign demonstrated not only how broadly the campaign touched China's urban society but also how deeply it was able to put individuals and their bodies under direct government control. The police apparatus, the residents committees, and other mass organizations that had existed before the anti-drug campaign was commenced, all contributed to the formation of a social control network that could encompass every aspect of an individual's life. The anti-drug campaign of 1952 took advantage of this existing network to accomplish its goal, and it also provided an opportunity for the authorities to consolidate this network further. Individuals were simply overwhelmed by this power. During the campaign, there were numerous cases of daughters being mobilized against their drug-trafficking fathers, or sisters against opium-smoking brothers, or wives against husbands (Chen Shouqian 1993, 238). Social control was so strong that it could break connections even between family members.

Thanks to a hegemonic discourse against drugs that was already well established in modern China, the Communists realized that they would certainly gain sympathy from the public by executing drug kingpins. By holding mass rallies and public trials, the Communists used this long-existing political ritual mainly to generate psychological pressure on the public, making the people acknowledge or accept the Party's power, consciously or unconsciously. This political ritual proved so effective that the Communists didn't have to use state violence excessively to achieve their goal. The drug-suppression campaign was both a part of a state-building process, and a successful means of showing the social control and mobilization power the state had gained.

7

Facing Drugs Again: Anti-Drug Discourse in Contemporary China

In targeting drug traffickers and makers for punishment, the campaign of 1952 basically eliminated the backbone of the drug problem in urban China, which had been rampant for more than a century. By the late 1950s, the opium problem was solved in most parts of China, except in several minority areas where the campaign was postponed. From the late 1950s on, China claimed it was a "drug free" country, and it enjoyed this reputation for more than two decades by virtue of the combination of the extremely tight control of individual life, and its virtual isolation from the rest of the world. Following the disastrous Cultural Revolution of 1966–1976, China finally adopted an open-door policy in late 1978, when it entered a reform era. At the very same time, drugs began to re-emerge in the country, creating a political embarrassment. Trying to keep the "drug-free" identity intact, the Chinese government was very reluctant to acknowledge the issue in public and, even after admitting it, had a difficult time to explain its appearance under Communist rule. It was not until the end of the 1980s that a new, nationwide, anti-drug campaign was launched.

THE GOLDEN TRIANGLE AND CHINA'S CURRENT DRUG PROBLEM

Except in some remote border areas, the anti-opium campaign of 1952 was very effective. In certain areas of Yunnan province, which had been a major opium-producing area before the Communists took over, the opium problem lingered for a much longer time. In Baoshan Prefecture, one of the two primary fieldwork sites for this study, following the rehabilitation rounds of 1952 and 1954, two more rounds were needed to cure remaining addicts in 1964 and 1965 (Huang and Dong 1991, 1). Yet according to my informants, in some areas inhabited by minority peoples where modern medical care was hardly found, opium continued to be commonly used as everyday medicine. A few old opium addicts even managed to sustain their addictions by getting opium from across the border or by secretly planting a small number of opium poppies in deep forests.

It was not until the end of the 1970s that people in the border areas, especially in southwestern Yunnan, encountered large amounts of opium and heroin entering China again. This time the drugs came primarily from the notorious Golden Triangle. Broadly speaking, the Golden Triangle consisted of poppy-growing border areas of Burma, Thailand, and Laos, with about 92,000 square miles and 3.7 million people. Within the Golden Triangle, Shan State in Burma produced the most opium. According to statistics, in the early 1980s, the poppy-growing area in the Golden Triangle comprised 67,000 acres. Thailand and Laos had only 3,500 acres each within their borders, the remaining 60,000 acres, or about 90 percent, were in Burma (He Ping 1995).

Though opium production in the Golden Triangle began in the nineteenth century, when Burma became colonized by the British, its production, when compared to the amount produced by then-British India and China, accounted for only a small portion of world production at that time. The French colonialists advocated opium planting in Laos in the 1940s before their retreat. After World War II, the chaos of the political situation in Southeast Asia provided a rare opportunity for the various local powers in the Golden Triangle to increase opium production. By the end of 1950s, opium production reached 700 tons in the Golden Triangle, amounting to 50 percent of all the illicit opium production in the world. The Vietnamese War during the 1960s and 1970s increased both the demand for narcotics among American troops in Vietnam and the inflow of American dollars to drug traffickers, pushing the yearly opium production to over 1,000 tons in the Golden Triangle (Liu Wei 1995).

Besides colonialist and American connections, there was also a Chinese connection in the making of the Golden Triangle. After being defeated by the Communists in 1949, the remaining Nationalist Eighth Army escaped to Burma. Supported by the CIA, they established their base in northeast Burma, forced local peasants to pay taxes for planting opium poppies, and even used their power to buy opium at very low prices in order to resell it and buy new arms. In 1951, the airport of Mengsa in the southern Shan State was rebuilt by the Nationalist Army, and it was used not only to get arms and logistics supplies from American military planes but also to export opium outside the Golden Triangle (He Ping 1995, 3). The involvement of the Nationalist Army escalated the scale and the degree of organization of the opium trafficking in the area. It was not until 1961 that the

Nationalist Army's influence was finally reduced when it was routed by a joint attack from the Burmese Army and the People's Liberation Army, the latter of which was allowed into Burma to attack the remaining Nationalist Army under an agreement between Burma and China. The surviving Nationalist forces either went to Taiwan or escaped into Thailand (He Ping 1995).

The drug kingpin Luo Xinghan, a Chinese Burmese, controlled the Golden Triangle from the 1960s to early 1970s; he was succeeded by Kun Sha, who was said to have been an ethnic Chinese with many Chinese assistants. In the 1960s and 1970s, a number of Chinese rusticated youth in Yunnan went to Burma, and some of them joined the guerrilla forces of the Burmese Communist Party. In 1989, the Burmese Communist Party broke down into four separatist factions that occupied the northern part of the Shan State. Three of the factions relied mainly on opium and heroin revenue for their survival; their involvement in drug trafficking became a major headache to the Yunnan province across the border (Chen and Li 1994, 28).[22]

At one point there were three drug-transit routes from the Golden Triangle to the main consumer markets in North America and Western Europe. The first route was transit of opium and heroin into Thailand, from Bangkok to Hong Kong, then to Japan and the United States. In the second route, drugs were transported to Rangoon, then to Kuala Lumpur, Singapore, and from there to their destination in North America. The third route was through northwest Burma to India or Sri Lanka, then to European countries. After China adopted its open-door policy and relaxed the control of border trade, the drug traffickers wasted no time in establishing the fourth traffic route, from the Golden Triangle to Yunnan, then to Hong Kong and the rest of the world.

The geographic conditions and intimate ethnic relations along the Sino-Burmese border also contributed to the rapid spread of drug trafficking through China. Yunnan has a 2,500-mile borderline with Burma, Vietnam, and Laos, and in most parts there are no natural barriers separating them from China. Usually villagers in China can look at foreign villagers across the border. In some cases, two villages on either side of the border even share the same well as a common water source. Thirteen nationalities inhabit both sides of the border, sharing the same or similar language, religious beliefs, customs, and traditions. Intermarriage and trading across the border are long-standing practices for these peoples. Together, such factors have made the task of controlling drug trafficking extremely difficult.

As drug-transit activities increased, so did the number of addicts. For example, in Baoshan, heroin was first intercepted in 1985, and seven heroin addicts were first found in 1987. But by the end of 1988, the number was more than one hundred. By April 1990, the number was approximately 1,000; by August of that year, the addicts numbered 2,625. Considering that these numbers represented known addicts registered by the public security authorities, the actual numbers most likely were much higher (Huang and Dong 1991, 1, 4). Another illustration comes from the Panlong district of Kunming, where the first heroin addict was found in December 1988. Though there were only two heroin addicts by mid-1989, by April of 1990 the number had increased to 509. It was this alarming situation that drove the Chinese government to launch a new anti-drug campaign at the end of the 1980s.

POLITICIZING AND DEPOLITICIZING THE DRUG ISSUE

The tone of anti-drug discourse altered after the Communists took power in 1949. Though blaming all previous rulers and the imperialists for creating an opium epidemic, they rarely identified the opium problem as a threat to the vitality of the Chinese nation, viewing it instead as a social problem harmful to people's health and to the party's efforts to "accelerate production." The logic was simple. To the Communists, the crisis of national survival had been averted forever by their triumph over the Nationalists. They had every confidence that they could wipe out opium in a new China.

In practice, the desire for a new China identity led the Communists to a series of campaigns in the early 1950s to stamp out prostitution, gambling, and drugs. As discussed in chapter 6, their desire to uphold a new China identity led them to keep the campaign of 1952 invisible to the outside world. After having kept China a drug-free country for nearly two decades, an achievement of which they were extremely proud, the Chinese government was unwilling to admit the resurgence of the problem until the mid-1980s. The unwillingness was largely a result of the worldwide politicization of drugs in the preceding years.[23]

The Chinese government found it very difficult to take the steps to acknowledge and address the drug problem. Since the late 1950s, China declared itself drug-free. This declaration was not only kept proudly by the Chinese government as a symbol of the new China identity, but had also been used to illustrate that only under the system of socialism and the rule of the Communists could the drug problem be solved. After so many years of representing drugs as a problem belonging either to old regimes or foreign imperialists, the re-emergence of drugs in the southwest border areas put the Chinese government in an embarrassing position. Its decision not to discuss the issue in public was a reflection of this and of its hope that the problem could be solved in a short period of time before it spread to other parts of the country.

The situation in Ruili is typical of the way this issue was handled. Ruili was a small county (now a city since 1994) located due southwest of Yunnan on the Sino-Burmese border. Among its 80,000-plus population, 61 percent are Dai, Jingpo, and other non-Han people. Because of its location, it was one of the first areas affected by drugs coming from the Golden Triangle. The county set up a "three-way suppression" ("suppressing planting, smoking, and trafficking drugs") office in 1983 to deal with the drug problem; and in 1984, established a permanent county rehabilitation center. A year later, four township rehabilitation centers and twelve rehabilitation classes at village levels were added. And a more advanced Drug Dependence Rehabilitation Center was established in April of 1989. The anti-drug appropriation increased from 7,000 *yuan* ($4,200) in 1985 to 1,150,000 *yuan* ($300,000) in 1991(Ruili County Government 1991). Much work appeared to have been done by the government.

But as admitted by the county government report, the county Party Committee and government were under tremendous pressure regarding the drug issue. After the myth that only socialism could solve the drug problem evaporated, the new declaration to "solve this problem one more time under the leadership of the Communist Party" turned out to be an empty promise in the face of a worsening drug problem. Even as it had no ready answer to this ideological dilemma, a new set of conflicts emerged. In the 1980s, the reform supporters and those opposed to reform had not settled their struggle on the approach that China should adopt. Consequently, the conservatives blamed the reform and its open-door policy for having brought drugs into Ruili and China.

To make matters worse, the local authorities found their anti-drug voices much weakened not only by the untenable ideological implication but also by the limits set by the higher authorities on the coverage of drugs in the media. Though local newspapers in Dehong Dai and Jingpo Autonomous Prefecture (where Ruili is located) and Baoshan Prefecture were among the first to be allowed to carry drug-related news, there were no news reports involving drugs in the local newspapers prior to 1988. But the rapid spread of drug addiction became an everyday issue involving many families. According to official statistics, the peak number of addicts reached 2,687 before 1992, an astonishing 3 percent of the total population in Ruili county (Ma Duan 1992). Some people thought the local authorities had turned blind eyes to the problem and done little to stop it. Local authorities felt "wronged" in front of accusations and pressure, but they were not allowed to address the drug issue via public media—an awkward position for the local authorities to deal with.

The dilemma was solved when the highest authority of China decided to depoliticize the drug issue and to treat it as a concrete social evil after the Tiananmen Incident of 1989.[24] One of the first nationwide mass campaigns the government conducted was called "wiping out pornography and six evils." The "six evils" were drugs, abduction of women, secret societies, superstition, pornography, and gambling. Though the campaign was said to serve the aim of constructing a socialist spiritual civilization (a new ideological framework set up in the open-door era), the campaign touched several concrete social problems of great concern to ordinary people, thus diluting much of the ideological implications. For example, when asked about the damages the six evils had caused, the deputy chief of Baoshan Prefecture answered: "Number one is damaging social order; the second is damaging the health of the masses, especially the teenagers and the youth;[25] number three is damaging the construction of socialist spiritual civilization; and number four is damaging the image of socialism" (*Baoshan Bao* 12/06, 1989). Although the ideological implication was not totally disconnected, the emphasis was placed on the first two points.

The down-to-earth approach of the campaign provided a much needed guide to local authorities to carry out anti-drug work. In Yunnan, drug suppression became the first priority of the "wiping out pornography and six evils" campaign and, most often overshadowed the other "evils." In Baoshan, a discussion session was held on the six evils that focused on the evil of drugs, singling out the threats of drugs to youth in particular (*Baoshan Bao* 12/06, 1989). After mid-1989, local anti-drug activities were incorporated into a much larger nationwide campaign, which not only solved the ideological predicaments the local authorities once had faced, but also signaled that the Chinese government had finally foregrounded the issue of illegal drug use and trafficking for everyone in China and the world. The limit on news coverage was lifted, and the propaganda machine immediately launched into full swing to attack drugs.

But this anti-drug effort also put Yunnan in the spotlight of the national media. In the early 1990s, when drugs were still pretty much limited to the southwestern part of China, the rest of China had little exposure to drugs and their effects. Now heroin, a substance many people may never have heard of before, was responsible for the problem that opium had caused in the past. Understandably, the drug use and trafficking in Yunnan became a hot topic for media reports and an ideal "sell" for those for-profit street magazines. These negative reports, in turn, shaped people's perception of Yunnan in the early 1990s. In a short period of time, the reputation of Yunnan as a center of drugs, derived from its vast production of opium in the old days, was restored. It is a reputation that even today, the Yunnan people are trying to shed.

DEMONIZING DRUG OFFENDERS: PROSTITUTION, STDS, AIDS, AND DRUGS

As with opium, China's current popular discourse on heroin has often been ambivalent. On the one hand, heroin has been depicted as a drug with mysterious effects, able to make the user have unspeakable euphoric feelings, fulfill all wishes, and elevate out of the real world. On the other, it has also been described as untouchable and destructive, producing universal and irresistible dependency among all its users. Numerous stories have been written describing how heroin made good people turn evil, made a good woman a prostitute, and drove a healthy person to death. Yet, despite the stories describing the terrible fate of addicts, sometimes readers could easily come away with the impression that addicts were adventurous and curious people whose explorations just went sour.

In the early 1990s, drug addicts were sometimes romanticized in the popular discourse, a pattern that coexisted uneasily with the more general tendency to demonize them. Female addicts were often depicted as beautiful and attractive before they fell to heroin, whereupon most of them became prostitutes and ready and indiscriminate sexual subjects in exchange for heroin. In fact, in the Chinese press, female drug addicts were often described as the most shameless human beings on the earth when they succumbed to their desire for drugs. In reality, most drug addicts had little formal education, as shown in a report by the Baoshan Women's Association that 97 percent of female drug addicts had completed less than the ninth grade (Baoshan Women's Association 1991); there were, however, doctors, artists, teachers, writers, and even policemen who became heroin addicts by first experimenting with the drug only to have their careers and lives ruined. Another group susceptible to drug abuse, wealthy private entrepreneurs, were said to squander their personal fortunes in pursuit of drugs.

It was the issue of prostitution that added a new, evil dimension to drugs and extended the harm of drug addiction beyond the individual or family level. The reappearance of prostitution, like drugs, was a national disgrace to some people, who saw it as a by-product of the open-door policy. But by the time of the late 1980s, prostitution had become widespread in China, especially in the south-eastern coastal areas, and female drug addicts simply enlarged the growing numbers of existing prostitutes, rather than being themselves the cause of the re-emergence of the prostitution.

Nonetheless, prostitution touched another sensitive issue, the spread of sexually transmitted diseases (STDs). In 1964, China declared that STDs had been eradicated, only to find out that they had returned in the 1980s. In Baoshan, the situation was alarming: in 1985, there were only 5 STD cases reported; by June of 1989, the total number of cases had reached 155; and the number rose to 263 by October 1990. The riskiest groups for contracting STDs were prostitutes and drug addicts (Zhang Jing 1991, 63). By spreading STDs, drug addicts were seen as posing a threat not only to individuals but also to society as a whole.

Yet it was the relationship between drugs and AIDS that culminated the demonization of drug addicts. The first AIDS case was reported in China in 1985. In 1986, Chinese health authorities set up monitoring stations for AIDS in Beijing and several big cities. From 1985 to September 1990, AIDS-prevention institutions conducted HIV blood-serum tests on 300,000 high-risk people nationwide and found 446 cases with the positive HIV antibody and five AIDS patients (Cui 1990, 32). Both Yunnan residents and drug users occupied a large percentage of the total number, as shown in Table 7.1 and 7.2.

According to the above incomplete statistics, by September 1990, Yunnan had nearly 97.6 percent of total Chinese HIV positive cases, all of which were drug users. The link between drugs and AIDS made Yunnan, already depicted as a drug-ridden area, an even more stigmatized place. Several widely circulated stories told of people from other parts of China who refused to shake hands with Yunnanese at national conventions for fear of being infected by AIDS, or who

Table 7.1. Positive HIV Carriers and AIDS Cases by Group, 1985–1990

Group	1985	1986	1987	1988	1989	1990*	Total
Drug user	0	0	0	0	146	222	368
Blood disease patients	4	0	0	0	0	0	4
Returned Chinese	0	0	0	0	2	3	5
STD patients	0	0	0	0	1	0	1
Foreigner	1	1	9	7	23	27	68
Total	5	1	9	7	172	252	446

*January to September only.
Source: *Beijing Review*, Nov. 26–Dec. 2, 1990, p. 32.

Table 7.2. AIDS Patients and HIV Carriers by Region, 1985–1990

Region	Total testing positive	Foreign AIDS patients	Chinese AIDS patients	Foreign carriers	Chinese carriers
Yunnan	389	1	1	20	367
Beijing	19	1	1	14	3
Henan	10	0	0	10	0
Zhejiang	9	0	0	4	5
Shanghai	8	0	0	8	0
Guangdong	4	0	0	4	0
Guangxi	3	0	0	3	0
Hubei	2	0	0	2	0
Fujian	1	1	0	0	0
Hebei	1	0	0	0	1
Total	446	3	2	65	376

Source: *Beijing Review*, Nov. 26–Dec. 2, 1990, p. 32.

declined to accept cigarettes offered by persons from Yunnan for fear that they might contain heroin.[26] Since drugs were linked to AIDS, the people's view toward drugs became more negative and emotional, which derived in part from the discourse on AIDS in China during the late 1980s and early 1990s.

From the very beginning, AIDS was depicted as a "new incurable disease" that threatened the whole world (*People's Daily* 09/07, 1983). But to ordinary Chinese, AIDS was seen as a "foreign" disease, especially related to the decadent lifestyle of Westerners, which included homosexuality and drug abuse. *Popular Medicine*, China's mostly widely read medical magazine, carried a number of articles discussing AIDS in the late 1980s and early 1990s. One article claimed that AIDS infection had only two modes: the "Western Way," which was mainly through homosexuality and drug abuse; and the "African Way," which was mainly through heterosexual activities. In the end, the author attributed Asians' different moral ideas as an important reason why fewer of them were AIDS patients (Hao 1988, 32).

From this point of view, the ideal way to deal with this "foreign" plague was to prevent AIDS from entering China's gate. Perceiving the West as a promiscuous world, another article on how to ward off AIDS from entering China categorized the Chinese studying abroad as a high-risk group. In the author's opinion, the most dangerous thing was to have a homosexual relationship with a Westerner. If infected, the student studying abroad not only would ruin himself but also would become a person condemned by history for bringing back AIDS to China. Based on the same logic, the author also appealed to the authorities to keep an eye on foreigners coming from areas that have AIDS, to require that foreigners have a test certificate on AIDS, and that they be monitored so they would not patronize prostitutes in China (Feng 1988, 19).

Other measures proposed by the same author included the prohibition of prostitution and homosexuality, and a ban on foreign blood products and used clothes from entering China. Absent from the list was the suppression of drug abuse. The cause of AIDS from drug abuse was mentioned in China, but it was illustrated mainly by the foreign cases. In the November 1988 issue of *Popular Medicine* an article entitled "Be Careful of Getting Infected with AIDS by Using Drugs" pointed out the high risk of sharing needles among intravenous drug users. But in the end, the author observed optimistically that since China had basically wiped out drug abuse, this way of spreading AIDS had been in fact eliminated among Chinese people (Jia Yicheng 1988, 22).

It is hard to determine whether these two authors were actually unaware of the re-emergence of drug addiction in China by 1988, or whether they deliberately avoided this sensitive topic in order to pass media censorship. At that time, the drug problem in the southwestern part of China was still not permitted to be exposed in the nationwide media. But two things were certain: (1) the Chinese knew that drug abuse, prostitution, STDs, and homosexuality were among the main channels to spread AIDS; and (2) AIDS was depicted mainly as a terrible "foreign" disease resulting from a dangerous "foreign" lifestyle. One article was devoted to answering the question of whether the contacts in ordinary daily life could spread AIDS. The inquiry came from a person who had just come back from a scholarly trip to the United States. In America, he had gone to restaurants, had shaken hands with Americans, and had shared towels with others. These activities now made him fear that he might be in danger (Fang 1988, 33). This case demonstrated that many Chinese perceived AIDS as a disease of foreign origin.

Under these circumstances, it was not surprising that people from other regions refused to shake hands with people from Yunnan when Yunnan's connection with drug abuse and AIDS was exposed to the public. AIDS had suddenly become very "Chinese," with most cases related to drug users in Yunnan, not to foreigners or people returning from abroad. In facing AIDS—the "plague of the twenty-first century"—China also experienced a period of panic like that in many Western countries. When drugs were related not only to individual loss of life and fortune, to prostitution and STDs, but also to AIDS, the Chinese view toward drug offenders became more negative. Drug offenders began to be treated like criminals who had committed unpardonable crimes. It was in this context that, in the next anti-drug campaign, both drug addicts and drug traffickers were demonized and became subject to stern punishments.

HISTORY, PATRIOTISM, AND DRUG-FREE CHINA

The other important factor to shape the contemporary discourse on drugs is the history of the Opium Wars. The drug issue, as already discussed, has always been related to modern Chinese history, especially to the history of the Opium Wars. It behooved the Communists to use the history to legitimate their anti-drug efforts—as did the Qing rulers and the Nationalists. Coincidentally, 1990 was the 150th anniversary of the First Opium War, and this opportunity was fully taken advantage of by the government. Various propaganda machines were mobilized to build momentum for the newly launched anti-drug campaign.

But the approaches to this event differed between the central and local authorities. In 1990, only one year after the Tiananmen Incident, the central authority was still preoccupied with how to remedy the legitimacy crisis they faced. The government referred to history to illustrate that, starting from the First Opium War, China had experienced a series of defeats and humiliations from Western imperialists, a situation that changed only after the Communists established the People's Republic. The government narrated the whole of modern Chinese history to demonstrate that only under the leadership of the Communists and by following socialism could China be saved. Thus, the anniversary was used by the central authority as part of its efforts to conduct a patriotic education campaign nationwide.

But to local authorities in Yunnan, the 150th anniversary was related directly to their efforts to suppress drugs. In May and June, various memorial activities were held in Baoshan and Dehong, including discussion sessions, mass gatherings, film receptions, and public exhibitions. The history of the First Opium War was used to make a general point that China was humiliated and weakened by the imperialists and opium, and that all Chinese should today make the country stronger and not abuse drugs lest history repeat itself. In Dehong, the imposition of the death sentence on fourteen drug traffickers was actually proclaimed at memorial gatherings of the Opium War in several counties (*Dehong Tuanjie Bao* 06/28, 1990). In Baoshan, the local leader proclaimed that it was time to fight a new "Opium War" and vowed to win this time (*Baoshan Bao* 06/30, 1990).

With the launching of the anti-drug campaign and the approaching of the return of Hong Kong to China, the name of Lin Zexu was mentioned more frequently in the 1990s. One memorial activity for the 150th anniversary of the Opium War in Baoshan was a month-long show of patriotic films, beginning with the film *Lin Zexu*. The film, made in the late 1950s, depicts Lin as an upright

Mandarin official sent to Guangdong to stop the illegal and immoral opium trade conducted by the British. The British use his decision to burn seized foreign opium as an excuse to launch the First Opium War, in which China's defeat under corrupt and incompetent Qing rulers results in a series of humiliating unequal treaties with foreign imperialists. As the first person to stand up against the foreign aggressors, Lin was hailed as a national hero in the film.

In 1997, Hong Kong, a colony the British had seized from China as the result of the First Opium War, was returned to China. A new film, *The Opium War,* was shown in China and the Chinese communities around the world. The film has been hailed as another patriotic film, and many have related the film to the increasing momentum that Chinese nationalism has gained in recent years. As we have seen, the history of the Opium War and the opium-burning action by Lin Zexu have been used to legitimize anti-opium campaigns by rulers and regimes prior to the Communists. The historical memory of the Opium War and the image of Lin Zexu have become a part of modern Chinese nationalism. The question examined in what follows is: In what way are the Communists using nationalism differently from their predecessors in the current anti-drug campaign?

To pursue this inquiry, one must explore the multiple inherent forms of Chinese nationalism. James Townsend points out three forms in China today: State nationalism, ethnic nationalism, and patriotism (Townsend 1988, 1992). State nationalism, adopted by both the Nationalist and Communist regimes, emphasizes that the Chinese nation includes the Han as well as non-Han people, as part of the effort to give China a new identity as a multinational country. Ethnic nationalism, often treated in a negative way in China, refers to either Han nationalism or non-Han nationalism, based mainly on ethnic identity. Though state nationalism is the official nationalism in China, and ethnic nationalism attracts the most scholarly attention, it is patriotism that occupies a pivotal position with regard to both the daily practices of Chinese nationalism and in the current anti-drug campaign.

The Communists' teaching of modern Chinese history has involved a concerted effort to rally ordinary people around them. After 1989, in their deepest crisis of legitimacy ever faced, and as an integral part of their efforts to promote patriotism and socialist spiritual civilization, the Communists launched a campaign calling on Chinese people to study modern Chinese history beginning with the First Opium War. Deng Xiaoping once said, "To know some Chinese history is the spiritual motivation to develop China" (Deng Xiaoping 1993, 358). Current leader Jiang Zemin went even further: "To inherit and develop the tradition of patriotism under the new historical conditions requires conducting broad and deep education on patriotism. This education shall start with children and teenagers. All people, especially the numerous youth, have to seriously study the history of the motherland, especially the history from the modern era" (Jiang Zemin 1990, 29). On one occasion, Jiang even promoted the idea that the history of modern China should be taught starting in kindergarten (Jiang Zemin 1991, 43).

Why does the state promote patriotism by resorting to the history of modern China? Using Rousseau's phrase, Eric Hobsbawm calls patriotism a "civic religion" (Hobsbawm 1990, 85); and points out further that "the original, revolutionary-popular idea of patriotism was state-based rather than nationalist, since it related to the sovereign people itself, i.e. to the state exercising power in its name" (Hobsbawm 1990, 87). Given the importance and scope that patriotism has in contemporary Chinese nationalism, Hobsbawm's comments help to contextualize the particularity of current Chinese patriotism and its relation to the anti-drug crusade.

Patriotism is "state based" foremost in contemporary China. It is manifested in state-censored official discourses and state-sponsored mass movements. In 1991, the propaganda department of the CCP and several other ministries instructed local authorities to use historic relics to conduct patriotic and revolutionary tradition education. In 1993, fifty "good" films were selected to be used to conduct patriotic education in primary and middle schools. In 1994, an *Execution Outline of Patriotic Education* was issued. Besides emphasizing loyalty to country and fraternity with the people, which make up the core of patriotism, official discourse often attempted to represent the Communist Party as an integral part of patriotic feelings. Thus the equation was drawn in the form: patriotism = love of motherland = love of the people = love of the Communist Party = love of socialism (the state).[27]

Within this new framework, history is used mainly as an illustration of the rationality and legitimacy of the present state or regime. In the official narrative of modern Chinese history, the whole history of the past two centuries proves one point: only socialism can save China. History is used to remind people that only Communist new China can free the Chinese people from being humiliated by imperialists, keep China sovereign, and lead China to its prosperity and modernization. The party argues that these promises deserve the people's support. History has been manipulated by the state to avert the people's discontent from the current situation China faces. At the same time, the emotion-laden, historical memories are used to build patriotism—the form of nationalism that China has needed most since 1989.

In post-Mao China, when the open-door policy (mainly vis-à-vis the West) is being repeatedly emphasized, and when the value of Western culture is becoming more acceptable, the target of Chinese nationalism and patriotism has become blurry. The Us/Them dichotomy, although it continues to exist, is having a difficult time in getting its desired momentum nowadays. To solve this problem, a new demarcation is necessary—that of the "Past/Present." The Past/Present emphasizes China's miserable past under regimes before the Communists as well as the remarkable improvements since 1949, yet it downplays the disasters such as the Cultural Revolution brought to the Chinese people by the Communists.

Within this context, the issue of drugs is inseparable from the interplay of the history of the Opium Wars and the rhetoric of patriotism. Thus abuse of or trafficking in drugs is not only individuals committing something harmful to themselves by ruining their health and fortune, it also affects their families by destroying happiness, and society at large by spreading AIDS and STDs. Most important to this rhetoric, drug use and traffic have constituted a very unpatriotic action that has allowed drugs, which had caused so much humiliation to China, to reappear. Though drugs had been depoliticized and treated as a social problem, under the shadow of modern Chinese history, this social problem has regained its particular symbolic meaning. The history of the Opium Wars has become a standard narrative in almost all articles and editorials promoting drug suppression. History has become a part of today's official anti-drug discourse in China and also a catalyst of patriotism, but its actual effect on current anti-drug campaigns remains to be seen.

INTERNATIONALIZING AND ETHNICIZING DRUGS: SEEKING ALTERNATIVE EXPLANATIONS

A consistent argument of contemporary anti-drug discourse is to emphasize the problem's foreign origin. By emphasizing that drugs come from abroad—that China is only a transit country of international drug kingpins in the Golden Triangle, that China is also a victim of international drug smuggling—the Chinese authorities give an answer, at least in part, to the difficult question of why China has a drug problem today.

As mentioned before, when the authorities first acknowledged drugs had come back to China again, addressing the preceding question was an ideologically sensitive matter. To those local officials in the southwestern border areas where the drug problem had become an everyday-life issue, blaming its foreign origin was a ready explanation for why the problem reemerged; simultaneously, recalling that the history of the Opium Wars explained why China should fight against drugs. These two components became standard features in official anti-drug discourse at different levels.

According to Yu Lei, Secretary-General of the National Narcotics Control Commission, China's drug problem was inseparable from every aspect of international drug connection. First of all, the illicit drug demand in Europe and America stimulates the production of and trafficking in illicit drugs. Second, many foreign nationals are directly involved in drug smuggling through China; in 1991, a total of 829 foreign traffickers were caught in China, a 10 percent increase from 1990. He specifically pointed out that there had been several cases involving British, German, and American nationals smuggling marijuana from China to Japan, which was a new trend of international, illicit drug trafficking through China (Yu Lei 1992).

Though China has had sporadic poppy cultivation in mountainous and forest areas in recent years, the quantity is negligible. In 1991, only more than 300 *mu* of opium poppy were found and eliminated nationwide. In border areas like Yunnan, local authorities have been effective in enforcing a ban on opium planting along the Chinese side of the border. These days virtually all heroin comes from the Golden Triangle outside China. To the Chinese government, there is every reason to believe that China is indeed a victim of international drug trafficking. So in his speech at the press conference of the International Day Against Drug Abuse and Illicit Trafficking, Yu emphasized that "what should be especially pointed out is the fact that the source of the Chinese domestic drug problem is abroad and the transit drug problem is the major one that China is facing in its fight against illicit drug abuse and trafficking." Besides, he continued, "China is suffering more and more from the continuous increase of the international transit drug problem. Since the mid-1980s, the number of drug addicts has increased in border areas, and drug abuse problem appears in interior areas where there is transit drug activity" (Yu Lei 1992).

Based on this, China reacted strongly to the term "China White" used by the American media to describe heroin in the American market, and denied any suggestion that the drug came from China. The Chairman of the National Narcotics Control Commission, Wang Fang, wrote an article in the *People's Daily* rebutting the use of this term by the American media, pointing out that China did not make heroin and was itself a victim of transit drugs. According to Wang, the international drug traffickers' use of China to smuggle heroin from the Golden Triangle was determined by the geographical proximity of China. Never should the original source of heroin and the transit places of illicit drugs be mixed up. Responding to Americans' accusations that China had not fought drugs vigorously, Wang declared that China had intercepted a great quantity of heroin for which the final destination was the United States (*People's Daily* 06/25, 1992).

As long as China's illicit drug problem is a result of international factors, the final solution of the problem also depends on the disappearance of the international origin of drugs. To support this claim, Chinese authorities have publicized a number of cases in which they have successfully seized illicit drugs through international cooperation. And the depiction of the Golden Triangle in the Chinese media has remained the same—that of a land controlled by powerful drug kingpins and the major cause of China's ever-deepening drug problem. In the southwestern part of China, to attribute the drug problem to this international source is a very convenient and convincing explanation for the Chinese authorities.

But this interpretation has been challenged by a new development in China's war on drugs. In the open-door era, China has witnessed a booming economy, made possible mostly by huge investment of foreign capital. The inclusion of the Chinese economy once again in the outside capitalist world may be the real reason why China has drug problems again. As modern commodities, drugs have to have producers as well as consumers. China failed to realize that its integration into the world economy could make it both a place of drug production and consumption. In recent years, the situation of transit drug trafficking has not been lessened, and drug-making and consumption in China has increased dramatically, especially since 1992, when China launched an all-out drive to establish a market economy.

In fact, since the adoption of the open-door policy, accelerating economic development has been the highest priority on the local governments' agenda. In recent years, drug traffickers have begun to appear in the country, disguised as businessmen. In the name of investment, they have established various kinds of companies. Sometimes they have even donated a large amount of money to the local charity, thus establishing good relationships with local officials and in turn being treated as VIPs. How Fujian province has been transformed by the Taiwanese into a major producing and trafficking center of methamphetamine is a good example of the penetrating power of international capital flow and market mechanism.

Methamphetamine was first made by the Japanese during World War II for the purpose of enhancing the endurance capability of its troops. Because it is in the shape of transparent crystal or white power, the drug is usually called "ice" by its users. In the 1980s, the Japanese introduced the drug-making methods to South Korea and made it a new producing center. When the South Korean authorities launched a major crackdown around the 1988 Seoul Olympic Games, drug makers transferred their operations to Taiwan, which made using "ice" a serious social issue there. In October 1990, Taiwan started to consider "ice" a controlled narcotic drug, and a crackdown on its production and consumption followed. Coincidentally, Fujian province, which directly faces Taiwan across the strait, was making every effort to attract more Taiwanese investment. Since the mainland Chinese had little knowledge of "ice" initially, Taiwanese "ice" makers were able to set up drug-making facilities in the coastal areas in the name of investing in the chemical industry. Most of the produced "ice" was trafficked to Taiwan, Japan, Hong Kong, the United States, and Southeast Asia.

Since 1991, the amount of produced "ice" and the scale of drug trafficking has increased dramatically in Fujian. By 1995, the authorities had intercepted 2,600 kilograms of "ice," but the police estimated that there were more than 5,000 kilograms that had been smuggled out. According to statistics of Taiwan police, during 1993 and 1994, a total of 7,357 kilograms of "ice" was intercepted, most of it from Fujian. More alarmingly, not only has Fujian become an "ice"-producing center but also, as with heroin, it is an emergent "ice"-consuming market. In 1992, the Fujian authorities caught the first case of "ice" use by local residents, who were said to be seduced by the Taiwanese. But by 1995, "ice" users had been found in all major areas within the province, and some of them had even formed user groups usually comprising a dozen addicts each (Niu and Cai 1997, 243–47). Though the international connections are still present, all these new developments have made the claim that China is only a transit point of drugs more and more untenable.

The internationalizing of the drug problem is visible in current Chinese anti-drug discourse, but the ethnicizing of the drug problem has recently become a subtle component. For geographical reasons, minority people in the border areas of Yunnan were among the first exposed to drugs being transported through China. Many villages along the border, especially those of Dai and Jingpo, were overwhelmed by drugs pouring into China. For example, Jiexiang township of Ruili is on the Sino-Burmese border, and 91 percent of its 13,000 total population are Dai people. In 1991, there were 493 known drug addicts, or 3.8 percent of the total population. By December 1991, among 202 drug addicts who had not yet been rehabilitated, 198 were Dai people and only 4 were Han Chinese (Jiexiang Township 1992).

Though it is true that drug abuse was a serious problem in some minority areas in western Yunnan in the 1980s, there was no media coverage of the problem before the early 1990s. By the time the Chinese news media was allowed to report publicly cases of drug abuse and trafficking, the heroin problem had already spread well beyond the border areas; the Han people had always comprised the majority of drug addicts and traffickers. Although the Chinese government gives some preferential treatment toward minority people, such as allowing them to have two children in the case of family planning, it did not treat drug trafficking as a nationality problem, but rather as a social problem. There was no leniency given at all to minority offenders.[28] Therefore, neither minority traffickers nor the connection between drugs and ethnic minorities was initially singled out to attract special attention from the general public.

This situation changed after a large-scale anti-drug raid in the Pingyuan area of Wenshan Zhuang and Miao Autonomous Prefecture in Yunnan during September to November of 1992 (for more detail see chapter 9). Recently, along with the spread of drugs in China, drug-trafficking activities have increased in northwestern China, where the Hui and other Muslim people live in compact communities. Cities like Xian and Lanzhou, distribution centers of opium before 1949, are becoming new centers of heroin trafficking. More and more Hui and other minority peoples involved in trafficking have been exposed, sometimes misleading the public that the Hui and other Muslim communities all over the Southwest and Northwest are likely to be involved in large-scale drug trafficking. Though this trend of ethnic stereotyping in media representations of the drug trade is still very subtle, it is alarming and worth following closely.

In summary, the anti-drug discourse in contemporary China has become more complex and conflicting than it had been before the 1980s. Lost is the discourse's insistence on the incompatibility of drugs with a socialist new China. Newly present are multiple reinterpretations of the drug problem in China. The new historical context has made the contemporary anti-drug discourse less consistent than the mainstream anti-opium discourse had been before 1949. After the Tiananmen Incident of 1989, the Chinese government was forced to disconnect drugs from ideological questions, to depoliticize the drug phenomenon as mainly a social problem, and to incorporate it into the party's efforts to eliminate pornography and other social evils. But in a society in which many phenomena have been over politicized, the process of depoliticization of certain social issues has never been completed. Drug suppression has been repoliticized by the state in order to conduct patriotic education by linking it to the history of the Opium Wars, sometimes resulting in the sugar-coating of anti-drug discourses with state-sanctioned, nationalistic sentiment.

The anti-drug discourse has been compounded by other issues, such as prostitution, STDs, and AIDS, which contribute to the demonizing of drug offenders in contemporary China. Facing an alarming situation, the authorities have tried to offer alternative explanations as to the cause of the emerging drug epidemic, often blaming international drug kingpins in the Golden Triangle for smuggling drugs through China. Recently, more media exposure about the Hui people involved in massive-scale drug trafficking has provoked an unfavorable profile of Chinese Muslims. The diversified anti-drug discourse allows different people in different localities the opportunity to adopt their own interpretations. It is in this very context that the current anti-drug campaign is being carried out and has withered gradually since its inception in the early 1990s.

8

A "People's War" without People: Anti-Drug Campaigns in the 1990s

There were two watershed incidents in China's war on drugs in the 1990s. One was the legitimacy crisis government faced after the Tiananmen Incident of 1989. The government launched the anti-drug campaign as a part of a broad campaign to clean up a variety of social "evils" in its effort to re-establish its legitimacy in the wake of the crisis. From 1990 to 1992, anti-drug campaigns were carried out vigorously in Yunnan and several other heavily affected provinces, which saw another wave of massive use of state violence in China. The other watershed came in 1992, when China's paramount leader Deng Xiaoping decided to embrace a full-swing market economy in China. Along with the unprecedented economic boom came the spread of drugs not just in the coastal areas but all over the country. Though the government has tried to conduct a "people's war" on drugs, the old strategy seems not to be working well under the new social circumstances. By the end of the 1990s, the prospect of the government's outright success in the war on drugs in the short run has become more and more unlikely.

DRUG TRAFFICKERS, STATE VIOLENCE, AND GOVERNMENT LEGITIMACY

From the scene of executions of drug traffickers described at the very beginning of this book, the extensive use of state violence is the most striking aspect of the current anti-drug campaign. The campaign was launched by the Chinese govern-

131

ment after the Tiananmen Incident as a part of a nationwide campaign for wiping out the "six evils"—a time in which the Communists were experiencing their most serious legitimacy crisis. By using brutal state violence against student demonstrators, the Communist Party lost its ideological appeal to the majority of China's urban population. The task of re-establishing legitimacy while consolidating a weakened power base became the most urgent task facing the Chinese authorities. Deng Xiaoping directed the new Communist Party leadership, formed after the Tiananmen Incident, to "concentrate their attention on several things that can make people satisfied and happy" (Li Ruihuan 1990).

Based on the experience gained in the campaign of 1952, the Communists knew that attacking concrete social problems such as drugs and prostitution could evoke sympathy from the general public; at the same time, these campaigns could be used by the authorities to achieve their overall goal. As a result, six evils, more directly related to the people's everyday concerns and less with ideological color, were sorted out as targets of the nationwide campaign. For example, while speaking about suppressing pornography, Li Ruihuan, a member of the standing committee of the Politburo of the CCP, proclaimed that the campaign "was helpful to the construction of the socialist spiritual civilization, to smoothly carrying out the works of the reform and open-door policy, and was paid fully attention to and was supported by the whole society. Numerous people cheered this campaign, saying it is an important task achieved by the Communist Party for the people." Li even cited General Secretary Jiang Zemin as saying: "Suppressing pornography has gained not only great sympathy from the public but also has greatly pleased the people" (Li Ruihuan 1990)!

Whereas pornography suppression was carried out principally in coastal areas, the anti-drug task became the priority of the authorities of southwestern China. In the context of post-Tiananmen China, the authorities employed the drug issue to enhance state power, as manifested by the dramatic increase in the application of capital punishment for drug trafficking. On June 26, 1990, the 150th anniversary of the First Opium War, sixteen drug traffickers were sentenced to death in Dehong Prefecture in public trials, as compared to only one death sentence in a similar public trial held in August 1989 (*Dehong Tuanjie Bao* 06/28, 1990; 08/10, 1989). Also on June 26, 1990, fourteen traffickers were executed in Kunming after a public trial during which 520 kilograms of heroin and 480 kilograms of opium were burned (Yao Jianguo 1991, 20).

In fact, before the end of 1990 China had no specific law for dealing with drug trafficking. According to article 171 of the Chinese penal code, producing, selling, and trafficking in opium, heroin, and other narcotics were subject to less than a five-year prison term, and habitual offenders and smugglers of large quantities could get prison terms of more than five years. The article was revised by the Standing Committee of the National People's Congress (NPC) in 1982, and prison terms of more than ten years, life in prison, as well as the death penalty were added to the list of punishments of drug traffickers (NPC 1982). Even so,

A scene of one of the mass anti-drug gatherings in China in the late 1990s

drug trafficking was listed as a type of economic crime, and specific punishments for offenses of different degrees were not clearly defined.

The situation changed after the issuance of the *Decision to Suppress Narcotics* by the Standing Committee of the NPC on December 28, 1990 (hereafter called Decision), which gave definite, quantitative criteria for types of punishments rendered to different offenders. According to the Decision, a person producing or trafficking in more than 1,000 grams of opium or more than 50 grams of heroin was subject to more than fifteen years in prison, life in prison, or the death penalty. More than a seven-year prison term was to be administered to people producing or trafficking in 200 to 1,000 grams of opium, or 10 to 50 grams of heroin. For those with offenses involving less than 200 grams of opium or less than 10 grams of heroin, less than a seven-year prison term or custody was to be applied (NPC 1990).

Since most current trafficking cases involve heroin, the weight of 50 grams has become a critical factor in determining whether a trafficker will receive the death penalty. In the draft of the Decision, the criteria of the death penalty were originally set at more than 1,500 grams of opium or more than 100 grams of heroin each (*People's Daily* 10/26, 1990). Yet the numbers were reduced to 1,000 and 50 grams, respectively, when the Decision was proclaimed two months later, and after the Decision was issued, the number of traffickers executed increased substantially (see Table 8.1). In the whole province of Yunnan, a total of 401 drug traffickers were sentenced to death in 1991, which was eight and one-half times the number

Table 8.1. Executions of Drug Traffickers in Dehong and Baoshan

Date	Dehong	Baoshan
1989	1	0
June 26, 1990	16	1
June 26, 1991	31	0
October 26, 1991	37	25
June 26, 1992	34	35
July 6, 1993	17	0

Sources: These numbers are cited from local newspapers of *Dehong Tuanjie Bao* and *Baoshan Bao*. The dates of editions in which reports appeared are June 27, 1991; October 29, 1991; June 27, 1992; July 8, 1993, of *Dehong Tuanjie Bao*; and October 29, 1991; June 30, 1992, of *Baoshan Bao*.

in 1990 (*World Journal* 03/28, 1992). In 1992, the number of death penalties increased to 464 (*World Journal* 03/22, 1993).[29] According to Chinese law, only the Supreme People's Court has the authority for final approval of execution. Since the High Court of Yunnan Province had so many capital punishment cases, it was granted authority to render final approval of the death penalty by the Supreme People's Court in June 1991 (*People's Daily* overseas edition 03/29, 1992).

The number of executions carried out in Yunnan during 1991 and 1992 almost equaled the total number of death penalties rendered nationwide in the anti-drug campaign of 1952. It was an example of another wave of the use of extensive state violence to suppress internal problems by the Chinese government following the Tiananmen Incident. So why was the use of state violence against drug traffickers accepted and supported by the public, even though they had witnessed the terror of state violence at Tiananmen only a year previously? This support was well illustrated by a commentary of *Baoshan Bao* on October 29, 1991. Three days before, in the biggest public trial ever held in Baoshan since 1949, more than 160 kilograms of illicit drugs were reduced to ashes and 25 drug traffickers executed. The article's title was "all people are happy about using draconian punishment," which revealed the paper's position. Even slogans like "Hail to burning! Hail to killing" were used to express the writer's approval of the public trial. Such slogans reflected the local people's extremely negative attitude toward drug offenders in that area.

In fieldwork in Yunnan for this study, informants were often asked what they thought was the most effective way to solve the drug problem. Surprisingly, they repeatedly said that the government should kill all those involved in drug trafficking because those were the people responsible for the spread of drugs in Yunnan. One government official even related in a very serious way, that he thought that not only did drug traffickers deserve to die but also addicts with no hope of rehabilitation, because such addicts had become useless to an already overpopulated society. His position was reminiscent of a similar, stringent approach to punish opium addicts suggested by Huang Juzi one and one-half centuries earlier.[30]

It would be a very challenging task to explore the Chinese view of the applicability of state violence. Why does their attitude toward state violence differ so dramatically in the cases of the Tiananmen Incident and of drug suppression? One explanation is that the Chinese have different criteria for the applicability of state violence toward different social groups. College students are viewed as the backbone of China's efforts to become modernized in the near future, whereas drug traffickers and abusers are labeled as evil or useless members of society. Furthermore, the actions taken by the students in 1989 were widely believed to be for the good of the country, but traffickers are thought to be spreading drugs that pose great threats to individual well-being. The denotation of "usefulness" versus "useless," "righteous" versus "evil," between students and drug traffickers may have contributed to creating such a vast gap in people's attitudes toward state violence against these two different groups.

The policymakers have taken full advantage of the public's strong anti-drug sentiment. Public trials and executions not only have been held on a grand scale but they have also been made into a political ritual that shows how much coercive power the state possesses. A public trial is usually participated in by thousands of people. With many paramilitary policemen standing by with loaded rifles, drug offenders are placed on a platform, and the confiscated drugs are placed in specially made big pots, before being destroyed. As described before, the session usually starts with anti-drug speeches by government officials, followed by public trials during which a number of death penalties are proclaimed and the public burning of confiscated drugs occurs. Participants become emotionally charged at the scene. The convicted drug traffickers are then loaded on trucks and sent to the execution ground, escorted by large numbers of armed police. The motorcade often goes through the main streets of the city, drawing tens of thousands of bystanders. It is not difficult to see that the current anti-drug campaign bears a striking similarity to that of 1952. The government not only inherits the form of conducting mass campaigns to solve drug problems, but also uses the public trials and public gatherings to gain momentum for the campaign. Yet there is also a striking difference between the two campaigns. The 1952 public trials and gatherings successfully shook up drug offenders and mobilized the most urban population, but they have become merely annual public shows in the 1990s, while the drug problem continues to worsen. Although the central authorities have succeeded in using public trials and anti-drug gatherings to get people's sympathy, they have had little success in mobilizing the whole country and the people to participate in this "people's war" against drugs.

A "PEOPLE'S WAR" WITHOUT MASS MOBILIZATION

Conducting a mass campaign has been a traditional way of solving social problems by the Communists (Dirlik 1975; Bennett 1976). From the very start of the current campaign, the highest authorities vowed to solve the drug problem by launching another "people's war," which required both broad participation by the general public and coordinated efforts from the authorities at different levels. Since the anti-drug campaign has been a part of broad efforts to re-establish government legitimacy since the Tiananmen Incident, there is no evidence that the central government was not serious about carrying out the campaign.

The central government clearly acknowledged that the success of the campaign depended on the participation of various sectors of society. As a "people's war," the anti-drug campaign was supposed to be fought jointly by the public security bureaus, educational institutions, propaganda organs, factories, business circles, as well as workers' unions, women's associations, and youth organizations. In cases such as public trials and anti-drug gatherings, members from all walks of society could be found, and many anti-drug activities were held by these sectors in response to a call from higher authorities. But, as discussed below, the intensity of mobilization has not been in any way comparable to what the government achieved in the early 1950s. This is in part due to the different roles played by different players in the campaign.

A residents committee is the lowest administrative unit in the city. As mentioned in chapter 6, its duties are to assist in maintaining public order in its area, to arbitrate domestic conflicts or disputes in the neighborhood, to propagandize government policies, to conduct a hygiene campaign, and to check on adherence to family-planning rules. The work of the residents' committees usually touches the daily lives of residents on the street and was instrumental in exercising extremely tight social control of the urban population in China till the 1980s.[31] To control drug abuse and the spread of drugs in the cities, the residents committee is the most important organization that needs to be mobilized.

Wuguo Road is a street in Panlong district, near the downtown area of Kunming. The residents committee has about 500 households under its jurisdiction. During an interview, its director, Mrs. Duan, acknowledges that there are eight heroin addicts on the street and her residents committee has its own way of handling the drug problem. Once a person is found to be a drug addict, a help group, usually consisting of a local policeman, an official of the committee in charge of public security, and parents of the addict, would be established. The help group visits the addict every half month, persuading him/her to get rid of the habit. Their advice is very much in conformity with the general anti-drug discourses of contemporary China, but the emphasis is on the damage drugs do to the addicts themselves and their families rather than on the history of the Opium Wars.

When an addict is released from the rehabilitation center, it is the residents committee's responsibility to keep him/her from abusing drugs again. After a while, the residents committee sends the former addict's urine sample for urinalysis. If the result is negative, the addict is proclaimed rehabilitated, and the residents committee helps him or her find a job. The task of the residents committee is very comprehensive. But when asked about the result of their work, Mrs. Duan concedes that in reality their work has not been as effective as reported.

There are various obstacles that impede the residents committee's efforts. Sometimes the parents of addicts are too embarrassed to admit that their children are abusing drugs, so it is very difficult to get their assistance at first. Compared to other problems, this one is relatively easy to solve, because the majority of parents can be persuaded to be supportive. But some other difficulties are out of the residents committee's reach, added Mrs. Duan. For example, rapid urban development has made many old residents move out of the area, making efforts to track ex-addicts sometimes impossible. Furthermore, in past times, everyone belonged to a certain work unit, so that the residents committee could ask an addict's unit for assistance. Right now so many people are on their own that there is no way to ensure their participation in anti-drug meetings. There are only four people in the residents committee, and they have to bear a heavy workload. Truly, they just cannot do the anti-drug task in the way they have been asked to do it, according to Mrs. Duan.

School is another place pivotal to the current anti-drug campaign. Since the majority of drug abusers are youngsters, educating students in middle and high schools is viewed as a priority. A textbook on narcotics-prevention education was sponsored by the National Narcotics Control Commission in 1992, which had 6 million copies printed in the first edition. The Commission requires narcotics-prevention education in middle and high schools nationwide. In addition, Yunnan issued its own anti-drug textbook in 1993. In 1994, however, during an extensive survey by the author of this book on drug education in Yunnan, interviews conducted at seven middle and high schools in Kunming, Baoshan, Mangshi, Ruili, and Longling revealed that drug education in these schools was far from systematic, and sometimes neglected altogether.

Among the seven schools, not a single one had the drug education course in its curriculum. The textbook on narcotics suppression was given to students in Kunming and Ruili only as after-school reading material. In schools of Baoshan, Longling, and Mangshi, the textbook was totally ignored. Though teachers were asked to teach students not to abuse drugs, according to a teacher at Ruili First Nationality Middle School, there was no concrete measure to judge whether drug education was carried out in the schools.

When asked why Yunnan—the region of China with the most serious drug problem—had not started an anti-drug course in its high schools, several teachers gave a variety of reasons. First, the local public education officials had different views about incorporating an anti-drug course into the middle school's regular curriculum. According to Mr. Wang, a teacher at Kunming No. 5 Middle School, the main reason that middle schools in Kunming did not have drug education courses was the concern that it might have adverse effects. It was argued that since there were very few cases of middle school students abusing drugs, too much discussion of drugs might trigger students' curiosity to try drugs. In any case, adolescent drug addicts were mostly drop-outs. Once they dropped out, the school had no responsibility to oversee their drug problem. Nonetheless, Mr. Wang admitted that in the previous three years, more than 40 students had dropped out, or about 10 percent of the 460 students he had taught.

To exclude those drop-outs in the counting of drug addicts has been a common strategy by middle school administrators to downplay the drug issue in their schools. Every school alleged that there was no single *in-school* student using drugs, but they "heard" some other schools had such students. The drop-out factor may explain why they could make this claim. Mr. Cheng, a researcher at the Yunnan Education Commission, offered another reason why drug education was not getting enough attention in middle schools, pointing out that middle and high schools focus on how to make students pass the college entrance examinations. Everything else with no direct relation to this goal is likely to be left out. From this point of view, it is understandable that, though some schools handed out textbooks on drug education to students for self-study, they considered this action itself to be enough and were not willing to do more for fear of distracting the students' ultimate efforts to enter colleges.

There have been, however, efforts made by individual teachers and schools to educate students to fight drugs. At Longling Middle School, students were shown anti-drug videotapes, were asked to participate in public trials, and took part in lectures given by drug enforcement officials. The school also viewed smoking cigarettes as a stepping-stone on the path to smoking heroin. If caught smoking a cigarette, the student was put into a "study session" for introspection and at the same time had to pay 2 *yuan* as a fine. If caught twice, the student's parents were asked to deposit 100 to 300 *yuan* as so-called discipline guaranty money. Considering that Longling was an extremely poor county, this amount of money was very substantial for an average family. In this way the school tried to pressure parents to prevent their children from using drugs.

Combining anti-drug efforts with financial penalties has been widely used by work units nowadays. The higher units often give anti-drug quotas (such as to rehabilitate a definite number of addicts in a limited period of time) to the lower units. The lower units are also required to make contracts with and pay deposit money to the higher units, promising to reach their quotas. For example, Yunnan Tin Company incorporated the achievement of drug suppression in its criteria of examining whether the lower units had fulfilled the requirements of the "economic responsibility contract system." Since the company was huge and had tens of thousands of employees, it established its own rehabilitation center to which all drug addicts were sent. The addicts, along with their parents and the subunits to which they belonged, had to make a contract with the company and to deposit 200 *yuan*, promising to be rehabilitated within a limited time. If the addict failed to do so, the money was taken away by the company as a fine (*Yunxi Bao* 1991).

In the countryside, this method is also widely adopted. In Gangmeng Township of Yingjiang county, if drug addicts failed to be rehabilitated, both addicts and their cooperatives were subject to fines.[32] If the recidivism rate of a cooperative surpassed 30 percent, the cooperative would be fined 100 *yuan* by the township authority; the fine increased to 200 *yuan* if the recidivism rate surpassed 40 percent (*Dehong Tuanjie Bao* 08/15, 1991). In some villages, the penalty was more severe. For example, Yingpan village in Longchuan county of Dehong Prefecture set up its own rehabilitation session for twelve addicts. According to newly made village rules, after finishing the session, those twelve persons were to be under the supervision of the whole village. Anyone who fell to the craving again would not only be fined 1,000 to 2,000 *yuan* but also lose membership in the cooperative and be expelled from the village (*Dehong Tuanjie Bao* 06/11, 1994).

The practice of relating anti-drug activities to financial gain or loss reflects a much broader trend in the social mentality of contemporary China. Due to the lack of rehabilitation facilities and the lack of expertise in government-sponsored rehabilitation centers, many rehabilitation centers without official licenses have been set up. At a time when the main interest of the Chinese is to get rich first, it has turned out that many "private," "individual," or "underground" rehabilitation centers are merely money-generating machines, with no credibility in conducting rehabilitation services. As pointed out by Gu Yingqi, Vice Minister of the Ministry of Health, some of those private centers have become new drug-distributing places to addicts (*World Journal* 12/05, 1992).

SHOULDERING THE BURDEN: THE CENTRAL
AND LOCAL AUTHORITIES ON DRUGS

The changing relationship between the central and local authorities has also detracted from the current campaign's status as a "people's war." Using the widespread indifference toward mass campaigns by the Chinese people after the Cultural Revolution as a general frame of reference, it is time to examine the actual relationships between different agencies involved in the anti-drug campaign. As shown by the campaign of 1952, a successful nationwide campaign demands well-coordinated actions between the central and local authorities. For this purpose, the National Narcotics Control Commission was established in November 1990 to lead the war on drugs nationwide. Since Yunnan was the place where most drug-abuse and drug-trafficking cases occurred, Yunnan's anti-drug actions were pivotal to the success of the whole campaign.

Drugs had reappeared in Yunnan long before 1990, and in several border areas the problem had become so serious that it attracted a lot of public attention. In an effort to alleviate misunderstanding and in response to pressure from the public, the Yunnan government was initially very enthusiastic about starting a massive anti-drug campaign, and in a short period of time, the drug issue became a hot topic in the media. Cases of drug trafficking and abuse were publicized to an unprecedented degree, and Yunnan was proudly called China's anti-drug outpost.

At the same time, the media also exposed Yunnan as a center of drugs, and more frighteningly, of AIDS. When people of other provinces refused to shake hands with people from Yunnan for fear of becoming infected with AIDS, the Yunnan authorities were prompted to re-examine their stand on publicizing drug issues.

The case of Baoshan is a good example. Baoshan Prefecture has Baoshan city and four surrounding counties under its jurisdiction, among which two counties share a border with Burma. According to public records, Baoshan had heroin addicts since 1987 and intravenous heroin addicts since 1988, which were fairly late initial dates for Yunnan (Huang and Dong 1991, 1). Despite this, anecdotal reports depicted Baoshan as the "capital of drugs" in China, which led to it being chosen as a primary field site for this study.

This puzzle was solved only in an interview with a government official, who related to this author that in the early 1990s, it was rumored that the United Nations Drug Control Programme (UNDCP) and the Chinese government would provide huge amounts of money to places in Yunnan with serious drug problems. Having been a very poor area for many years, the local authorities tried very hard to compete with other locales for the alleged money; they did so by deliberately exaggerating the drug problem in Baoshan. As a result, on June 25, 1990, in the meeting commemorating the 150th anniversary of the Opium War, a high-ranking official proclaimed that Baoshan was the number-one drug center in Yunnan (*Baoshan Bao* 06/30, 1990). In the end, the promised money never materialized. "We made a big mistake, a stupid mistake by portraying our hometown as the capital of drugs. With this reputation, how could those foreign investors dare to come to make the investments we need? We had to do something to rebuild our image in front of the eyes of the world," said the official. Since then, Baoshan has been very careful in reporting drug-related news.

At the provincial level, Yunnan was aware of the dilemma it faced. The People's Congress of Dehong Prefecture passed its own anti-drug regulations in August 1990, four months before the same action was taken by the National People's Congress. But Dehong's regulations were at first rejected by the Provincial People's Congress, out of concern for Yunnan's image. Following the initial wave of the drug campaign in the early 1990s, though officially Yunnan has retained its firm stance against drugs, out of the same concern, the reports on drugs in Yunnan have become less mysterious, exotic, or eye-catching, and increasingly matter-of-fact in tone.

The campaign also reveals the conflicts between local and higher authorities and between different government agencies involved. In the mid-1990s, at the time of this study, the morale of policemen of the public security bureau, the main force in the anti-drug campaign, was very low in places like Longling. At times, they were unable to get their previous month's wages because of the county's financial difficulty, and they often complained about their out-of-date equipment and accused provincial officials of keeping most new cars for their personal use. They reported that, while pursuing traffickers, the police's old domestic-made cars were often outrun by the traffickers' foreign Jeeps. On several occasions, the public security authorities could not get needed information on traffickers because the local stations simply had run out of money to pay for communication expenses.

How to run rehabilitation centers is another issue that stirred discontent among local public security authorities. Though the authorities have spent much energy on rehabilitating drug addicts, little progress has been recorded, and the growth in the number of addicts is far higher than those cured.

There are several levels of rehabilitation institutions in China. The lowest level is the rehabilitation session set up by small work units or townships and villages. Next are the temporary rehabilitation centers, which are usually established in big work units or counties with moderate drug problems. The permanent rehabilitation centers in cities and counties occupy the next level, where addicts might stay for between three months and one year. The highest level is called reform-through-labor rehabilitation centers, where recidivists who were rounded up are placed for up to three years. The rehabilitation session and temporary centers were common during the early 1990s when the campaign started, but are rarely seen today. Only the last two types of rehabilitation centers are supported by government funds. At first, the rehabilitation center was supposedly to be run jointly by civil administration, public health departments, and public security bureaus, but today it has been left to the authorities of public security alone.

Sometime rehabilitations at the local level has been conducted in an old-fashioned way. A well-publicized case in Dehong Prefecture happened in Longba Township of Longchuan county. The township had conducted rehabilitation drives since 1989 but with little success. Frustrated with the high recidivism rate, the authority of Bangwan village invented a special rehabilitation method, which was called the "wooden cage method." It literally put the addict in a wooden cage about three meters long, by a little more than one meter wide and high, to go through the agony of withdrawal. In front of more than one thousand spectators, seven addicts were put into cages under twenty-four-hour surveillance by forty-eight security guards. Supported by the township authorities, this method was followed by other villages, and two dozen more wooden cages were made and put into use (*Dehong Tuanjie Bao* 12/07, 1993; 02/08, 1994).

Due to government financial difficulties, rehabilitation centers often operate in the red. Among four permanent rehabilitation centers visited for this study, Ruili center was best staffed and equipped because the center was set up with assistance from UNDCP as a showcase to the outside world. But even with so much attention, the center faced financial difficulties, too. According to the center director, the large number of addicts accepted meant that the center needed more subsidies, because the appropriation from the government was not enough. The center had over 100 *mu* of fields, so those addicts capable of working were asked to grow rice and cultivate litchi trees, as well as to look after a fishpond. The proceeds were used to improve addicts' diet as well as to make up the budget deficit.

At Baoshan Education-Through-Labor Rehabilitation Center, almost everyone had to work on an affiliated lime kiln every day. In the spring of 1994, there were only 73 inmates, far less than its planned capacity of 300 to 500, and well below the 1,784 drug addicts qualified to be sent there. To enable the center to reach its full capacity, a total of 6.2 million *yuan* was needed, but, by 1994, only 1.8 million *yuan* had been appropriated. Those parents who were anxious to have their children rehabilitated had to use back-door connections to get them in. Even then, they were asked to pay 2,000 *yuan* to cover expenses. This rule effectively excluded many poor families from sending addicts to the center.

The conditions of permanent rehabilitation centers have varied from one to another. Of the four centers visited for this study, the Baoshan center had the poorest conditions. The center had two barracks, and in each room there were more than ten addicts living together. All slept on the floor because there were no beds. The room was dirty and foul smelling. There was a so-called rehabilitation room for those experiencing withdrawal symptoms, where they were put into confinement and restrained by chains. There had been one doctor providing medical service in the center, but he had left recently due to the harsh working conditions. In contrast, the rooms at the Tengchong center were relatively clean, and there was even an entertainment room for addicts to watch TV or play Ping-Pong. There was also one doctor on the staff.

The function of such rehabilitation centers has been to provide a place where drug addicts can be put into confinement and cut off from heroin. Comprehensive modern drug-rehabilitation methods, which involve physiological, psychological, and medical treatments, are unavailable. China set up a national rehabilitation center in Beijing in the early 1990s, but their rehabilitation experts have rarely come to Yunnan. Local people once mentioned sarcastically, "Beijing center has experts but no addicts; our center has addicts but no experts."

Local centers have used only two methods to rehabilitate addicts. One is compulsory, which means putting addicts into confinement until they pass the period of withdrawal. The other one is through education, including lectures and work. Each rehabilitation center visited had an education program that covered the history of the Opium Wars, the history of Yunnan's opium epidemic, and the damage that drugs brought to the society and the whole country as the standard content of the lectures. The education efforts were incorporated into the addicts' daily lives by local rehabilitation centers. In Tengchong center, all addicts had to stand in line and sing a "rehabilitation song" together before breakfast. The song put new words into the lyrics of a popular song so that everybody was able to sing it. Its theme was teaching addicts to rid themselves of the bad habit and become new people once they rehabilitated. After breakfast, the whole group was divided into different teams to do some manual work, such as planting vegetables and cleaning the surroundings. The afternoon was usually devoted to an education session, during which addicts were lectured by administrators of the center. But the main focus was on each addict telling of individual experiences and then trying to find ways to rehabilitate that person. The staff of Baoshan Education-Through-Labor Center often visited inmates' families, held discussions with family members, and asked them to visit their relatives at the center. On holidays, the center sent inmates out to celebrate with other people, making inmates feel they were not abandoned by society. The staff sometimes even acted as mediators, asking the wives of recovering addicts not to seek a divorce from their addicted husbands. As an administrator said, "Big theory is not as effective as a family letter to these addicts."

Generally speaking, the local public security authorities in Yunnan have done a good job in running rehabilitation centers under difficult conditions. But why has their good work had little effect on curbing the increase of drug abuse? It is true that now the rehabilitation centers are dealing mainly with heroin addicts, who are extremely difficult to rehabilitate. Yet what makes the situation even worse is the failure of the society to mobilize fully the sufficient resources to handle the problem. The high demands of the central authorities and the limited resources of the local governments often make the goals unrealistic. As a result, many addicts are left out of rehabilitation. Plus the wide availability of drugs on the streets has made the recidivism rate extremely high in many places. In 1990 the recidivism rate of 598 addicts "rehabilitated" in Baoshan was 85 percent. The recidivism rate of 132 female addicts was an amazing 100 percent (Baoshan Women's Association 1991, 4, 10).

A PROTRACTED WAR: ANTI-DRUG CAMPAIGN IN THE LATE 1990s

By all accounts, the current campaign of the war on drugs is in retreat. When the campaign was launched at the beginning of the 1990s, the goals were to curb the momentum of drug trafficking within two to three years and to prevent drugs from spreading to interior China (*Liaowang Weekly* 07/22, 1991). When it became clear that these goals were unreachable within those two years, the strategy of the campaign was forced to change to fighting a "protracted war." To make the situation even worse, the drug abuse problem has spread to the whole country.

Shanghai, the biggest city in China, has seen the number of drug addicts increase rapidly since 1992. In the first half year following its establishment in July 1992, the municipal rehabilitation center treated only 12 addicts. The number increased to 94 in 1993 and 162 in the first half of 1994 (Zhao and He 1994). Liaoning province in the northeast China has witnessed an explosion of drug addicts. In its capital city Shenyang, there were 117 registered addicts in 1993. The number increased to 1,740 in 1994, and by the first half of 1996, the number was conservatively estimated as between 40,000 and 50,000. And, to the government's surprise, the secret drug and opium dens that had long ago disappeared have recently reappeared (Wei 1996, 6).

Since the early 1990s, the coastal and border areas of China have been hit extremely hard by drugs. Shenzhen, China's first Special Economic Zone, has become somewhat synonymous with China's economic take off in the reform era. Along with its rapid growth, however, the city has seen a dramatic increase in drug trafficking and consumption. For example, there were 20 drug trafficking cases from 1981 to 1990, averaging two cases per year in Luohu district, Shenzhen's main business center housing permanent residents of more than 300,000. In the first half of 1996, the trafficking cases caught by the police reached 202, involving 440 people, and another 773 were caught using drugs. Though the authorities launched three waves of massive arrests of drug offenders over six months, according to police, the crackdowns would not be able to stop the spread of drugs in the area in the long run (Xiao 1997, 430–39).

It is evident that China is rapidly becoming a drug-consuming market in the 1990s. It has evolved from the end of the 1970s, when drugs from the Golden Triangle were transited through China to Hong Kong for American or West European consumers, but the Golden Triangle drug producers and Chinese traffickers consumed very little of the drugs. As drugs have become more available and affordable, however, the number of drug abusers has increased rapidly. Table 8.2 shows an alarming picture of the official government statistics, the actual figure of addicts is estimated at four times the number of registered addicts. In other words, China has more than two million drug addicts today.

A related statistic is that the number of HIV positive and AIDS cases has also increased dramatically in recent years. According to the statistics from the end of September 1998, China had 11,170 HIV positive cases, among which there were 338 with AIDS (*People's Daily* 11/06, 1998). The apparent ineffectiveness of government efforts to curb the spread of drug abuse has prompted public disputes on how to handle the drug issue. In a commentary entitled "Are We Doing Enough to Prevent the Spread of the 'White Peril'?" in the *Liaowang Weekly*, a magazine that often reflects points of view of the highest authorities of China, the author proclaimed that the "white peril" has posed a threat directly or indirectly to everyone, and that everyone is a potential victim. Criticizing the prac-

Table 8.2. Registered Drug Addicts in China, 1990–1998

Year	Number
As of June 1991	70,000
June 1992	148,000
December 1992	250,000
1994	380,000
1995	520,000
1997	546,000
1998	596,000

Sources: *Renmin Gongan Bao* (People's Public Security News), November 7, 1992, June 26, 1993; *Liaowang Weekly*, March 4, 1996, 8; *China Daily*, August 16, 1997; *China Daily*, June 11, 1999.

Chinese police officials inpsecting seized opium and heroin

tice of not reporting drug-related news in the early stages of the drug problem and calling it a lesson to be learned, he suggested a propaganda initiative to make the danger of drugs known to all people (Ye 1996, 8).

It was in these ever-worsening circumstances that the Chinese government decided in 1996 to conduct a "special struggle against drugs" in 1997. A commentary issued by the *People's Daily* on April 22, 1997, outlined the proposed campaign. From its title "Conducting a People's War to Suppress Drugs," one can tell that there was not much new in the government's strategies: conducting propaganda campaigns to the public, starting with elementary and middle school students; mobilizing all societal forces to help accomplish the campaign's goal; and using the work of drug suppression as a criterion by which to evaluate performance by cadres at different levels. Insisting on the "people's war" strategy, which had worked very well in the 1950s, the authorities failed to respond to the new situations that have made conducting a mass campaign against drugs very difficult in China today.

First of all, having been through a string of disastrous mass campaigns, from the Great Leap Forward to the Cultural Revolution, ordinary people have not only lost interest in but also have become suspicious of new mass campaigns conducted by the authorities. As an old political slogan, the "people's war" does not possess the appeal it once had. Additionally, the authorities have lost a great deal of mobilization power in society. As shown, before the open-door era, almost every aspect of individual life—be it at home, on the street, or at work—was under tight control by institutions like residents' committees, work units, schools, and other mass organizations. But these institutions have changed, and their individual agendas often get more priority than the government's anti-drug initiatives.

The only unqualified success in the campaign may be the authorities' use of state violence against drug traffickers. The public executions demonstrate the state's power and at the same time make people "satisfied and happy" in a manner that relates to its crisis-handling mentality after the Tiananmen Incident of 1989. Having been portrayed as something harmful, dangerous, and unpatriotic, trafficking in drugs has become an unpardonable crime. This kind of discourse escalates the pitch of anti-drug sentiment at the public trials. But drugs mean different things to different people. Though there are many agencies involved in today's campaign, each reinterprets the existing anti-drug discourses in accordance with its own agenda, making the anti-drug discourse more diverse and inconsistent.

For example, though the history of the Opium Wars is being used in the discourse, and mentioning history serves as a "standard" start of anti-drug narratives, the nationalistic component in anti-drug discourse has now lost the prominence it once had. Though nationalism played an important role to mobilize anti-opium campaigns from 1924 to 1952, China then had visible Western powers to blame, be they the British, Japanese, or Americans. Today, as far as drugs are concerned, China's only clear mechanism for stirring nationalistic emotion is referring to the Opium Wars.

The latest anti-drug campaign, begun in April 1997, was intended to be conducted in a way similar to the campaign of 1952. According to the plan, the campaign would finish in September. By the end of June, it was reported that, according to incomplete statistics, 55,211 drug offenders had been arrested—about two-thirds of the arrests made in 1952. The government set up 187 new rehabilitation centers and had more than 30,000 addicts going through compulsory rehabilitation. In addition, more than 400 kilograms of "ice" drugs and 1,623 kilograms of heroin had been confiscated. But apparently the campaign was not able to achieve its goals. Acknowledging the serious drug problem China was facing, in August the National Narcotics Control Commission decided to extend the campaign to the end of 1997 (*People's Daily* 08/16, 1997). So far, no follow-up reports on the result of the campaign have been found. One thing for sure is that the campaign did not achieve the level of effectiveness comparable to 1952's,

*Posters from China's large-scale anti-drug
exhibition held in 1998 in Beijing*

and that further campaigns are needed to curtail, if not solve, the drug problem in contemporary China.

In the summer of 1998, the Chinese government launched another anti-drug drive by hosting a large-scale, anti-drug exhibition in Beijing. The exhibition lasted more than two months and attracted 1,660,000 visitors, including President Jiang Zemin and other high Chinese leaders. The authorities were pleased with the unprecedented publicity on the exhibition and the favorable public response toward the government's drug suppression policies (*People's Daily* 07/31, 1998). From the viewpoint of public relations, the government surely scored a victory by holding the exhibition. But it is an open question as to how long the effect of a successful propaganda drive can last to help forge a "people's war" on drugs in the late 1990s. Given the weakening of the authority's mobilization ability, the diminishing appeal of nationalistic anti-drug discourse, and the integration of China's economy into the world capitalist system, the success of an anti-drug campaign these days remains to be seen.

9

Anti-Drug Campaigns and Ethnic Minorities in Southwestern China: 1950s and 1990s

Until the 1950s, the southwestern part of China was a major drug-producing area. Many non-Han, minority peoples lived there, often in remote, isolated, mountainous areas, which provided safe havens for poppy planting and opium production. The anti-drug campaign of 1952, carried out mainly in cities, towns, and drug-distribution centers, did not enter most of these areas, and it was not until the mid-1950s that anti-drug campaigns were seriously conducted there, although in a way quietly different from that in the Han areas.

Since the late 1970s, the southwestern part of China has been the area most affected by drugs. Along with the Han Chinese, ethnic minority peoples have been involved in both drug addiction and trafficking, in some cases to an extreme degree. This chapter focuses on how and why drug suppressions have been conducted differently in minority areas in both the 1950s and 1990s by analyzing three cases: two anti-opium campaigns in the Liangshan Yi and Aba Tibetan areas in the mid- and late 1950s, and a 1992 drug crackdown in a Hui community in Yunnan. Two comparisons will be made: the campaigns in the Yi and Tibetan areas versus those conducted in the Han areas; and the first two campaigns in the 1950s versus the crackdown in 1992.

OPIUM AND LIANGSHAN YI SOCIETY

By all accounts, the introduction of opium into the Liangshan Yi area had such a profound effect that it changed many aspects of the Yi society in just a few decades. Opium not only was a part of the Yi people's everyday life, but also became a catalyst of the dramatic social changes that the Yi society experienced from the early to the middle years of this century. To discuss the anti-opium campaign in the Yi area, it is necessary to trace out the origin, spread, and effect of opium in Liangshan.

The Liangshan Yi Autonomous Prefecture is located in the southwestern part of Sichuan province. The area's current jurisdiction is about 63,000 square kilometers encompassing nineteen counties, with the prefecture capital in Xichang City. It is the largest Yi-inhabited area in China, with a total Yi population of 1,350,000 recorded in the early 1980s (Editors of Liangshan 1985, 1–2). Before 1978, the Liangshan Yi Autonomous Prefecture referred to a much smaller mountainous area between the Dadu and Jinsha Rivers, about 19,000 square kilometers with only nine counties under its jurisdiction. In 1978, the former Xichang Prefecture was incorporated into the Liangshan Prefecture, making today's Liangshan larger and more populous. And both Liangshan and Xichang belonged to the Xikang province until it was dismantled and incorporated into Sichuan province in 1955. In the mid-1950s, the total population of Liangshan was 973,000, of which 706,000, or about 72 percent, were Yi (Cheng 1987, 152). Since the Yi population in the Xichang Prefecture was a small percentage, the following discussion focuses on Liangshan before 1978, unless otherwise specified.

Chinese scholars agree that the existence of slaves was one of the main characteristics of the old Yi social system before it was fundamentally changed by the "democratic reform" carried out by the Communists in the 1950s (Wang Yingliang 1987, 49–52).[33] Yi society had a rigid hierarchy that was divided into two groups: black Yi and white Yi. The black Yi (about 7 percent of the population) made up the aristocratic ruling class, and the white Yi held subordinate status. Within the white Yi, however, there were three subgroups: Qunuo, Anjia, and Jiaxi. Qunuo (about 50 percent of the population) was defined as semi-independent peasants, who owned some land and production implements.[34] Anjia (about 33 percent) and Jiaxi (about 10 percent) were slaves. The Jiaxi—many of them captured Han Chinese—had the lowest social status of the three, and lacked any personal or economic independence from their owners. The black Yi owned slaves, as did some rich Qunuos. In fact, a Qunuo might be richer than a black Yi, but the lines of the hierarchy could never be crossed, as manifested by the fact that there was absolutely no intermarriage between the black and white Yi.

Clan organizations had a dominant role in the Yi society. A unit was composed of the black Yi clan and its subordinate Qunuo, Anjia, and Jiaxi. The clan organization was not limited to black Yi, however; Qunuo had their own clan organizations, though they lacked clear territorial boundaries and were not closely organized like those of the black Yi (Hu 1987, 32). Many clans were often involved in various kinds of feuding, which were extraordinary in frequency and scale. As Lin Yaohua pointed out: "Clan feuding is a pivot of Lolo [an old name of Yi] culture, around which are linked the different parts of their social life. . . . Anyone entering the Lolo area cannot fail to observe the prevalent phenomena of fighting and killing between Lolo clan enemies. . . . There is not one branch or lineage among the Lolo families in Liang Shan [old spelling] that is in complete amity with its neighbors or without some involvement with hostile families surrounding them" (Lin Yaohua 1961, 111). Frequent clan feuds also made Yi society very militarized, and fighting was the main channel for protecting a group's self-interests.

The Yi people maintained a strained relationship with the Han people living in adjacent areas. Liangshan area was surrounded by high mountains that had been used by the Yi to resist the Han. Historically, Han rulers had used military force to suppress large-scale resistance by the Yi from time to time, but they were unable to maintain control of Liangshan for long. Indeed, the Yi used their strong fighting power (originally mobilized by clan feuds) to descend from the mountains and capture Han villagers, taking them away as slaves. As a result, by the 1940s, the area under Yi control was in fact much larger than it had been 100 years previously (Hu 1987, 19). This dominance of the Yi was a rare exception in the relationship between the Han and other nationalities in southwest China, in which the Han usually played the dominant role.

All these social aspects were affected by the introduction of opium into the Liangshan area in the early twentieth century. According to several sources, opium poppy planting was begun around 1910 by the Han people as a way of evading the anti-opium campaign conducted by the Qing dynasty (Shao 1987b, 51; Zhan 1987, 144; Du 1987, 220). By 1930, poppy planting was widespread in the counties of Liangshan (Editors of Liangshan 1985, 90). In Jinyang county, the spread of opium coincided with the rise of Long Yun as the ruler of the neighboring Yunnan province in 1928. A member of a local black Yi clan, Long Yun became the ideal protection his clan members needed to conduct their opium business. Even under pressure from Jiang Jieshi during the Six-Year Opium Suppression Plan, Long Yun never loosened his grasp on opium revenues. Not surprisingly, around 1930, the Long family started recruiting Han Chinese from Yunnan to their hometown to plant poppies. The Long family not only extracted taxes as high as 33–50 percent of the total poppy output, but also controlled the local opium market using its political clout (Shao 1987a, 49).

The period of 1930 to 1950 was the heyday of opium production in Liangshan. By 1950, in the area of the current Liangshan, 50–80 percent of the households, both Yi and Han, engaged in poppy planting; and 50–60 percent of the local populations smoked opium (Sun, Shi, and Zhu 1993, 198). In Jinyang county, 40 percent of arable land was used to plant poppies from 1940 to 1950 (Shao 1987b, 51), and simultaneously the price of opium increased dramatically. Around 1930, one *liang* (about 50 grams) of opium could be exchanged for 0.15 *liang* of silver. Around 1940, the rate increased to 6 *liang*, and by 1943, 1 *liang* of opium had a value of 10 *liang* of silver (Shao 1987b, 52).[35] The increased income from the opium enabled the Yi to buy grains, salt, and sugar from Han areas, and this meant the Yi had to devote more land to poppy planting to maintain their needs, thus deepening their dependency on the Han for these basic necessities of life (Shao 1987b, 53–54). The crop shortage was a chronic problem facing the majority of the population.

Opium changed not only the Yi's economic life but their political and social landscapes as well. Though the black Yi received the big share of the opium wealth, the massive inflow of silver enriched the entire Yi society, which in turn played a big role in the further stratification of the Yi social hierarchy. For example, it became common for rich Qunuo to use newly accumulated money to buy land and slaves. Before the mid-1950s, one-fifth of the households of Qunuo had slaves. Even a small portion of Anjia had their own land and owned Jiaxi. Conversely, both Anjia and Jiaxi were able to use silver to redeem themselves from their black Yi masters, moving themselves one rung up in the social hierarchy. For example, it cost twenty to forty ingots of silver (one ingot of silver was about 10 *liang*), for an Anjia to pay off service and become a Qunuo. This practice raised the number of Qunuo to about 60 percent of the total population by the mid-1950s (Wang Yingliang 1987, 71–73). Meanwhile, the number of Anjia and Jiaxi also increased dramatically as a direct result of the constant campaign to capture and enslave the Han people (Du 1987, 231).

This was all made possible by opium. Along with opium came the inflow of rifles and handguns to the Liangshan Yi area. Guns started to replace traditional weapons, such as bows, arrows, poles, and knives in 1911, about the same time opium was introduced to the area (Lin Yaohua 1961, 116). Local Han warlords were actively engaged in exchanging rifles for opium in order to make huge profits. For example, in the early Republic period, one German-made rifle could be bought with 20 *liang* of opium in the Han area, but in the Yi area it was worth 200 *liang* of opium (Du 1987, 224). Opium markets in Liangshan were also used to exchange guns. About 20–30 guns could change hands in a town market on a fair day (Shao 1985b, 52). By 1950, there were about 100,000 guns of various kinds in the hands of over 600,000 Yi people, or about one gun in every household (Editors of Liangshan 1985, 91).

The prevalence of guns had several effects on the Liangshan Yi society. Weapons dramatically increased the fighting power of the black Yi, enabling them to consolidate their ruling position. In addition, the possession of modern weaponry changed the nature of clan feuds, making them more frequent and more deadly. The fighting evolved to the degree that a feud could involve hundreds, or even thousands, of people and last from days to months. From 1940 to 1950, two branches of a clan fought a lengthy intraclan feud that caused the deaths of more than 200 Qunuo and 20 black Yi on both sides (Editors of Liangshan 1985, 88). Although the white Yi of the defeated side became slaves of the victorious side, capturing Han people from areas adjacent to Liangshan remained the main source of new slaves.

The large quantity of guns possessed by the Yi made them militarily superior to other ethnic groups, and the nearby Han and Tibetans became easy targets. The Yi's slave-capturing activities ranged from large-scale assaults by several clans against the Han area, to guerrilla-war-type strikes by small groups. In 1919, over 1,100 Han people, including 380 Han soldiers, were captured in a district of Leibo county alone (He Yaohua 1987, 135). Some of the captured were put on the slave market in exchange for opium, guns, and silver. It was estimated that before 1950, among the total Yi population of over 600,000, about 10 percent were Han-turned-slaves (Hu 1987, 20). This fact could explain why the slave population increased so fast in the years after opium was introduced into Liangshan, and why the hatred and distrust between the Yi and Han had become so deeply rooted by the time the Communists arrived in 1950.

ANTI-OPIUM CAMPAIGN IN LIANGSHAN: 1950–1959

Opium brought silver, guns, and slaves into Liangshan. It caused a series of political, economic, and social upheavals in the Yi society and was intertwined in almost every aspect of Yi life. No place in China was influenced and transformed more deeply and in such a short period of time than was Liangshan by opium. It was in this historical context that the Communists, after the establishment of the People's Republic, launched an anti-opium campaign in the Liangshan Yi area.

From the very beginning, opium suppression was carried out separately in the Han and Yi areas of Liangshan, and with very different approaches. The Han area comprised the majority of the former Xichang Prefecture, which was a stronghold of the Nationalist Army in early 1950. The People's Liberation Army (PLA hereafter) entered Xichang at the end of March and within three months destroyed the Nationalist Army (Lin Yaohua 1995, 203). By mid-1950, the Xichang Prefecture was under the control of the Communists.

The anti-opium issue seemed to be a priority on the agenda of the newly established government. On July 20, Xichang Military Administrative Committee issued its first decree on the opium issue, forbidding poppy planting, ordering the closure of opium dens, and requiring the rehabilitation of all opium addicts. Yet these measures were enforced within the Han area only. From April 1950 to December 1951, 1,376 opium dens were closed in Xichang, and more than 130,000 *liang* of opium was seized. Poppy planting was under control after the Land Reform was carried out during the winter of 1951 and the spring of 1952 in the core area of the prefecture (Sun, Shi, and Zhu 1993, 200).

Though contained, by the middle of 1952 opium was still a headache to the authorities. According to information collected in preparation for the anti-drug campaign of 1952, Xichang still had more than 5,000 poppy planting households, 1,705 drug traffickers, 745 opium dens, about 10,000 addicts, and more than 20,000 *mu* of poppy fields. Targeting drug trafficking and traffickers, Xichang authorities conducted the campaign of 1952 in the same way the campaign was carried out in the rest of the country. Massive propaganda drives were initiated. The authorities held more than 2,000 public meetings participated in by more than 500,000 people. After three waves of massive arrests, more than 70 public trials were held, in which 26 drug offenders were sentenced to death and more than 300 were sent to prison (Sun, Shi, and Zhu 1993, 202–203).

The effectiveness of the 1952 campaign in the Han area was compromised in the following years, because opium produced in the Yi area found its way back to the Han area through both Han and Yi traffickers. So in 1954, local authorities decided to deal with the resurgence of opium on two fronts. In addition to cracking down on opium trafficking by Han Chinese in the Han area, the authorities also tried to cut off the outflow of opium from the Yi area. Yi traffickers, however, were only subject to "education," compared to the severe punishment the Han traffickers faced. By the end of 1954, after 466 arrests, the authorities claimed that the resurgence of opium in the Han area had been suppressed (Sun, Shi, and Zhu 1993, 204–205).

Why these different approaches? There was a well-defined official policy that differentiated the Han area from the Yi. Since opium played such an important role in Yi life, the Communists were very cautious initially in dealing with the Yi. In two opium-suppression decrees issued on September 1, 1950, and February 23, 1952, the Xikang provincial government clearly proclaimed that anti-opium campaigns would not be carried out in ethnic minority areas (Sun, Shi, and Zhu 1993, 205–206). In fact, given that many of those areas were not under total control of the Communist rule in the early 1950s, this factor might also have reflected authorities' limited power at the time. For example, though the government of the Liangshan Yi Autonomous Region was established in October of 1952, the government did not start to establish its administrative apparatus until 1953. There was strong resistance to both the PLA and the government working teams entering the Yi area. In September of 1954, more than 3,000 Yi attacked the Han intruders and were counterattacked by the PLA. It was not until July 1955 that the entire Liangshan area was finally under the control of the PLA (Lin Yaohua 1995, 208–212).

Thus, the Liangshan Yi area was not touched by the anti-opium campaign of 1952. In the following years, the authorities tried to accomplish their goals step by step. Major attempts to curtail opium planting and trafficking were first carried out in Yi areas within the Xichang Prefecture where the Han constituted the majority. Before April 1954, when opium was found being brought by Yi or other ethnic minorities into the Han area, the authorities would merely point out the harmful effects of opium to the traffickers, asking them to take opium back.[36] In areas with large opium outflows, the authorities also tried to persuade Yi clan heads to tell their subordinates not to sell opium in Han areas. After April 1954, however, the authorities started to seize opium brought in by minority people in order to prevent the drug from being reintroduced. The seized opium was eventually turned over to the local government of the opium owner, and the government would work with the opium owner's clan head on the issue. Finally, by the second half of 1954, the authorities started to confiscate opium brought into Han areas, provided that taking this kind of action would not strain the relationship between the Han and the Yi (Sun, Shi, and Zhu 1993, 204–207).

Suppressing poppy planting in the Yi area turned out to be a much tougher issue than curtailing the outflow of opium. As pointed out earlier, many Yi depended on the opium income to acquire food and other life necessities. Without the transformation from opium planting to crop cultivation, it would be very difficult for the Yi to stop planting poppies. This issue touched the interests of Yi of varying social status, especially those black Yi with large investments in poppy planting fields and slaves. Understandably, the authorities approached this issue carefully. They worked to educate and persuade Yi voluntarily to increase crop cultivation and to decrease poppy planting. Without resorting to any form of coercion, the propaganda and persuasion seemed to work quite well in several Yi areas. By the end of 1954, the Yi had voluntarily uprooted 16,000 *mu* of poppy land out of a total of more than 20,000 *mu* in four counties (Sun, Shi, and Zhu 1993, 207–208).

In contrast, the authorities met with strong resistance when they used force to uproot poppy fields in the Yi area. After achieving the encouraging eradication of the poppy in two Xichang counties in 1954, the Prefecture authorities asked that the task be carried out in five other counties and set the spring of 1955 as the deadline for eradicating poppy planting in both Han and Yi areas. To meet the deadline, poppy uprooting was carried out hurriedly by force, an action that became the catalyst of a large-scale riot in Miyi county in January 1955. Led by several Yi clan heads, more than 800 people, armed with over 300 guns, took part. They attacked eight districts and townships, killing more than a dozen government cadres, including the district party secretary and the vice director of county public security bureau. The riot lasted five months and was eventually dissipated by means of political maneuver and military suppression. Immediately following the outbreak of the riot, the Prefecture authorities ordered the poppy-uprooting working teams to be dismantled, and the forced eradication of opium in the Yi area was halted (Sun, Shi, and Zhu 1993, 208).

It was not until after 1956 that authorities had both the resolve and means to solve the opium issue—indeed, before 1955, the Liangshan Yi area was not under total control of the local government. The upper class Yi, many of whom were heads of clans and held a lot of slaves, still had tremendous influence and power over the local society. Before 1954, the most effective way for the authorities to gain influence in the area was to serve as mediators between feuding clans. From 1950 to 1954, government working teams mediated more than 10,000 clan feuds.

In the time period, working teams were ordered not to liberate slaves nor to propagandize the Land Reform.[37] They did not forbid mercenary marriage, nor conduct opium suppression or confiscation of opium by the Yi (Lin Yaohua 1995, 205–206). In other words, the authorities left the main parts of Yi society intact.

Allowing a slave-based society to remain intact within a socialist China, however, was not congruent with Communist ideology. After consolidating their presence in the Yi area for several years, the authorities finally launched a so-called democratic reform in 1956. The democratic reform was actually a revolution forced upon Yi society. It demanded the confiscation of slave owners' land and the distribution of it among the public. It also forbade ownership of slaves and granted the liberation of all slaves. Slave owners, most of them black Yi, resisted the democratic reform by revolting against the government. The riots started on December 24, 1955, and were finally put down in October 1957.

From many aspects, the democratic reform reflected the same techniques that the Communists had used in other areas to establish their rule. It involved: (1) mobilizing, organizing, and arming the masses; (2) defining individuals' class status; (3) confiscating slave owners' lands, guns, and means of production; and (4) consolidating grassroots-level organizations and establishing a local government. As a result of a massive propaganda campaign and the mass mobilization, 220,000 Labor Association members and 110,000 Self-Defense Teams members participated in the democratic reform and fought alongside 10,000 PLA troops and 5,000 militia members against rioters. In this process, the authorities cultivated 35,000 activists, including 2,300 Yi cadres. The Communist Party recruited 2,380 new members, 8,060 Communist Youth League members, and established 251 party committees and 363 Communist Youth League branch committees. By doing so, the Liangshan Yi area was finally under the firm control of the Communists (Lin Yaohua 1995, 223–29).

The fundamental changes in the Yi society from 1956 to 1958 provided a new opportunity for the authorities to carry out opium suppression in the Yi area. At the beginning of the democratic reform, poppy planting was resurrected amid riots and social chaos. According to statistics, from the winter of 1956 to the spring of 1957, there were 10,000 *mu* of poppies in Liangshan and 8,000 *mu* in Xichang. Since slave owners were the main cultivators of the poppy, however, when their land was confiscated, poppy ceased to be planted. Authorities had considerable leverage over the newly liberated slaves to prevent them from planting poppies: after all, they had just received land from the government and did not want to jeopardize their acquisitions. Suppressing opium planting in accordance with the process of democratic reform was clearly elaborated by the government document of 1957. By the second half of 1957, the authorities had eradicated 7,000 *mu* of poppy fields in Liangshan and 4,700 *mu* in Xichang—70 percent and 55 percent of the total acreage, respectively (Sun, Shi, and Zhu 1993, 209).

On July 23, 1957, in the third meeting of the Third People's Congress of the Liangshan Yi Autonomous Prefecture, a resolution forbidding opium planting was passed, signaling the formal start of an anti-opium campaign in the Yi area. The resolution clearly stipulated that no nationality would be allowed to plant poppy, that no person would be allowed to sell stock opium within or outside the Yi area, and that no opium den would be allowed to stay in business. Offenders would be subject to punishment according to law. It was the first time the authorities did not differentiate between the Han and Yi when dealing with the opium issue. Yet the resolution warned that the Han Chinese would face more severe punishment if they were to plant or traffic opium in the Yi area (Sun, Shi, and Zhu 1993, 210).

The final phase of opium suppression in Liangshan was carried out from 1958 to 1959. This time the initiative was quite similar to the campaign of 1952, with drug traffickers and opium-den operators the main targets, including both Han and other ethnic minority drug offenders. In the Yi area, the campaign was carried out concurrently with the campaign to suppress counter-revolutionaries, conducted in minority areas in the second half of 1958 and 1959. A total of more than 3,000 counter-revolutionaries and criminals were arrested, some also guilty of drug offenses. In addition, the authorities tackled 17 opium cases and made 27 arrests. As far as poppy planting was concerned, the 85 percent of Yi households that had joined cooperatives by the spring of 1958 enabled the eradication of all poppies in Liangshan during the campaign. Meanwhile, with the seizure of 56,000 *liang* of stock opium in the Liangshan Yi area and another 55,000 *liang* in the Xichang, opium was finally declared to have been wiped out in the Liangshan area (Lin Yaohua 1995, 229; Sun, Shi, and Zhu 1993, 210–12).

OPIUM SUPPRESSION IN ABA TIBETAN AREA IN THE 1950s

The Aba Tibetan Autonomous Prefecture was located in the northwestern part of Sichuan province, where the Tibetan, Qiang, and Han comprised the majority of the population.[38] According to a survey conducted in 1952, there were about 190,000 Tibetans in this area (including 50,000 to 60,000 Tibetan that spoke Jiarong dialect), accounting for about 48 percent of the area's total population of 400,000 (Research Office 1985a, 2; 1985b, 178). Within Aba, an area of 82,000 square kilometers that covered thirteen counties, Tibetans were concentrated mainly in the western and northwestern parts, while the Han and the Qiang were in the east and southeast parts, adjacent to the Han-dominated area of Sichuan province (Editors of Aba 1985, 1, 11).

It is believed that opium planting started in 1862 in Maogong [Xiaojin] county and gradually spread to neighboring counties. The British and their missionaries have been accused of initially bringing opium into Maoxian county and of being involved in opium transactions after they established a church in 1909 (Yang Chengguang 1993, 316–17). Since the Qing dynasty established an "official" opium outlet in Maoxian in 1909, opium consumption appears to have been common in the area. Qing's campaign against opium was rigorous at the time, yet the government's initiatives had little success in this area where Qiang people were in the majority. In March 1911, the "official" opium outlet was destroyed by hundreds of Qiang people (Editors of Aba 1985, 83).

After the fall of the Qing dynasty, poppy planting started to spread to the whole Aba area, though poppy planting in the eastern and southeastern parts was more visible than in the western and northeastern parts of Aba. Before 1950, about 40 percent of the land in Maogong county was used for opium planting. The percentage of opium planting fields reached 90 in Tibetan-dominated Maerkang county (Yang Chengguang 1993, 316), although the number may have been a bit exaggerated. According to a survey in one district of Maerkang during several years before 1950, out of a total of 32,180 *mu* of arable land, 3,400 *mu*, or 10.6 percent, were devoted to opium planting. The planting in Maerkang started in 1935, and reached its peak during 1947–1949 (Sichuan Nationality Survey Team 1985a, 258, 260; Maerkang Working Committee Survey Team 1985, 281). Coincidentally, 1935 was the start of the Six-Year Opium Suppression Plan under the Nationalists. It is possible that the opium cultivators in the Han area were under pressure and turned to the Tibetan area as a safe haven for opium.

The introduction of opium into the Tibetan area in Sichuan (mainly the agricultural area) brought a series of changes to the local society. First of all, opium became a catalyst of commercial exchange, something that had barely existed in the mostly self-sufficient Tibetan economy. Maerkang, the current capital of Aba Prefecture, transformed itself from a small village to a bustling commercial market due to the opium trade. Though Han and Hui businessmen from both Sichuan and Gansu provinces dominated opium transactions, Tibetan businessmen and stewards of Lamaist temples were also involved in exchanging opium for salt, tea, and other everyday necessities (Sichuan Nationality Survey Team 1985a, 261–62). Similar to what had happened to the Liangshan Yi society, opium also brought more guns into the Aba area. This in turn made the opium business very risky, and opium businessmen became easy targets of bandits. For example, in the winter of 1949, more than 100 merchants lost their lives during ambushes in one town of Wenchuan county alone (Editors of Aba 1985, 122).

But the opium did not enrich and empower the ordinary Tibetan to the same extent that it had the Yi in Liangshan. At the beginning of opium planting in Maerkang, one silver *yuan* could buy several *liang* of opium. Later, the price was hiked as high as two dozens silver *yuan* for one *liang* of opium, but usually the price was kept at the level of ten silver *yuan* for one *liang* of opium (Sichuan Nationality Survey Team 1985a, 260). The huge opium profit materialized mostly in the process of commercial exchange. If Aba opium reached Gansu, the price would be quadrupled and go even higher if it made it to the Xinjiang province. Though the profit was extremely high, except for chieftains (*tusi*), headmen, Lamaist temples, and a small number of wealthy people, the majority of Tibetans were not involved in opium business transaction due to its capital-intensive nature (Sichuan Nationality Survey Team 1985b, 334).

Despite the vast quantities of guns that came into Aba areas, the Tibetans never presented a strong military threat to neighboring peoples. This was mainly a consequence of demographics. There were fewer than 200,000 Tibetans living in an area of 82,000 square kilometers, and a quarter of that population raised animal stock, making for a scattered population. In addition, Han Chinese were well represented in Maogong and Jinghua [Jinchuan] counties, two of the most notorious opium production areas; Han Chinese accounted for 75 percent and 69 percent of the total population, respectively, whereas the Tibetan population was about 20 percent and 29 percent, respectively (Research Office 1985b, 181). The Han and Hui opium merchants controlled the transaction of opium; the Tibetans' role was limited to that of opium producer.

Before the arrival of the Communists, the Tibetan population in the region was subject to the rule of Tibetan chieftains, Lamaist Temples, and the Nationalist government, depending on the area.[39] To ordinary Tibetans, participating in poppy planting did not translate into an improvement in their financial situation. In fact, some poppy-growing Tibetans in the Nanping area found themselves among the poorest because of the heavy burden of taxes and extortion from the Han secret-society members of "Gelaohui." The senior members of Gelaohui used to give "gifts," such as a pair of straw sandals or a pack of cigarettes, to the Tibetans in spring, asking them to hand over a half-dozen *liang* of opium in return when poppies were harvested. On occasion, the Tibetans were even forced to plant poppies by the Han Chinese to avoid the penalty of a so-called lazy tax. But, sometimes after the Tibetan planted poppies, they were ordered by the authorities to uproot it in the name of opium suppression. The uprooting of opium often met with strong resistance. A county magistrate of Songpan, for instance, was killed when he tried to eradicate poppy by force (Research Office 1985a, 21).

Facing complex social and ethnic problems, the Communists used caution in dealing with the opium issue in the Aba area. They tackled the issue step by step, and differentiated Tibetan from Han and other ethnic groups. The strategy adopted was similar to the one used in the Liangshan Yi area, reflecting a consistent policy on opium suppression in the so-called minority areas by the People's Republic.

The step-by-step strategy was mainly due to Aba's status as one of the last areas to come under the control of the Communists. The PLA troops entered Maoxian county in January 1950 and established the Maoxian Prefecture in February, which held jurisdiction over six counties in the eastern and southeastern parts of the current Aba Prefecture.[40] It took the authorities almost three years to establish the Sichuan Tibetan Autonomous Region (the name was changed to the Aba Tibetan Autonomous Prefecture of Sichuan Province in December 1955) at the end of 1952. Yet it was not until mid-1953 that the remnants of the Nationalist Army and bandits were completely cleared out of the area (Editors of Aba

1985, 110–20, 12–29). Opium suppression was first carried out in the area under government control. In September 1950, the authority of the Maoxian Prefecture issued a directive on opium suppression, and by the end of November, opium-suppression committees had been set up in Maoxian, Wenchuan, Lifan, and Songpan counties. According to the authorities, opium planting, smoking, and trafficking were all to be stopped (Yang Guangcheng 1993, 319–20).

The result of suppression was visible, though not as quick as the authorities would have liked in the first few years. In Songpan county, because so much land had been used to plant poppies, before 1950 the food crops produced could only support the population for four months of the year. In 1950, the number increased to five months, then to six and eight in 1951 and 1952, respectively, with the conversion of poppy fields to plant crops (Research Office 1985a, 43). Progress was also made in reducing the numbers of addicts and traffickers, as illustrated by Table 9.1.

It took much longer to eradicate the opium problem in Aba than in the rest of country.[41] In 1951–1953, opium suppression was carried out in Aba in areas cleared of the remnants of the Nationalists. In 1954, the campaign was conducted in the Chuosijia and Heishui counties, signaling the extension of the campaign to the whole Aba area. In the same year, the Land Reform was carried out in the Han and Qiang areas, thus reducing poppy planting further. From 1956 to 1959, the democratic reform deprived landlords of their land holdings in Tibetan communities. In 1959, the whole area was collectivized, and poppy planting was virtually eradicated in Aba. For the authorities, the remaining task was to seize opium still in people's possession. The detailed plan for this was laid out in 1959, and the task was finally accomplished in 1963 (Editors of Aba 1985, 139–40; Yang Guangcheng 1993, 321–22).

The step-by-step strategy was used concurrently with another strategy of differentiating and stratifying different ethnic groups in the opium suppression. Theoretically, with the exception of the Han Chinese, all ethnic groups belonged to minority nationalities and were entitled to certain rights under the so-called nationality policy of the Communist Party. The policy permitted local authorities to adopt different means and paths to achieve the party's goals in minority areas.

Table 9.1. Numbers of Drug Addicts and Traffickers in Maoxian, Wenchuan, Lifan, and Songpan Counties, 1950–1952

Year	Drug addicts	Drug traffickers	Long-distance traffickers
1950	16,672	17,444	760
1951	9,007	9,507	499
1952*	883	8,815	318

*By March.
Source: Yang Chengguang 1993, 320.

Interestingly enough, in the anti-drug campaigns of 1950s, differentiation was made between not only the Han and non-Han, but also between the three other main ethnic groups—Tibetan, Qiang, and Hui—in the Aba area.[42]

Before 1950, the majority of Aba-produced opium was trafficked to the Gansu and Sichuan, which were controlled by Hui and Han trafficking groups, respectively. From the very beginning, Han and Hui were the main targets of opium-suppression policies. At the end of 1951, the public security bureau of the then-Maoxian Prefecture ordered the crackdown on Han and Hui traffickers. Yet, in dealing with Tibetan and Qiang opium merchants who sold in the Han area, the local authorities were instructed to use "persuasion" only and to let the chieftains and headmen handle the issue. Paradoxically, as far as the opium trafficking was concerned, the Hui were obviously deprived of their right to be members of the minority nationalities, and the Qiang enjoyed the same lenient treatment like the Tibetan. But since the majority of Qiang lived in Maoxian (currently the Maowen Qiang Autonomous County), and had close contact with the Han, the authorities did not differentiate the Qiang from the Han when they conducted the Land Reform in the fall of 1954, thus finally subjecting them to the same standard of opium suppression as in the Han area.

Tibetans were on the top of ethnic stratification, and enjoyed more tolerance in the opium suppression attempts. The national anti-drug campaign of 1952 interfered with only the Han Chinese in Aba. The local authorities presented suggestions on forbidding poppy planting to the provincial authorities on September 28, 1952, but the latter were cautious and waited more than a year to instruct the local authorities to carry out anti-drug campaigns through a combination of propaganda and education, and to pay attention to people's real-life difficulties in the process. Furthermore, the instructions emphasized that opium suppression should strictly limit its strike target to the Han and Hui opium traffic groups, especially those Han traffickers from outside Aba (Yang Guangcheng 1993, 321). The authorities clearly realized that in some areas, opium was still the main source of income for many ordinary households. Without full control of that area and without replacing poppies with crops, the Communists knew that conducting opium suppression would have provoked strong resistance, even riots, as happened in the Liangshan Yi area. It is understandable that only after the democratic reform and the collectivization in Tibetan areas was opium planting finally stopped in 1959.

DRUG CRACKDOWN IN PINGYUAN HUI COMMUNITY IN 1992

On the evening of August 30, 1992, a motorcade of over 100 military vehicles left Kunming and headed to the Pingyuan area, which was about 200 kilometers from the Sino-Vietnamese border. It was reported that this action even attracted attention from the intelligence agencies of foreign countries. In fact, about 2,000 on board were not soldiers but rather police and paramilitary policemen who were about to take part in the largest, single, anti-drug crackdown since the end of the 1950s. By the dawn of August 31, the whole Pingyuan area was under a siege, which lasted for 80 days. At 7:00 A.M., the raid formally started. The police arrested a dozen big drug traffickers, but met with strong resistance. Two alleged traffickers were shot to death and three policemen were killed in the action. The raid was halted the next day, but the siege went on.

According to the commander-in-chief of the crackdown, the halt of the raid was ordered for several reasons. First, the community was enraged by the siege and was geared up to fight, as were the policemen who had just seen their fellow policemen die. This could have caused the situation to veer out of control. Second, since the community was heavily armed, the raid would face continued resistance, leading inevitably to heavy casualties on both sides, including innocent people caught in the crossfire. Third, heavy casualties in the Hui community would have caused irreparable political damage to the authorities (Fan 1993, 86). After all, Pingyuan was a minority area to be handled with special care.

Pingyuan was located at the juncture of Wenshan and Yanshan counties of the Wenshan Zhuang and Miao Autonomous Prefecture in south Yunnan. Broadly speaking, Han, Zhuang, Miao, Yi, and Hui peoples inhabited the area, with a population of about 80,000. The targeted area comprised seven villages and the Pingyuan township, with a population of 15,000, of which 80 percent were Hui (Bai 1993). Almost all members of the Pingyuan Hui community were Muslims, deeply devoted to their religious practice. These characteristics warranted that the authorities deal with the community within the framework of both the nationality and the religion policies of the Communist Party.

The authorities had prior experiences in dealing with Muslim communities in Yunnan. In an area where the majority of the population did not follow Islam, the relationship between Hui and other peoples, especially the Han, had not been smooth. Yunnan's Hui population amounted to 535,000 in 1992 (Yunnan Yearbook 1993, 398), and they usually lived in compact communities, which led to strong solidarity among the Hui. During the Cultural Revolution, when the government's radical policies forbade Hui religious beliefs, the government met with strong resistance and had to use military force to put down Hui uprisings. The Shadian Incident was a well-known, bloody suppression by the PLA in 1975, in which reportedly more than 1,600 Hui people were massacred in Shadian, a Hui village in the neighboring Honghe Prefecture, not far from Pingyuan (Gladney 1991, 137–40). It was not until after 1978 that the incident was redressed and the tension between the Hui and Han people in Yunnan lessened, but the roots of distrust remained.

During the Cultural Revolution, the Pingyuan Hui community was subjected to the radical policies and its resistance—branded as "counter-revolutionary revolt"—was suppressed by military force (Zhao Tingguang 1995). Since the end of the Cultural Revolution, the authorities examined the situation and, in an effort to avoid repeating mistakes, took a more cautious approach in dealing with the Hui communities in Yunnan. Meanwhile, the Pingyuan Hui Muslims took advantage of community solidarity to advance their interests in their interactions with the Han and other peoples, which soon posed a problem for the authorities.

Since the mid-1980s, the area had become a smuggling center for gold, silver, knives, and pornographic materials. Due to high profits in drug trafficking and gun smuggling, the area became a notorious distribution center for illicit opium, heroin, and guns, selling drugs and guns to more than 24 provinces throughout the country. To protect their lucrative business, traffickers bought large quantities of guns and ammunition to arm themselves, making it extremely difficult for authorities to enforce law and order. In fact, since the early 1980s, Pingyuan had gradually become a place out of the reach of local authorities. The local residents did not pay taxes, did not apply for residence registration and resident identification cards, did not register their marriages, did not obey family-planning rules, and did not have their vehicles registered. And though land ownership was illegal in China, land was bought and sold openly in the Pingyuan area (Bai 1993).

The situation was compounded by the role played by some local religious leaders. When the authorities would attempt to enforce the law, local mosques would sound alarm bells to summon hundreds of villagers to surround policemen when they entered villages. On a couple of occasions, policemen were humiliated when they had to surrender their guns before being allowed to leave Pingyuan. In 1987, even the Pingyuan public security bureau was attacked by villagers.

Besides the tense relationships with the Han, the Pingyuan Hui community also had a rough relationship with the Zhuang, Miao, and Yi peoples. On March 3, 1991, a Pingyuan youth was beaten up in a failed robbery attempt by several youth of a nearby village. Several dozens of Pingyuan villagers went to the village to seek revenge, but were detained by angry villagers. Local leaders of Pingyuan organized 1,000 villagers who marched to the neighboring village, only to meet a 2,000-men-strong "united protection team" organized by the nearby villagers of the Zhuang, Miao, Yi, and Tu people. This incident almost provoked a large-scale feud among several minority peoples (Luo Ping 1993, 20). Thus, solving problems in Pingyuan involved not only the issue of religion but also that of relationships between the Hui and Han, as well as the Hui and other minority peoples. With the lesson of the Shadian Incident in mind, the authorities were very hesitant to confront the Pingyuan issue. Over the years, Pingyuan became a safe haven for rampant drug-trafficking and distribution activities.

In August 1991, the Provincial Party Committee sent a working team to Pingyuan in a last attempt to solve the problems. This matched the CCP's pattern on enforcing its policies, which worked well in mobilizing and organizing the ordinary people in the Yi and Tibetan areas in the 1950s. But the working team met with hostility from the first day it entered Pingyuan. Over the next year, the working team heard gunfire almost every night. Its compound was the target of snipers' shots. On March 30, 1992, a high-ranking prefecture party cadre, along with a member of the working team, was killed, and three policemen were seriously injured when they tried to arrest a fugitive. This incident not only shocked the provincial authorities but also the highest authorities in Beijing, and finally prompted the authorities to take decisive action.

At the beginning of August 1992, Beijing instructed Yunnan to define the problem of Pingyuan neither as a nationality problem nor a religious problem, but rather as the problem of serious criminal offenses of drug trafficking and gun smuggling. Since the situation was out of control, no time was to be wasted in attacking the problem (Luo Ping 1993, 22). Based upon these instructions, the Yunnan authorities launched a raid in the name of suppressing criminal activities, with big drug traffickers as the main targets of the first wave of the raid.

After the August 31 military raid was halted, the policemen completed the siege and occupation of Pingyuan, and a propaganda campaign was initiated. Propaganda trucks with loudspeakers were dispatched more than 100 times to inform villagers of the government's policies in conducting this raid. More than 3,000 policemen and working team members were sent into the streets to post and hand out more than 10,000 copies of two announcements issued by the provincial authorities. These announcements ordered drug traffickers and gun smugglers to surrender themselves within a limited period of time, and promised extremely lenient treatment to those who followed orders (Luo Ping 1993, 23; Zhang Liyong 1993).

Not surprisingly, this propaganda campaign had little effect on the villagers, whose distrust of the authorities was deeply rooted. The authorities first had to convince mosque *ahungs* and religious leaders that the raid targeted neither Islam nor Hui people, but only drug traffickers. It was then through these religious leaders that the government policy reached the general public. During the raid, the authorities made a special effort not to provoke religious or ethnic conflicts. They did not allow other ethnic groups of the local area to take part in the raid nor did they permit troops to enter mosques to seize drugs and guns. They directed troops to follow Moslim dietary restrictions when stationed in the Hui villages, and not to use heavy weapons to contain drug traffickers' resistance, thus avoiding endangering ordinary people's lives and property (Zhao Tingguang 1995).

After a one-and-one-half-month siege, the authorities gained effective control over the Pingyuan area. A public trial participated in by 8,000 was held on October 14. At this event, two drug traffickers were sentenced to the death penalty and immediately executed, and 22 others were arrested. At the same time, five were released due to their voluntary surrender to the authorities. The siege culminated in another grand public trial held on November 12, at which 12,000 people were present. Among the five people given the death penalty were the vice-director of the Pingyuan township and the general steward of a mosque, who had been leaders of the local community. To the authorities, the execution of these five people represented the destruction of the old political and religious power structure that had made the Pingyuan area so uncontrollable before.

Though on a much smaller scale, the raid and siege of Pingyuan were good examples of the interaction between the anti-drug campaign and the process of state building. From the very beginning, the ultimate purpose of the authorities was to restore their control of political and religious power in the name of cracking down on drug trafficking. According to statistics given by the authorities, about 10 percent of the adult population in Pingyuan were criminals. In the crackdown, a total of 854 drug traffickers and gun smugglers either were arrested or turned themselves in. Among them, 46 percent, or 393 out of 854, could be given the death penalty, according to the existing law. But by the end of the siege, only seven had been sentenced to death, another seven got prison terms, plus another thirty were put on probation. The vast majority of criminal offenders were set free (Luo Ping 1993, 24; Zhao Tingguang 1995). As one of the raid commanders put it, "The purpose of conducting the raid was not to kill a few more people, but to solve the problem completely. The purpose was not to pursue a short-lived effect, but to promote solidarity among different nationalities and to keep the society stable in the long run" (Zhao Tingguang 1995).

The authority of the government and regaining control of the local government materialized in the process of the drug crackdown. The Resident Committee, Village Council, Security Committee, and Women's Association—organizations that had not been able to be established before—were set up. The systems of resident registration, tax collection, marriage certification, vehicle registration, and family planning were demonstrated. It was reported that 89 percent of households turned over grain owed for past-due agricultural taxes in just two and one-half days. And by November 1, 137 couples registered marriages that had never been on the books (Zhang Liyong 1993). More significantly, with the arrest and execution of those Hui leaders who had been dominant influences in the community, the Communists were able to establish pro-authority people into leading positions.

By all accounts, the raid of Pingyuan was a huge success for the government. The result of the crackdown was stunning. The list of seizures included a total of 1,074 kilograms of heroin, opium, and other illicit drugs; 964 guns of various kinds; more than 40,000 rounds of ammunition; 278 grenades and mines; over 10 million *yuan* cash; 2,500 grams of gold; 14,400 grams of silver; 60 automobiles, and 34 motorcycles (Zhao Tingguang 1995). More important, a Shadian-type confrontation was avoided. Though the villagers were heavily armed, after the first day, the raid was carried out without the authorities firing another gunshot. By so doing, they minimized casualties and avoided escalating the raid into a large-scale conflict between the troops and villagers; yet at the same time, the authorities successfully restored control of the local government and the Hui community. The success of the raid also demonstrated a departure from the usual practice of the authorities not to publicize cases involving sensitive nationality and religious issues. The drug crackdown in Pingyuan was made public on national television and in newspapers, and subsequent stories covering this raid in popular newspapers and street magazines exposed the Hui community in an

*Police and local minority militia members engage in anti-drug
activities in the southwestern border area of China*

unfavorable way and gave the general public the impression that most Hui people in Pingyuan were drug traffickers.

In summary, from the birth of the People's Republic, the Chinese government tackled the opium problem within the framework of its nationality policies, which included conducting the suppression step-by-step and applying different treatments to different ethnic groups. Though subjecting one ethnic group to the same harsh policy applied to the Han, the authorities used lenient policies with other groups.

The standard of ethnic stratification is intriguing. Ostensibly, it seems the more Hanicized an ethnic group was, the more likely it would get the same treatment as the Han as far as opium was concerned. In the cases of Aba, Tibetan, Qiang, Hui, and Han, they were treated differently along this ladder of ethnic stratification in the opium suppression of the 1950s. Yet this pattern needs further scrutiny. Even though Hui traffickers in Aba were listed along with the Han as the main targets, the authorities refrained from dealing with trafficking problems in Pingyuan as aggressively as they did with Han traffickers. Little special consideration was paid, however, to the Zhuang, Miao, and Yi people living in the same area, who were less Hanicized than the Hui.

In actuality, the application of different policies had more to do with the level of the government's actual control over particular ethnic groups in particular areas at particular times. Both the Yi in Liangshan and the Tibetans in Aba were not under firm control of the newly established People's Republic, so the authorities had to conduct the opium-eradication campaigns step-by-step in connection with the completion of political and social transformation in these areas. In Pingyuan, the same cautious policy was adopted because of the difficulty in controlling the Hui community and the potential for widespread casualties. The standard of ethnic differentiation was set mainly according to the degree of potential threat posed to the authorities.

Detaching the drug problem in the Pingyuan Hui community from issues of religion and nationality signaled a major shift in Beijing's way of handling the drug issue in minority areas. In the name of a drug-trafficking crackdown, the authorities achieved two major goals: wiping out a drug-distribution center, and destroying the community power base that was beyond the government's control. Though the authorities used the same follow-up techniques as those of 1952, the success of this raid was accomplished neither in connection to other mass campaigns nor based on the mobilization of the general public. Instead, it could only be done through a long-term siege and occupation of the community with a massive presence of force. The loosening of government control and the lack of mass participation in this campaign reflect the general picture of China's anti-drug campaigns since the 1980s.

10

Conclusions

The main aim of this study has been to construct a cultural history of anti-drug campaigns in modern China. The intention has been not only to combine anthropological study with history, but also to write a cultural history that "is a chronicle of intentions, contingencies, and relationships: among people, in a culture, over time" (Fox 1991, 95), a history different from traditional cultural history in which "structural or normative principles prefigure events and humans" (Fox 1985, 206). As pointed out in the introduction, the static concept of culture and the model of subculture—two methodological weapons mostly used in anthropological studies on drugs—are not applicable to the study of anti-drug movements in modern China. Their complexity is far beyond the grasp of the organismic concept of culture, which makes most anthropological studies on drugs seem teleological and tautological in explaining the phenomenon of drugs. A new approach has to be found.

In fact, in the period of the roughly 100 years that this book covers, Chinese society and culture have experienced a series of dramatic changes that make meaningless and irrelevant the question of what Chinese culture is precisely. There is not an abstract, coherent, static "Chinese culture" that can be readily pulled out of the concrete historical contexts and applied to explain why the Chinese use a certain kind of drug, how they perceive and define drugs, or how they conduct anti-drug campaigns. Chinese culture should be seen as being constantly in the making by people in social actions. A cultural history of the anti-drug campaigns is manifested through specific anti-drug initiatives people proposed, negotiated, and carried out in particular historical contexts, in which the "culture" of the anti-drug campaigns was made and defined by people's concrete actions.

It is from this point of view that, in this study, no megatheory has been used to provide one-size-fits-all explanations (as many social scientists are eager to

169

do) to the several anti-drug campaigns explored. These campaigns occurred in different contexts, and a single explanation would be overly generalized or reductive. Yet this does not mean that important theoretical issues do not arise from the different campaigns. Nationalism, the relationship between state and society, and the anti-drug campaigns and state building are three issues given special attention in this study.

Anti-drug crusades are closely intertwined with nationalism in modern China. Nationalism provides motivation, legitimacy, and the requisite emotional charge for the Chinese to take an anti-drug stance. Nationalism plays a major role in the making of a mainstream, anti-drug discourse in modern China, in the interpretations of the history of the Opium Wars, in the mobilization of the social elite and general public in the cause of drug suppression, and even in the linking of drugs to the survival of the Chinese nation in the face of foreign aggression and threat. However, the complexity and changeability of nationalism can only be fully appreciated if its multiple forms and multiple meanings in modern China are explored. To avoid adopting nationalism as a concept of universal applicability—a mistake often committed by Western scholars—this study has also shown that the manifestations of nationalism in anti-drug campaigns are complex and multifaceted, subject to different interpretations by the different parties involved in different contexts of anti-drug campaigns.

A little elaboration is needed here. Though being drug free was linked as a prerequisite to becoming a new citizen of the Republic established after the fall of the Qing dynasty, this new citizenry—a component of modern nationalism—has not been emphasized since the early Republic. When the Shanghai elite used nationalism to mobilize the private sector to form the NAOA in 1924, its direct aim was to gain equal status for the Chinese delegation among others in the International Opium Conference as a way to restore China's equality with the Western powers. The participation of Chinese Christians in the anti-drug campaigns was a part of their efforts to indigenize Christianity and gain independence from foreign missionaries. To the Nationalists and the Communists, nationalism was directly tied to anti-imperialism in conducting drug-suppression campaigns. In today's China, nationalism has been deliberately channeled to patriotism in the anti-drug crusade, which is playing a unique role in the changed historical context of China in the 1990s. It is clear that over the course of the century, the components, emphases, and targets of Chinese nationalism have been under constant change and reconstruction. The fluidity and complexity of Chinese nationalism require the exploration of its influences on the anti-drug campaigns from a historical perspective.

As far as the issue of the relationship between the state and the society during the anti-drug campaigns is concerned, this study employs the concept of public sphere to describe the fact that the anti-drug campaign has always generated much attention from the general public in modern China. How does the drug issue define a public sphere in modern Chinese society? This question brings back the role of nationalism in the making of a strong anti-drug discourse in modern China. Nationalism not only mobilized China's private sector to participate in the anti-drug movements in the early days of this century, but also provided the necessary legitimacy and protection to individuals for broad participation through the hegemonic anti-drug discourse that it had helped to forge. Those who participated in anti-drug campaigns risked little but gained much prestige; those involved in the drug business lost credibility in the public. Emphasizing the damage drugs do to the health of individuals, to the strength of state, and even to the survival of China as a modern nation-state, this anti-drug discourse was very widely accepted and echoed in the first half of this century. In addition, the symbolic meaning opium possesses relates the drug issue directly to China's humiliating experiences with the West. In this context, the history of the Opium Wars has been interpreted in a nationalistic tone, making drugs an explosive public topic in modern China.

It was through such public discourse, along with the historical situation of China in the 1920s, that it was possible for the Shanghai elite to play a prominent role in anti-drug campaigns. The Chinese bourgeoisie was experiencing rapid growth in its wealth and power; the Chinese state had fallen into the hands of warlords; thus there was no central government truly in control of the whole country. Confident Shanghai elites were thus eager not only to engage in controlling the Chinese economy, but also to be active players on the political and social fronts. The formation of the NAOA was a manifestation of the growing attention given by the Shanghai elite to this social issue of both national and international significance. Assisted by its rich resources and skillful use of the media, the NAOA was extremely successful in mobilizing public opinion and creating a public sphere for the anti-drug cause.

But this in no way means that drug use as a domain of the public sphere has been homogenous in its composition. Though the anti-drug discourse has enjoyed a dominant position, there have been other kinds of discourses on drugs in modern China that portray smoking opium as fashionable or as a form of high pleasure associated with the individual's special class status in the society. Both nationalism and drugs mean different things to different people. Anti-drug discourses are often interpreted in multiple ways to accommodate different needs of different groups. Even within the NAOA, division and conflicts occurred on what policy should be adopted to suppress drugs in the early 1930s. All of these factors contributed to make the anti-drug issue a public sphere in which both society and state negotiated and maneuvered themselves in an advantageous position according to their different agendas.

Thus in the anti-drug campaigns, the relationship between state and society has always been ambivalent and not smooth. Both the Nationalists and the Communists deliberately incorporated anti-drug campaigns into their efforts of state building, which included to enhance the authority of the central government, to tighten social control, and to legitimate state violence. Generally speaking, after the Nationalists entered Nanjing, the state played a dominant role in setting opium policy and conducting nationwide, anti-drug crusades, and the role of the private sector gradually diminished during the tenure of the Nationalist rule until it scarcely existed at all under the Communists.

The Six-Year Plan gives a clear example of how the anti-opium crusade served the purpose of state building. Jiang Jieshi maneuvered the drug-suppression campaign to achieve his larger political agenda. By making opium suppression a part of the NLM, he aimed not only to bring everyday lives of individuals under rigid ideological control, but also to deprive regional powers of their legitimacy in conducting the opium business. Carrying out the Six-Year Plan was designed to make the central government the only authority to exercise an opium monopoly; at the same time, it cut off the main revenue resource from regional powers in southwestern China, thus subordinating them to the central government.

The Communists successfully conducted an anti-drug campaign in the early 1950s to consolidate their newly gained power. In the campaign, their ideological articulation of a new socialist China was accompanied by nationalism, which was used to mobilize anti-American sentiment and to keep the campaign invisible to the outside world. Their success not only derived from the use of the mass propaganda and mobilization, but also from the ability of the state to conduct a revolution in social organization, which enabled the state and the party to penetrate and control all aspects of people's everyday lives. In this process, China's private sector was overwhelmed by and incorporated into the state. The unprecedented degree of social control kept the drug problem out of China until the end of the 1970s.

In reality, the state is not the sole player in anti-drug crusades. Quite often, it has to negotiate with the private sector of society as well as with different sectors of itself. A dilemma arose from the fact that opium tax revenue was such a vital part of government's revenue, that few regimes could afford to abandon it and live up to the public, anti-opium stance. To solve this dilemma, regimes explored multiple interpretations of the anti-drug discourse and made them resonate with existing public anti-drug sentiment, thus at least generating a fig leaf to their revenue-generating deeds. It was in this context that the private sector had more maneuvering room in its relationship with the Nationalist state. The NAOA's relationship with the Nationalists involved negotiations and cooperation, as well as confrontation, in which the NAOA sometimes even exercised powerful influence over the government's opium policy. Jiang Jieshi also met with strong resistance from regional powers, and his aims of drug suppression were never fully realized.

The complexity of the role of the state also manifests in the fact that the state is never a singular entity. This study has not reified the state as a monolithic entity by emphasizing diverse purposes behind the state's will to conduct anti-drug campaigns. There are divisions within the state, as shown by the fact that many local party committees and governments were against the opium policy adopted by the highest authority of the Nationalists. In the current anti-drug campaigns, the differing priorities between the central government and local authorities, the divisions between different government organs, and the lack of mass participation by China's social institutions are also important, and are documented in this study.

It is appropriate here to offer some thoughts on the current drug situation in China. The comeback of drugs (heroin instead of opium, this time) in the late 1970s smashed the myth of the superiority of socialism in fighting drugs. Facing an ideological dilemma, the state was forced to depoliticize the anti-drug discourse and to begin seeking new interpretations. Its attempts have included demonizing drug offenders, blaming international or ethnic groups for the drug problem, and treating drugs as an inevitable vice that comes with modernization. Though old components of anti-drug discourses are still being used in the current campaign, the altered social conditions have made both anti-drug discourse and practices appear scattered and disoriented. There is strong evidence that the state is not winning its fight.

The recent loosening of social control may be a reason why the government does not have the same success it had in the early 1950s. In recent years, China has become not only a transit point of international drug trafficking but also a site of drug production as well as a drug-consumption market. This development has occurred while China is being incorporated into the world economic system, and international capital has come to play a crucial role in making drugs available in China—reminiscent of the role capitalism played in making opium a commodity and an epidemic in pre-1949 China. Examining how sugar became an important common necessity (or drug) in capitalist Europe, Sidney Mintz has demonstrated the close relationship of an originally luxurious and exotic substance to the capitalist world system (Mintz 1985). Will heroin produce another drug epidemic in China, and will China become a huge drug-consumption market? And how will China conduct anti-drug campaigns in the future? No matter the approach, answers to these questions need to be based on an understanding of the drug problem within the historical context of reform and global capitalism in China in the last two decades of the twentieth century. Since the latest transformation in Chinese society is still unfolding, it will be another one or two decades until there are clearer answers to the above questions. It is an intellectual challenge for all to decipher.

Notes

1. In this manuscript, the term "drugs" generally refers to opium before the 1960s and to heroin after the 1980s, if not otherwise specified.

2. The concept of subculture is well received by many anthropologists, because it fits well into traditional ethnographic study methods and can give a detailed picture of the subject being studied. A few exceptions exist. For detail, see Dreher 1982; and Wormsley, pp. 197–218.

3. For a detailed discussion of the concept of hegemony and its application in anthropology, see Kurtz 1996, pp. 103–35.

4. A special issue of *Modern China* was devoted to the symposium, to "'Public Sphere'/'Civil Society' in China?" *See Modern China* 19 no. 2 (April 1993).

5. All quotations from Chinese materials are my translations if not otherwise specified.

6. For a detailed history on the debate over opium policy among the Chinese ruling elites, see Polachek 1992.

7. In fact, this kind of argument has been mentioned from time to time until today. For a recent version, see Newman 1995, pp. 765–94.

8. This book also uses "anti-opium" and "anti-drug" alternately, because either opium or narcotics suppression can be encompassed in the phrase "*jindu*," which means literally "poison suppression" in Chinese. Nonetheless, when narcotics other than opium are involved, the term "anti-drug" covers all substances.

9. Based on *Judu Monthly*, *Shenbao*, and other NAOA publications.

10. Xiong was once prime minister of the Republic, Tao was one of the most famous educators in modern China, and Fan was a prominent politician.

11. The official stance on this issue can be seen from this excerpt from the Chinese delegation's Memorandum to the President of the First Opium Conference when it withdrew from the Conference:

As the Chinese delegation has always said, it recognizes that the existence of contraband trade in opium constitutes an impediment to the effective operation of messages for the total suppression of the legalized use of prepared opium, but it does not admit that this impediment is such as to prevent and excuse the Powers concerned from taking immediate steps to enforce measures that will, if allowed free play, lead, within a definite or reasonably brief period of time, to the total prohibition of the legalized smoking of opium. With such measures in existence, even though their operation be somewhat retarded by illicit trade, the Powers will be in a position to increase their efficiency in exact proportion as the retarding influences, of which contraband is but one, are lessened or wholly removed. (League of Nations, 1925a, 170)

12. I want to thank Dr. Edward Slack, Jr., for providing me these useful materials.

13. Those ten provinces were: Henan, Hubei, Hunan, Anhui, Jiangxi, Jiangsu, Zhejiang, Fujian, Shanxi, and Gansu.

14. Though *jinyan* (opium suppression) and *jindu* (poison suppression) are often used alternately, they were differentiated this time with the latter designated specifically to morphine, heroin, and other narcotic drugs. The term "drug" is used in this chapter to correspond to the Chinese term "*du*."

15. Those added provinces were Sichuan, Yunnan, Guizhou, Chahaer, Suiyuan, Ningxia, Hebei, Shandong, and Shanxi and the cities of Beiping, Tianjin, and Qingdao.

16. For a general perspective on this period, see Teiwes 1987; and Lin, Fan, and Zhang, 1989. For more recent works on the abolition of prostitution, see Hershatter 1992; and Henriot 1995.

17. Besides original materials from the Archives of the Ministry of Public Security of China, one book used extensively is *Jinchang jindu* (Abolish prostitution and eradicate narcotics) (Ma Weigang 1993). Most papers in the volume are based on archival materials of various local bureaus of public security.

18. It has been revealed that, in their struggle of survival during the years of the Nationalist blockade of the Communist-controlled Shan-Gan-Ning Border Region during the Sino-Japanese War, the Communists did cultivate and sell opium outside their base in exchange for hard currency and strategic materials, yet at the same time maintained the prohibition of opium smoking and trade within the border region. This issue is still a forbidden topic in Chinese historiography, and we will not be able to have a clear view of it until more materials are available. For the most recent research based on secondary materials, see Chen Yung-fa 1995.

19. Except in 1960, China was listed as a principal source of heroin by the United States in its *Report on the Traffic in Opium and Other Dangerous Drugs* between 1953 and 1962.

20. In his report to Mao Zedong and the Central Committee on May 5, 1952, Tan Zhenglin, acting secretary of the East China Bureau of the CCP, summarized that the side effects of the Three Antis and Five Antis in Shanghai were "unemployment, increased inventory, decreased prices, and the irresponsible capitalists." Facing these unexpected consequences, the CCP decided to postpone conducting the Five Antis Movement in the medium and small cities in May 1952. See *"Zhonggong zhongyang guanyu 'wufan' dingan, butui gongzuo deng de zhishi"* (Directive on making final conclusion and refunding in the "Five Antis") May 9, 1952; and *"Zhonggong zhongyang guanyu tuichi xianquxiang de 'sanfan' he zhongxiao chengshi de 'wufan' de zhishi"* (Directive on the postponement of conducting the "Three Antis" in county, district, and township as well as the "Five Antis" in medium and small cities), May 23, 1952; in Document Research Office (1992, 181, 195–96).

21. See Teiwes 1987, 88, fn. 25. The number is consistent with newly revealed statistics from sources in the PRC, which say that by May 1951, 500,000 had been executed. See Lin, Fan, and Zhang 1989, 143.

22. For a detailed study on drugs in Burma and the Golden Triangle, see Renard 1996; and McCoy 1991, pp. 283–386.

23. According to an official of China's National Narcotics Control Commission, China started to inform the United Nations and other international organizations about its narcotics situation in 1984.

24. It should be pointed out that almost everything in China was overpoliticized under Communist rule. The term "depoliticization" is used here in the context of comparing the current situation with the overpoliticization of the past. As we shall see in the following paragraphs, the drug issue is not "depoliticized" totally by the Chinese authorities. From time to time, attempts to repoliticize it have been made.

25. "Health" denotes not only the physical but also the mental or spiritual health of people in the terminology of contemporary China.

26. The same stories were encountered many times during fieldwork. They were used by local people to show their resentment toward the "misunderstandings" others imposed on Yunnan people.

27. The Nationalists had the same pursuit of the Communists. John Fitzgerald (1996) discusses this issue in his book, *Awakening China: Politics, Culture, and Class in the Nationalist Revolution*.

28. In a personal interview, this issue was emphasized as a standard government policy by an official in the government of Dehong Prefecture.

29. In the Chinese penal code, between life in prison and the death penalty, there is a "death penalty with two-year reprieve." In 1991, a total of 142 traffickers received the death penalty with two-year reprieve in Yunnan. In 1992, the number increased to more than 600.

30. Since the drug issue is still a very sensitive topic in China, this book uses only pseudonyms to protect the informants. The specific time and location of interviews will not be provided.

31. For a detailed discussion on the history and function of the Residents Committee, see Franz Schurmann 1968, pp. 374–80.

32. Although in most parts of China the people's communes and cooperatives had been dismantled, cooperatives still existed in the area where fieldwork for this study was conducted in the mid-1990s.

33. To date, the most detailed description of Liangshan Yi society in English is *The Lolo of Liang Shan* by Lin Yaohua (Lin Yueh-hua), a Harvard-trained anthropologist. The book was originally published in Chinese by the Commerce Press in 1947 and has been translated into English. The English edition was published by HRAF Press, New Haven, Connecticut, in 1961.

34. This percentage is quoted from *A general description of the Liangshan Yi Autonomous Prefecture*. Editors of Liangshan 1985, pp. 60–62. A different estimate is that there were 7 percent of black Yi, 60 percent of Qunuo, 25 percent of Anjia, and 8 percent of Jiaxi. See Wang Yingliang 1987, pp. 52–53.

35. The actual price may have varied in different areas and during different times of the harvest season. According to Lin Yaohua, in March 1943, one piece of silver could buy three liang of opium. See Lin Yaohua 1961, p. 94.

36. In Xichang, besides Yi, lived Tibetan, Hui, and other ethnic minority groups who were also involved in opium planting and trafficking.

37. The Land Reform was carried out in the Han area before 1953.

38. The name of the prefecture was changed to Aba Tibetan and Qiang Autonomous Prefecture in the 1980s.

39. The Nationalists established the Sixteenth Administrative Region of Sichuan in 1935, which included five counties in eastern and southeastern Aba. An interesting episode of their attempt to increase influence in the northwestern part of the Tibetan-inhabited area involved Zhong Ketuo, the first secretary-general of the NAOA. In 1938, Zhong, as an assistant minister of the Ministry of Interior Affairs, led a delegation to "convey government policies and appreciation" into the current Ruoergai county. He was given the cold shoulder by the Tibetans and had a hard time finding any place to stay. Enraged that a local chieftain did not present a *hada* to his wife, Zhong forced his way into Lamaist temples and stayed there overnight with his wife—who, as a woman, was not allowed. Zhong tried to convene a meeting of twelve chiefs of local tribes, but not one showed up. He then tried to seize the head of the twelve chiefs as hostage, but ended up expelled by the Tibetans. See Research Office of Southwest Nationality College 1985, p. 22.

40. The six counties were Maoxian, Wenchuan, Lifan, Maogong, Jinghua, and Song-pan, which all previously belonged to the Sixteenth Administrative Region of Sichuan under Nationalist rule.

41. *A General Description of the Aba Prefecture* claimed that opium was basically erad-icated by 1953. This was obviously not the case according to recent available materials. See Editors of Aba 1985, pp. 125–26.

42. According to statistics from the early 1980s, the Tibetans were about 42.4 percent of the total population of 730,000. The Han Chinese were about 41.2 percent, the Qiang were 13.8 percent, and the Hui were 2.6 percent. See Editors of Aba 1985, pp. 11–12.

Bibliography

Agar, Michael H. 1973. *Ripping and Running: A Formal Ethnography of Urban Heroin Addicts.* New York: Seminar Press.

Alasuutari, Pertti. 1992. *Desire and Craving: A Cultural Theory of Alcoholism.* Albany: State University of New York Press.

Association for the Study of Southwestern Warlords, ed. 1983. *Xinan junfashi yanjiu congkan* (Series on the study of southwestern warlords). Vol. 2. Guiyang: Guizhou renmin chubanshe.

———, ed. 1985. *Xinan junfashi yanjiu congkan* (Series on the study of southwestern warlords). Vol. 3. Guiyang: Guizhou renmin chubanshe.

Bai Tieguo. 1993. Jinri Pingyuanjie (Pingyuan Today). *Yunnan Legal News*, July 30.

Baoshan Bao (Baoshan news). 1988–1995. Baoshan, Yunnan.

Baoshan Women's Association. 1991. Laizi "biancheng" de baogao (Reports from a "border city": A survey on drug addiction among women in Baoshan). In *Jindu* (Narcotics control), ed. Huang Shaozhi and Dong Zhiliang, 4–14. Baoshan, Yunnan: Propaganda Department of the Party Committee of Baoshan Prefecture.

Barnett, A. Doak, ed. 1969. *Chinese Communist Politics in Action.* Seattle: University of Washington Press.

Beijing City. 1952. Beijing shi guanyu jindu xuanchuan de qingkuang he chubu jingyan (The situation of conducting drug suppression propaganda in Beijing and some preliminary experiences). Declassified government document.

Beijing Review. 1990. Beijing.

Bennett, Gordon. 1976. *Yundong: Mass Campaign in Chinese Communist Leadership.* Berkeley: University of California Press. China Research Monographs, no. 12.

Bergere, Marie-Claire. 1986. *The Golden Age of the Chinese Bourgeoisie 1911–1937.* Cambridge: Cambridge University Press.

Blecher, Marc. 1989. China's Struggle for a New Hegemony. *Socialist Review* 19 (2): 5–35.

Cameron, Meribeth E. 1931. *The Reform Movement in China: 1898–1912.* University Series: History, Economics, and Political Science, vol. 3, no. 1. Stanford, Calif.: Stanford University Press.

Centenary Conference Committee. 1907. *China Centenary Missionary Conference Records.* Shanghai: Methodist Publishing House.

Central Committee of the CCP. 1952a. *Zhuanfa xibeiju guanyu jindu yundong de zhishi zhongyang bing guiding quanguo jindu yundong zhuyao you zhongyang gonganbu zhangwo* (Forwarding the directive on drug suppression movement by the Northwest

Bureau and the Central had decided that the National Anti-Drug Campaign should be handled principally by the Central Ministry of Public Security). Archives of the Ministry of Public Security, 1952–005.

——. 1952b. *Zhongyang pizhun Luo Ruiqing bayueershiqiri guanyu zhaokai gongshen dufan panchu shixing de baogao* (The Central approves the report by Luo Ruiqing on 27 August suggesting to put drug offenders on public trials and given the death penalty). Archives of the Ministry of Public Security, 1952–005.

——. 1952c. *Guanyu jindu de tongling* (Directive on eradication of drug epidemic). Archives of the Ministry of Public Security, 1952–016.

——. 1952d. *Zhuanfa xinanju "guanyu shenru sudu yundong de jinji tongzhi"* (Forwarding the "Urgent notice on deepening Anti-Drug Campaign" by the Southwest Bureau of the CCP). Archives of the Ministry of Public Security, 1952–005.

——. 1952e. Zhonggong zhongyang guanyu "wufan" dingan, butui gongzuo deng de zhishi (Directive on making verdicts and refunds in the "Five Antis," May 9, 1952). In *Jianguo yilai zhongyao wenxian xuanbian* (Selections of important documents since the establishment of the PRC). Vol. 3, ed. Documents Research Office of the Central Committee of the CCP, 181. Beijing: Zhongyang wenxian chubanshe, 1992.

——. 1952f. Zhonggong zhongyang guanyu tuichi xianquxiang de "sanfan" he zhongxiao chengshi de "wufan" de zhishi (Directive on the postponement of conducting the "Three Antis" in county, district, and township as well as the "Five Antis" in medium and small cities, May 23, 1952). In *Jianguo yilai zhongyao wenxian xuanbian* (Selections of important documents since the establishment of the PRC). Vol. 3, ed. Documents Research Office of the Central Committee of the CCP, 195–96. Beijing: Zhongyang wenxian chubanshe, 1992.

Central Department of Propaganda. 1952a. *Guanyu jindu xuanchuan de yige tongbao* (A general notice on anti-drug propaganda). Issued on August 14. Archives of the Ministry of Public Security, 1952–016.

——. 1952b. *Guanyu jindu xuanchuan de zhishi* (Directive on anti-drug propaganda). Archives of the Ministry of Public Security, 1952–016.

Chen Cunyi and Li Yirong. 1994. Miandian shanbei diqi riyi kuoda de dupin shengchan dui woguo goucheng de yanzhong weihai (The increasing production of drugs in the Northern Shan State poses a great threat to China). *Yunnan Gongan Yanjiu* (Yunnan public security study) (1): 28–30.

Chen Jing. 1995. Ma Mozhen jiaoshou fangtanlu (A conversation with Professor Ma Mozhen). *Beijing Dangshi Yanjiu* (Beijing party history study) (1): 43–45.

Chen Shouqian. 1993. Wuhan jindu yundong (Anti-drug campaign in Wuhan). In *Jinchang jindu* (Abolish prostitution and eradicate narcotics), ed. Ma Weigang, 229–46. Beijing: Jingguan jiaoyu chubanshe.

Chen Yung-fa. 1995. The blooming poppy under the Red Sun: The Yan'an way and the opium trade. In *New Perspectives on the Chinese Communist Revolution*, ed. Tony Saich and Hans van de Ven, 263–98. Armonk, N.Y.: M. E. Sharpe.

Cheng Xianmin. 1987. Liangshan Yizu renkou wenti qianxi (A preliminary analysis of Liangshan Yi population). In *Study of Southwest Nationalities* (Special Issue on Yi), ed. China Association for the Study of Southwest Nationalities, 151–79. Chengdu: Sichuan minzu chubanshe.

China Daily. 1997–1999. Beijing.

The Chinese Recorder. 1937. Vol. 68. Shanghai.

Coble, Parks M. 1980. *The Shanghai Capitalists and the Nationalist Government 1927–1937.* Cambridge: Council on East Asian Studies, Harvard University.

Cui Lili. 1990. AIDS Challenge for China. *Beijing Review,* Nov. 26–Dec. 2: 32.

Dehong Tuanjie Bao (Dehong solidarity news). 1988–1995. Dehong, Yunnan.

Deng Xiaoping. 1993. *Deng Xiaoping xuanji* (Selections of Deng Xiaoping). Vol. 3. Beijing: Renmin chubanshe.

Des Forges, Alexander. 1997. Opium and the Textual Construction of Turn-of-the-Century Shanghai. Paper presented to the conference on Opium in East Asian History. University of Toronto-York University Joint Center for Asia Pacific Studies, May 9–10.

Dirlik, Arif. 1975. Mass Movements and Left Kuomintang. *Modern China* (1): 46–74.

———. 1993. Civil Society/Public Sphere in Modern China: As Critical Concepts versus Heralds of Bourgeois Modernity. *Chinese Social Sciences Quarterly (Hong Kong),* (3): 10–17.

Dirlik, Arif, and Maurice Meisner, eds. 1989. *Marxism and the Chinese Experience: Issues in Contemporary Chinese Socialism.* Armonk, N.Y.: M. E. Sharpe.

Documents Research Office of the Central Committee of the CCP, ed. 1992. *Jianguo yilai zhongyao wenxian xuanbian* (Selections of important documents since the establishment of the People's Republic of China). Vol. 3. Beijing: Zhongyang wenxian chubanshe.

Dreher, Melanie Creagan. 1982. *Working Men and Ganja: Marihuana Use in Rural Jamaica.* Philadelphia: Institute for the Study of Human Issues.

Du Bose, Hampden C. 1910. *The Last Days of the Poppy.* Shanghai: Methodist Publishing House.

Du Yuting. 1987. Banfengjian banzhimindi de jiuzhongguo yu Liangshan de nulizhi (On the relations between the Liangshan Yi slavery and the semi-feudal, semi-colonial society of the old China). In *Study of Southwest Nationalities* (Special Issue on Yi), ed. China Association for the Study of Southwest Nationalities, 219–36. Chengdu: Sichuan minzu chubanshe.

Eastern Miscellany (*Dongfang zazhi*). 1906. Beijing.

Eastman, Lloyd E. 1974. *The Abortive Revolution: China under Nationalist Rule,* 1927–1937. Cambridge: Harvard University Press.

———. 1986. Nationalist China during the Nanking Decade 1927–1937. In The *Cambridge History of China.* Vol. 13, ed. Denis Twitchett and John K. Fairbank, 116–67. Cambridge: Cambridge University Press.

Editors of Aba. 1985. *Aba zangzu zizhizhou gaikuang* (A general description of the Aba Tibetan Autonomous Prefecture). Chengdu: Sichuan minzu chubanshe.

Editors of Liangshan. 1985. *Liangshan Yizu zizhizhou gaikuang* (A general description of the Liangshan Yi Autonomous Prefecture). Chengdu: Sichuan minzu chubanshe.

Everett, Michael W., Jack O. Waddell, Dwight B. Heath, eds. 1976. *Cross-Cultural Approaches to the Study of Alcohol.* The Hague: Mouton Publishers.

Fan Buchun. 1993. Zhengsu Pingyuanjie (Rectifying the Pingyuan area). *Jiefangjun Wenyi* (Art and Literature of the Liberation Army) (4): 78–95.

Fang Hanqi. 1981. *Zhongguo jindai baokanshi* (History of newspapers in modern China). Taiyuan: Shanxi jiaoyu chubanshe.

Fang Yu. 1988. Yiban shenghuo jiechu huibuhui ranshang aizibing? (Is it possible to get AIDS through contacts in everyday life?) *Popular Medicine* (9): 33.

Feng Xinwei. 1988. Ju "ai" yu guomen zhiwai (Ward off AIDS outside the gate of country). *Popular Medicine* (1): 19.

Fitzgerald, John. 1996. *Awakening China: Politics, Culture, and Class in the Nationalist Revolution*. Stanford, Calif.: Stanford University Press.

Fox, Richard G. 1985. *Lions of the Punjab: Culture in the Making*. Berkeley: University of California Press.

———, ed. 1991. *Recapturing Anthropology: Working in the Present*. Santa Fe, N.M.: School of American Research Press.

Fudan University. 1985. *Fudan daxue zhi, 1905–1949* (The history of Fudan University, 1905–1949). Shanghai: Fudan daxue chubanshe.

Gao Yanhong. 1983. Xinan junfa yu yapian maoyi (Southwestern warlords and opium trade). In *Xinan junfashi yanjiu congkan* (Series on the study of southwestern warlords), ed. Association for the Study of Southwestern Warlords, 49–60. Guiyang: Guizhou renmin chubanshe.

Gardner, John. 1969. The Wu-fan Campaign in Shanghai: A Study in the Consolidation of Urban Control. In *Chinese Communist Politics in Action*, ed. A. Doak Barnett, 477–539. Seattle: University of Washington Press.

Gladney, Dru C. 1991. *Muslim Chinese: Ethnic Nationalism in the People's Republic*. Cambridge: Council on East Asian Studies, Harvard University.

Government Administrative Council. 1950. Zhengwuyuan guanyu yanjin yapian yandu de tongling (General order on elimination of opium and narcotics by the Government Administrative Council). In *Jindu gongzuo shouce* (Handbook of narcotics control work), by Huang Shaozhi et al., 97–98. Shanghai: Shanghai sanlian shudian.

Gramsci, Antonio. 1971. *Selections from the Prison Notebooks*. New York: International Publishers.

Gu Changsheng. 1981. *Chuanjiaoshi yu jindai zhongguo* (Missionaries and modern China). Shanghai: Shanghai renmin chubanshe.

Habermas, Jurgen. 1989. *The Structural Transformation of the Public Sphere: An Inquiry into a Category of Bourgeois Society*. Cambridge: MIT Press.

———. 1991. "The Public Sphere." In *Rethinking Popular Culture: Contemporary Perspectives in Cultural Studies*, ed. Chandra Mukerji and Michael Schudson, 398–404. Berkeley: University of California Press,

Hao Lianjie. 1988. Aizibing de chuanbo fangshi dou yiyang ma (Does AIDS spread in the same way)? *Popular Medicine* (7): 32.

He Ping. 1995. Miandian dupin wenti de lishi yu xianzhuang (The drug problem in Burma: Its history and current situation). Paper presented to the conference on Stability and Development of the Border Areas in Yunnan, held in Kunming.

He Yaohua. 1987. Lun Liangshan Yizu de jiazhi zhidu (On the Yi lineage system in Liangshan). In *Study of Southwest Nationalities* (Special Issue on Yi), ed. China Association for the Study of Southwest Nationalities, 119–42. Chengdu: Sichuan minzu chubanshe.

Henriot, Christian. 1995. "La Fermeture": The Abolition of Prostitution in Shanghai, 1949–58. *The China Quarterly* (142): 467–86.

Hershatter, Gail. 1992. Regulating Sex in Shanghai: The Reform of Prostitution in 1921 and 1951. In *Shanghai Sojourners*, ed. Frederic Wakeman and Yeh Wen-hsin, 145–85. Berkeley, Calif.: Institute of East Asian Studies.

Hobsbawm, E. J. 1990. *Nations and Nationalism since 1780*. Cambridge: Cambridge University Press.

Howard, Paul W. 1997. Opium Suppression in Late Qing China: The Limits and Possibilities of Social Reform. Paper presented to the conference on Opium in East Asian History. University of Toronto-York University Joint Center for Asia Pacific Studies, May 9–10.

Hsu, Immanuel C.Y. 1995. *The Rise of Modern China*. New York and Oxford: Oxford University Press.

Hu Qingjun. 1987. Lun Liangshan Yizu de nuli zhidu (On the Yi slave-owning system in Liangshan). In *Study of Southwest Nationalities* (Special Issue on Yi), ed. China Association for the Study of Southwest Nationalities, 10–46. Chengdu: Sichuan minzu chubanshe.

Huang Juzi. 1838. Selections of Memorials to the Throne by Huang Juzi. In *Yapian Zhanzheng* (The Opium War). Vol. 1, eds. Ji Sihe, Lin Shuhui, and Shou Jiyu, 455–82. Shanghai: Shanghai renmin chubanshe, 1957.

Huang Shaozhi, Dong Zhiloang, and Wu Song, eds. 1992. *Jindu gongzuo shouce* (Handbook for narcotics control work). Shanghai: Shanghai sanlian shudian.

Huang Shaozhi and Dong Zhiliang, ed. 1991. *Jindu* (Narcotics control). Baoshan, Yunnan: Propaganda Department of the Party Committee of Baoshan Prefecture.

Huang Shaozhi and Dong Zhiliang. 1991. Jianjue zhizhi dupin weihai (Adopting effective means to curb the damage of drugs). In *Jindu* (Narcotics control), ed. Huang Shaozhi and Dong Zhiliang, 1–3. Baoshan, Yunnan: Propaganda Department of the Party Committee of Baoshan Prefecture.

International Opium Commission. 1909. *Report of the International Opium Commission, Shanghai China: February 1 to February 26, 1909*. Shanghai: North China Daily News and Herald Ltd.

Ji Sihe, Lin Shuhui, and Shou Jiyu, eds. 1957. *Yapian zhanzheng* (The Opium War). Vols.1 and 2. Shanghai: Shanghai renmin chubanshe.

Jia Yicheng. 1988. Shidu, dangxin ranshang aizibing (Be careful of contracting AIDS by drug abuse). *Popular Medicine* (11): 22.

Jiang Jieshi. 1944a. Xinshenghuo yundong de yaoyi (The essence of the New Life Movement). In *Xintun shinian* (Ten years of the New Life Movement). Vol. 3. ed. Promotion Committee of the NLM. Chongqing: Promotion Committee of the NLM.

———. 1944b. Tuixing xinyun yu jianshe Shaanxi (Conducting the NLM and constructing Shaanxi). In *Xiniun shinian* (Ten years of the New Life Movement). Vol. 3. ed. Promotion Committee of the NLM. Chongqing: Promotion Committee of the NLM.

———. 1944c. Xinyun duixiang yu shixing fangfa (Objects and implementation methods of the NLM). In *Xiniun shinian* (Ten years of the New Life Movement). Vol. 3, ed. Promotion Committee of the NLM. Chongqing: Promotion Committee of the NLM.

———. 1944d. Xunshi Guizhou gejie yao shixing xinshenghuo yundong (Instructions to all circles of Guizhou to carry out the NLM). In *Xiniun shinian* (Ten years of the New Life Movement). Vol. 3, ed. Promotion Committee of the NLM. Chongqing: Promotion Committee of the NLM.

———. 1944e. Xinshenghuo yundong liuzhounian jinian xunci (Instructional speech on the sixth anniversary of the NLM). In *Xiniun shinian* (Ten years of the New Life Movement). Vol. 3, ed. Promotion Committee of the NLM. Chongqing: Promotion Committee of the NLM.

———. 1944f. Xinshenghuo yundong qizhounian jinian xunci (Instructional speech on the seventh anniversary of the NLM). In *Xiniun shinian* (Ten years of the New Life Movement). Vol. 3, ed. Promotion Committee of the NLM. Chongqing: Promotion Committee of the NLM.

Jiang Qiuming and Zhu Qingbao. 1996. *Zhongguo jindu licheng* (Stages of drug suppression in China). Tianjin: Tianjin jiaoyu chubanshe.

Jiang Zemin. 1990. Aiguo zhuyi he woguo zhishi fenzi de shiming (Patriotism and the mission of intellectuals). In *The Readings on the Execution Outline of Patriotic Education*, ed. Propaganda and Education Bureau of the Propaganda Department of the Central Committee of the CCP. Beijing: Xuexi chubanshe, 1994.

———. 1991. Zhi guojia jiaowei lingdao tongzhi de xin (A letter to officials of the National Education Commission). In *The Readings on the Execution Outline of Patriotic Education*, ed. Propaganda and Education Bureau of the Propaganda Department of the Central Committee of the CCP. Beijing: Xuexi chubanshe, 1994.

Jiexiang Township Government and Party Committee of Ruili County. 1992. *Jiaqiang lingdao hengzhua jindu* (Strengthening leadership and enhancing drug suppression). Ruili, Yunnan.

Jin Shibao and Liao Yiwen. 1993. Guizhou sudu (Anti-drug campaign in Guizhou). In *Jinchang jindu* (Abolish prostitution and eradicate narcotics), ed. Ma Weigang, 267–92. Beijing: Jingguan jiaoyu chubanshe.

Jinchaji Border Region. 1939. Jinchaji bianqu xingzheng weiyuanhui guanyu yanjin bozhong yingsu de mingling (Order on prohibiting opium poppy cultivation by the Jinchaji Board Region Administrative Committee). In *Jindu gongzuo shouce* (Handbook of narcotics control work), Huang Shaozhi, Dong Zhiliang, and Wu Song, 79–80. Shanghai: Shanghai sanlian shudian, 1992.

Judu Monthly (Opium: a national issue). 1926–1936. Shanghai.

Judu Xinwen (Opium suppression news). 1928. Issue 66 (November 2). Shanghai,

Kapp, Robert A. 1973. *Szechwan and the Chinese Republic: Provincial Militarism and Central Power*, 1911–1938. New Haven: Yale University Press.

Kuang Shanjie and Yang Shurong. 1985. Sichuan junfa yu yapian (Sichuan warlords and opium). In *Series on the Study of Southwestern Warlords*. Vol. 3, ed. Association for the Study of Southwestern Warlords, 250–62. Guiyang: Guizhou renmin chubanshe.

Kurtz, Donald V. 1996. Hegemony and Anthropology: Gramsci, Exegeses, Reinterpretations. *Critique of Anthropology* 16 (2): 103–35.

Lai Shuqing. 1986. *Guomin zhengfu liunian jinyan jihua jiqi chengjiu* (The Six-Year Opium Suppression Plan of the National Government and its achievements). Taipei: Guoshiguan.

Lan Bo. 1993. Qingdao qingchu yandu jishi (Records on eliminating opium in Qingdao). In *Jinchang jindu* (Abolish prostitution and eradicate narcotics), ed. Ma Weigang, 390–97. Beijing: Jingguan jiaoyu chubanshe.

Lary, Diana. 1974. *Region and Nation: The Kwangsi Clique in Chinese Politics, 1925–1937*. London and New York: Cambridge University Press.

League of Nations. Advisory Committee on Traffic in Opium and other Dangerous Drugs. 1924. *Minutes of the Sixth Session. Geneva, August 4th–14th, 1924.* [C.397.M.146. 1924.XI]

———. 1925a. First Opium Conference. Geneva, November 3, 1924–February 11, 1925. *Minutes and Annexes* (C.684.M.244.1924.XI).

———. 1925b. Records of the Second Opium Conference. Geneva, November 17, 1924–February 19, 1925. Volume 1, *Plenary Meetings Text of the Debates*, Annex 7 (C.760.M.260.1924.XI).

Li Ruihuan. 1990. Zai quanguo "saohuang" gongzuo huiyi shang de jianghua (Speech at the national meeting on the work of "wiping out pornography"). In *Dehong Tuanjie Bao* (Dehong solidality news). October 30.

Li Xiaowei and Fang Shijiao. 1993. Jinyan yu jinzheng: Gansu lishi shang de jinyan sudu (Opium and opium suppression: Anti-opium campaigns in Gansu history). In *Jinchang jindu* (Abolish prostitution and eradicate narcotics), ed. Ma Weigang, 184–96. Beijing: Jingguan jiaoyu chubanshe.

Lian Xi. 1997. *The Conversion of Missionaries: Liberalism in American Protestant Missions in China, 1907–1932.* University Park: Pennsylvania State University Press.

Liaowang Weekly (Outlook). 1991–1997. Beijing.

Lin Ronghong. 1980. *Fengchao zhong fenqi de zhongguo jiaohui* (The rise of Chinese church in turmoil). Hong Kong: Tiandao shulou.

Lin Yaohua (Lin yueh-hua). 1961. *The Lolo of Liang Shan.* New Haven: HRAF Press.

———. 1995. *Liangshan yijia de jubian* (Tremendous changes of Liangshan Yi people). Beijing: Commercial Press.

Lin Yunhui, Fan Shouxin, and Zhang Gong. 1989. *Kaige xingjin de shiqi* (Times of marching in triumph). Zhengzhou: Henan renmin chubanshe.

Lin Zexu. 1839. Political Essays of Lin Zexu. In *Yapian Zhanzheng* (The Opium War). Vol. 2, eds. Ji Sihe, Lin Shuhui, and Shou Jiyu, 131–227. Shanghai: Shanghai renmin chubanshe, 1957.

Lindstrom, Lamont, ed. 1987. *Drugs in Western Pacific Societies: Relations of Substance.* ASAO Monograph no. 11. Lanham, Md.: University Press of America.

Liu Jialin. 1995. *Zhongguo xinwen tongshi* (A general history of Chinese press). Vol. 1. Wuhan: Wuhan daxue chubanshe.

Liu Wei. 1995. Jinsanjiao de lishi, xianzhuang he weilai (The Golden Triangle: History, current situation and its future). Paper presented to the conference on Stability and Development of the Border Areas in Yunnan, held in Kunming.

Lodwick, Kathleen L. 1996. *Crusaders against Opium: Protestant Missionaries in China, 1874–1917.* Lexington: University of Kentucky Press.

Luo Ping. 1993. *Yunnan Pinyuanjie yanda jishi* (Report of drug crackdown in the Pingyuan area of Yunnan). *Liaowang Weekly* (13): 20–24.

Luo Ruiqing. 1952. *Quanguo jindu yundong zhongjie baogao* (The sum-up report of the National Anti-Drug Campaign), December 14. Archives of the Ministry of Public Security, 1952-007.

Ma Duan. 1992. *Fayang chengji, zaijie zaili, nuli kaichuang jindu gongzuo xin jumian* (Keep working hard to make a breakthrough in the anti-drug campaign). Ruili, Yunnan.

Ma Fengcheng. 1985. Guizhou junfa yu yapian (Guizhou warlords and opium). In *Xinan junfashi yanjiu congkan* (Series on the study of southwestern warlords). Vol. 3, ed. Association for the Study of Southwestern Warlords, 349–63. Guiyang: Guizhou renmin chubanshe.

Ma Mozhen. 1993. *Dupin zai zhongguo* (Drugs in China). Beijing: Beijing chubanshe.

———, ed. 1998. *Zhongguo jindushi ziliao* (Materials of the history of drug suppression in China). Tianjin: Tianjin renmin chubanshe.

Ma Weigang, ed. 1993. *Jinchang jindu* (Abolish prostitution and eradicate narcotics). Beijing: Jingguan jiaoyu chubanshe.

MacFarquhar, Roderick, and John K. Fairbank, eds. 1987. *The Cambridge History of China.* Vol. 14. Cambridge: Cambridge University Press.

Madancy, Joyce A. 1997. Poppies, Patriotism, and the Public Sphere: Nationalism and

State Leadership in the Anti-Opium Crusade in Fujian, 1906–1916. Paper presented to the conference on Opium in East Asian History. University of Toronto-York University Joint Center for Asia Pacific Studies, May 9–10.

Maerkang Working Committee Survey Team. 1985. Zhuokeji dubu xiasizhai shehui diaocha (A social survey of four villages of the Dubu district in Zhuokeji). In *Sichuansheng abazhou zangzu shehui lishi diaocha* (A survey of Tibetan society and history in the Aba Prefecture of Sichuan province), ed. Sichuan Editors, 271–300. Chengdu: Sichuan Academy of Social Sciences Press.

Mao Tsetung. 1965. *On New Democracy. Selected Works of Mao Tsetung*. Vol. 2. Oxford: Pergamon Press.

Marshall, Mac. 1987. An Overview of Drugs in Oceania. In *Drugs in Western Pacific Societies*, ed. Lamont Lindstrom, 13–50. ASAO Monograph no. 11. Lanham, Md.: University Press of America.

McCoy, Alfred W. 1991. *The Politics of Heroin: CIA Complicity in the Global Drug Trade*. New York: Lawrence Hill Books.

Ministry of Public Security. 1952. *Guanyu Guangxi lijiangxian jindu gongzuozhong shanzi xingdong jinxing wenzi xuanchuan de baogao* (Report on taking unauthorized action and conducting propaganda in writing by Lijiang county in Guangxi province). Archives of the Ministry of Public Security, 1952-016.

Mintz, Sidney W. 1985. *Sweetness and Power: The Place of Sugar in Modern History*. New York: Penguin Books.

Modern China. 1993.

National Anti-Opium Association (NAOA). 1931. *Judu yundong zhinan* (Directory of the Anti-Opium Movement). Shanghai: National Anti-Opium Association.

National Opium Suppression Commission (NOSC). 1929. *Quanguo jinyan huiyi huibian* (Compilation of the documents of the National Opium Suppression Conference). Nanjing: National Opium Suppression Commission.

National People's Congress (NPC). 1982. Guanyu yancheng yanzhong pohuai jingji de zuifan de jueding (The decision to punish criminals causing serious damage to the economy by the Standing Committee of the Fifth National People's Congress). In *Jindu gongzuo shouce* (Handbook of narcotics control work), eds. Huang Shaozhi, Dong Zhiliang, and Wu Song, 113–17. Shanghai: Shanghai sanlian shudian, 1992.

———. 1990. Guanyu jindu de jueding (The decision to suppress narcotics by the standing Committee of the Seventh National People's Congress). In *Jindu gongzuo shouce* (Handbook of narcotics control work), eds. Huang Shaozhi, Dong Zhiliang, and Wu Song, 139–44. Shanghai: Shanghai sanlian shudian.

Newman, R. K. 1995. Opium Smoking in Late Imperial China: A Reconsideration. *Modern Asian Studies* 29 (4): 765–94.

Ning Gongshi. 1993. Nanjing de jindu gongzuo (Anti-drug work in Nanjing). In *Jinchang jindu* (Abolish prostitution and eradicate narcotics), ed. Ma Weigang, 363–80. Beijing: Jingguan jiaoyu chubanshe.

Niu Jigang, and Cai Xiaolin. 1997. Fujiansheng bingdu fanzui fengxi ji duice (An analysis of "ice" drug offenses in Fujian province and prevention strategies). In *Yanhai yanbian jingji kaifaqu xinde shehui wenti yanjiu* (Study on the new social problems in economic development zones on coastal and border areas), ed. Wang Dazhong, 243–49. Beijing: Zhongguo renmin gongan daxue chubanshe.

Northeast Bureau of the CCP. 1952a. *Zhonggong zhongyang dongbeiju dui jilin shengwei guanyu "sanfan" "wufan" zhong faxian daliang fanmai dupin de baogao de pishi* (Written comments by the Northeast Bureau of CCP to the report by the Party Committee of Jilin province concerning findings on massive drug trafficking in the campaigns of the "Three Antis" and "Five Antis"). Declassified government document.

——. 1952b. *Jindu xuanchuan gongzuo zhishi* (Directive on anti-drug propaganda). Issued by the Propaganda Department of the Northeast Bureau of the CCP on August 12. Archives of the Ministry of Public Security, 1952-016.

Northwest Bureau of the CCP. 1952. *Zhuanfa xinanju "guanyu shenru sudu yundong de jinji tongzhi"* (Forwarding the urgent notice on deepening anti-drug campaign). Archives of the Ministry of Public Security, 1952-005.

Park, William Hector, ed. 1899. *Opinions of Over 100 Physicians on the Use of Opium in China*. Shanghai: American Presbyterian Mission Press.

People's Daily (Renmin Ribao). 1983, 1989–1999. Beijing.

Polachek, James M. 1992. *The Inner Opium War*. Cambridge: Harvard University Press.

Popular Medicine (Dazhong yixue). 1986–1992. Shanghai.

Promotion Committee of the NLM, ed. 1944. *Xinyun shinian* (Ten years of the New Life Movement). Chongqing: Promotion Committee of the NLM.

Rankin, Mary B. 1986. *Elite Activism and Political Transformation in China: Zhejiang Province, 1865–1911*. Stanford, Calif.: Stanford University Press.

Reins, Thomas D. 1991. Reform, Nationalism and Internationalism: The Opium Suppression Movement in China and the Anglo-American Influence, 1900–1908. *Modern Asian Studies* 25 (1): 101–42.

Renard, Ronald D. 1996. *The Burmese Connection: Illegal Drugs and the Making of the Golden Triangle*. Boulder, Colo.: Lynne Rienner Publishers.

Renborg, Bertil A. 1947. *International Drug Control: A Study of International Administration by and through the League of Nations*. Washington, D.C.: Carnegie Endowment for International Peace.

Renmin Gongan Bao (People's public security news). 1992–1996. Beijing.

Research Office, Southwest Nationality College. 1985a. Caodi shehui qingkuang diaocha (A social survey of the grassland society). In *Sichuansheng abazhou zangzu shehui lishi diaocha* (A survey of Tibetan society and history in the Aba Prefecture of Sichuan province), ed. Sichuan Editors, 1–74. Chengdu: Sichuan Academy of Social Sciences Press.

——.1985b. Jiarong zangzu shehui qingkuang diaocha (A social survey of Jiarong Tibetan). In *Sichuansheng abazhou zangzu shehui lishi diaocha* (A survey of Tibetan society and history in Aba Prefecture of Sichuan province), ed. Sichuan Editors, 178–257. Chengdu: Sichuan Academy of Social Sciences Press.

Rowe, William T. 1993. The Problem of "Civil Society" in Late Imperial China. *Modern China* 19 (2): 139–57.

Ruili County Government. 1991. *Mobilizing All Forces to Eliminate Drug Trafficking and Consumption through the People's War*. Ruili, Yunnan.

Saich, Tony, and Hans van de Ven, eds. 1995. *New Perspectives on the Chinese Communist Revolution*. Armonk, N.Y.: M. E. Sharpe.

Schurmann, Franz. 1968. *Ideology and Organization in Communist China*. 2d ed. Berkeley and Los Angeles: University of California Press.

Second National Historical Archives. 1937–38. *Ershiwu niandu, ershiliu niandu jinyan nianbao* (Annual report of opium suppression, 1936 and 1937). Archive no. II (12) 334.

Shanganning Border Region. 1942. Shanganning bianqu jinyan jindu tiaoli (Ordinances on prohibition of opium and narcotics in the Shanganning Border Region). By Huang Shaozhi et al., *Jindu gongzuo shouce* (Handbook for narcotics control work), 74–77.

Shao Xianshu. 1987a. Jiefangqian Long Yun shili zai jinyang diqu de kuozhang huotong (The expansion of power of Long Yun in the Jinyang area before the liberation). In *Sichuan Guizhou Yizu shehui lishi diaocha* (A survey of Yi society and history in Sichuan and Guizhou provinces), ed. Yunnan Editors, 45–50. Kunming: Yunnan renmin chubanshe.

——. 1987b. Jiefangqian yapian zai jinyang diqu de zhongzhi, xiaoshou jiqi dui Yizu shehui jingji de yingxiang (The effects of opium planting and sales on the Yi society and economy in the Jinyang area before the liberation). In *Sichuan Guizhou Yizu Shehui Lishi Diaocha* (A survey of Yi society and history in Sichuan and Guizhou provinces), ed. Yunnan Editors, 51–54. Kunming: Yunnan renmin chubanshe.

Shenbao. 1919–1926. Shanghai.

Sichuan Editors. 1985. *Sichuansheng abazhou zangzu shehui lishi diaocha* (A survey of Tibetan society and history in the Aba Prefecture of Sichuan province). Chengdu: Sichuan Academy of Social Sciences Press.

Sichuan Nationality Survey Team. 1985a. Zhuokeji tusi tongzhi diqu diaocha (A survey of the area under the Zhuoheji chieftains). In *Sichuansheng abazhou zangzu shehui lishi diaocha* (A survey of Tibetan society and history in Aba Prefecture of Sichuan province), ed. Sichuan Editors, 258–70. Chengdu: Sichuan Academy of Social Sciences Press.

——. 1985b. Chuosijia shehui diaocha (A social survey of Chuosijia). In *Sichuansheng abazhou zangzu shehui lishi diaocha* (A survey of Tibetan society and history in the Aba Prefecture of Sichuan province), ed. Sichuan Editors, 332–53. Chengdu: Sichuan Academy of Social Sciences Press.

Spence, Jonathan. 1975. Opium Smoking in Ch'ing China. In *Conflict and Control in Late Imperial China*, ed. Frederic Wakeman, Jr., and Carolyn Grant, 143–73. Berkeley: University of California Press.

Su Zhiliang. 1997. *Zhongguo dupin shi* (The history of drugs in China). Shanghai: Shanghai renmin chubanshe.

Sun Xingsheng, Shi Tangxi, and Zhu Changhe. 1993. Jinyan jindu zai Liangshan (Anti-opium campaign in Liangshan). In *Jinchang jindu* (Abolish prostitution and eradicate narcotics), ed. Ma Weigang, 197–217. Beijing: Jingguan jiaoyu chubanshe.

Teiwes, Frederick C. 1987. Establishment and Consolidation of the New Regime. In *The Cambridge History of China*, Vol.14, ed. Roderick MacFarquhar and John K. Fairbank, 51–92. Cambridge: Cambridge University Press.

Townsend, James. 1988 Nationalism Chinese Style. *Antioch Review* (46): 204–20.

——. 1992. Chinese Nationalism. *The Australian Journal of Chinese Affairs* (27): 97–130.

Twitchett, Denis, and John K. Fairbank, eds. 1986. *The Cambridge History of China*. Vol. 13. Cambridge: Cambridge University Press.

U.S. Department of State (U.S.D.S.). 1985. *Records of the U.S. Department of State Relating to the Interior Affairs of China, 1930–1939.* Wilmington, Del.: Scholarly Resources. Microfilm.

U.S. Government. 1952. *The Report of the Government of the United States on the Traffic in Opium and Other Dangerous Drugs, 1951.* Washington, D.C.: United States Government Printing Office.

——. 1953. *The Report of the Government of the United States on the Traffic in Opium and Other Dangerous Drugs, 1952*. Washington, D.C.: United States Government Printing Office.

Wakeman, Frederic Jr. 1991. Models of Historical Change: The Chinese State and Society, 1839–1989. *Newsletter for Modern Chinese History* (11): 50–65. Taipei.

——. 1995. Licensing Leisure: The Chinese Nationalists' Attempt to Regulate Shanghai, 1927–49. *Journal of Asian Studies* 54 (1):19–42.

Wakeman, Frederic E. Jr., and Carolyn Grant, eds. 1975. *Conflict and Control in Late Imperial China*. Berkeley: University of California Press.

Wakeman, Frederic E. Jr., and Yeh Wen-Hsin, eds. 1992. *Shanghai Sojourners.* Berkeley: Institute of East Asian Studies.

Waley, Arthur. 1958. *The Opium War through Chinese Eyes*. New York: Macmillan.

Wang Dazhong, ed. 1997. *Yanhai yanbian jingji kaifaqu xinde shehui wenti yanjiu* (Study on the new social problems in economic development zones in coastal and border areas). Beijing: Zhongguo renmin gongan daxue chubanshe.

Wang Jinxiang. 1996. *Zhongguo jindu jianshi* (A concise history of drug suppression in China). Beijing: Xuexi chubanshe.

Wang Yingliang. 1987. Liangshan Yizu shehui de lishi fazhan (The historical development of Liangshan Yi society). In *Study of Southwest Nationalities* (Special Issue on Yi), ed. China Association for the Study of Southwest Nationalities, 47–74. Chengdu: Sichuan minzu chubanshe.

Wang Yongjun, ed. 1989. *Huangpu junxiao sanbai mingjiang zhuan* (Biographies of 300 famous generals from the Huangpu Military Academy). Nanning: Guangxi renmin chubanshe.

Wei Yunheng. 1996. Dupin huohai xiang Liaoning manyan (Drug evil is spreading to Liaoning). *Liaowang Weekly* 10 (March 4): 6–7.

Williams, Raymond. 1977. *Marxism and Literature.* New York: Oxford University Press.

Wong, R. Bin. 1997. Opium and Modern Chinese State Making. Paper presented to the conference on Opium in East Asian History. University of Toronto-York University Joint Center for Asia Pacific Studies, May 9–10.

World Journal (Shijie Ribao). 1992–1997. New York.

Wormsley, William E. 1987. Beer and Power in Enga. In *Drugs in Western Pacific Societies*, ed. Lamont Lindstrom, 197–218. ASAO Monograph no. 11. Lanham, Md.: University Press of America.

Wu Jiayu. 1983. Fujian jinyan yundong "qudu she" (Opium Suppression Campaign in Fujian and the "Anti-Opium Society"). *Fuzhou wenshi ziliao xuanji* (Selections of Fujian cultural and historical materials) (2): 15–18.

Xiang Baosheng. 1993. Jiu Tianjin de yandu ji yijiuwuernian de jindu yundong (Opium and narcotics in old Tianjin and the anti-drug campaign in 1952). In *Jinchang jindu* (Abolish prostitution and eradicate narcotics), ed. Ma Weigang, 336–62. Beijing: Jingguan jiaoyu chubanshe.

Xiao Wenliang. 1997. Luohu xiaqu fandu anjian de zhuyao tedian ji dafang duice (The main characteristics of drug trafficking cases in Luohu district and the ways to deal with the situation). In *Yanhai yanbian jingji kaifaqu xinde shehui wenti yanjiu* (Study on the new social problems in economic development zones in coastal and border areas), ed. Wang Dazhong, 430–39. Beijing: Zhongguo renmin gongan daxue chubanshe,

Xie Zaojing. 1982. Xinshenghuo yundong de tuixing (The implementation of the New

Life Movement). In *Collections on Modern Chinese History*. Vol. 8, ed. Zhang Yufa, 247–89. Taipei: Lianjin Publishing Company.

Xu Dingxing, and Qian Xiaoming. 1991. *Shanghai zhongshanghui shi* (History of Shanghai General Chamber of Commerce, 1902–1929). Shanghai: Shanghai Academy of Social Sciences Press.

Xu Zirong. 1952. *Zhongyang gonganbu Xu Zirong fubuzhang zai jindu gongzuo huiyishang guanyu kaizhan quanguo guimo de jindu yundong de baogao* (The speech on conducting a national anti-drug campaign by Vice Minister Xu Zirong in working conference on drug suppression). Archives of the Ministry of Public Security, 1952–005.

Yang Guangcheng. 1993. Aba de jinyan sudu (Anti-opium campaign in Aba). In *Jinchang jindu* (Abolish prostitution and eradicate narcotics), ed. Ma Weigang, 316–22. Beijing: Jingguan jiaoyu chubanshe.

Yang, Mayfair Mei-hei. 1989. Between State and Society: The Construction of Corporateness in a Chinese Socialist Factory. *The Australian Journal of Chinese Affairs* 22 (July): 31–60.

Yao Jianguo. 1991. Yunnan: China's Anti-Drug Outpost. *Beijing Review* (August. 26): 20–25.

Yapian liujie (Six Commandments of Opium). [1848]. Ningbo: Huahua Bible Publishing House.

Ye Jundong. 1996. Yufang "baihuo" manyan de xingdong zugou ma (Are we doing enough to prevent the spread of the "white peril")? *Liaowang Weekly* (March 4): 8.

Yip Ka-che. 1980. *Religion, Nationalism and Chinese Students: The Anti-Christian Movement of 1922–1927*. Bellingham Wash.: Center for East Asian Studies, Western Washington University.

Yu Ende. 1934. *Zhongguo jinyan faling bianqian shi* (History of China's opium suppression laws and regulations). Shanghai: Zhonghua shuju.

Yu Lei. 1992. Speech at the Press Conference of the International Day against Drug Abuse and Illicit Trafficking. June 26. Beijing.

Yunnan Editors. 1987. *Sichuan Guizhou Yizu shehui lishi diaocha* (A survey of Yi society and history in Sichuan and Guizhou provinces). Kunming: Yunnan renmin chubanshe.

Yunnan Fazhi Bao (Yunnan legal news). 1993. July 30. Kunming, Yunnan.

Yunnan Gongan Yanjiu (Yunnan public security study). 1994. Kunming, Yunnan.

Yunnan Provincial Government. 1950. Guanyu yanjin yapian yandu de zhishi (Directive on opium prohibition). *Yunnan Dangan Shiliao* (Yunnan archival materials), 1991 (4): 3–4.

Yunnan Ribao (Yunnan Daily). 1950–1954, 1989–1997. Kunming, Yunnan.

Yunnan Yearbook (Yunnan Nianjian). 1993. Kunming, Yunnan.

Yunxi Bao (Yunnan Tin Company news). 1991. December 1. Gejiu, Yunnan.

Zhang Chengjun. 1993. Xian de jinyan sudu (Anti-Drug Campaign in Xian). In *Jinchang jindu* (Abolish prostitution and eradicate narcotics), ed. Ma Weigang, 302–15. Beijing: Jingguan jiaoyu chubanshe.

Zhang Chengxu. 1987. Liangshan Yizu yige nuli shichang de diaocha baogao (A survey of a slave market in the Liangshan Yi area). In *Study of Southwest Nationalities* (Special Issue on Yi), ed. China Association for the Study of Southwest Nationalities, 143–50. Chengdu: Sichuan minzu chubanshe.

Zhang Jing. 1991. Xidu yu xingbing (Drugs and STDs). In *Jindu* (Narcotics control). ed. Huang Shaozhi and Dong Zhiliang, 63–67. Baoshan, Yunnan: Propaganda Department of the Party Committee of Baoshan Prefecture.

Zhang Liyong. 1993. Xingdong daihao 8.31 (Action code 8.31). *Kunming Daily.* Weekend Supplementary Issue, no. 7 (January 15).

Zhao Jingyi, and He Jianhua. 1994. Jindu Shanghaitan (Drug suppression in Shanghai). *Renmin Gongan Bao* (People's public security news). July 30.

Zhao Shikung. 1993. Xiaomie Guilin de fandu huodong (Eradicate drug trafficking in Guilin). In *Jinchang jindu* (Abolish prostitutions and eradicate narcotics), ed. Ma Weigang, 255–66. Beijing: Jingguan jiaoyu chubanshe.

Zhao Tingguang. 1995. *Zai xinde lishi shiqi chuli fuza shehui maodun redian de shijian tansuo* (A practical experiment of handling hot spot of complex social contradictions in the New Era). Kunming, Yunnan.

Zhao Yinglin. 1995. "Zhongguo de mogen" Chen Guanfu faji shilu (Success stories of the "Chinese Morgan" Chen Guangfu). In *Heimu Shanghaitan* (Black sides of Shanghai), ed. Zhou Da, 288–97. Beijing: Tuanjie chubanshe.

Zheng Guanying. 1988. *Zheng Guanying quanji* (Collected works of Zheng Guanying). Ed. by Xia Dongyuan. Shanghai: Shanghai renmin chubanshe.

Zhong Ketuo. 1929. The Destiny of the First National Opium Suppression Conference. In *Quanguo jinyan huiyi huibian* (Compilation of the documents of the National Opium Suppression Conference), ed. National Opium Suppression Commission. 4–7. Nanjing: National Opium Suppression Commission.

Zhou Da. 1995. *Heimu Shanghaitan* (Black sides of Shanghai). Beijing: Tuanjie chubanshe.

Zhu Qingbao, Jiang Qiuming, and Zhang Shijie. 1995. *Yapian yi jindai zhongguo* (Opium and modern China). Nanjing: Jiangsu jiaoyu chubanshe.

Index

About the Author

Zhou Yongming is assistant professor in the department of anthropology at the University of Wisconsin—Madison.